# THE HUMANISTIC TRADITION

THIRD EDITION

# 2 Medieval Europe and the World Beyond

# THE HUMANISTIC TRADITION

THIRD EDITION

## 2 Medieval Europe and the World Beyond

Gloria K. Fiero

New York  St. Louis  San Francisco  Auckland  Bogotá  Caracas
Lisbon  London  Madrid  Mexico City  Milan  Montreal  New Delhi
San Juan  Singapore  Sydney  Tokyo  Toronto

*McGraw-Hill*
*A Division of The McGraw·Hill Companies*

THE HUMANISTIC TRADITION, BOOK 2

Copyright © 1998 by The McGraw-Hill Companies, Inc.
Previous editions © 1995, 1992 by William C. Brown Communications, Inc.

Permissions Acknowledgments appear on page 171,
and on this page by reference.

Library of Congress Catalog Card Number: 97–071270

ISBN 0–697–34069–4

Editorial Director  *Phillip Butcher*
Senior Sponsoring Editor  *Cynthia Ward*
Director of Marketing  *Margaret Metz*
National Sales Manager  *Jerry Arni*

This book was designed and produced by
CALMANN & KING LTD
71 Great Russell Street, London WC1B 3BN

Editors  *Ursula Payne, Richard Mason*
Designer  *Karen Osborne*
Cover Designer  *Karen Stafford*
Timeline Designer  *Richard Foenander*
Picture Researcher  *Carrie Haines*
Maps by Oxford Illustrators Ltd.

Developmental Editing by M. J. Kelly for McGraw-Hill

Typeset by Fakenham Photosetting, Norfolk
Printed in Hong Kong

10  9  8  7  6  5  4  3  2  1

http://www.mhhe.com

*Front cover*
Main image: Head of Theodora, detail of *Empress Theodora and Retinue*, ca. 547 C.E.
Mosaic. San Vitale, Ravenna. Photo: © Dagli Orti, Paris.
Insets: (top) Red-figure *kylix* showing man and youth debating. The Metropolitan Museum of Art,
Rogers Fund, 1952 52.11.4. Photograph © 1984 The Metropolitan Museum of Art, New York.
(center) Sandro Botticelli, detail of *Birth of Venus*, after 1482. Tempera on canvas,
full image 5 ft. 9 in. × 9 ft. ½ in. Uffizi Gallery, Florence. Scala, Florence.
(bottom) Detail of *Seated Buddha*, from the Gandharan region of Northwest Pakistan,
ca. 200 C.E. Gray schist, 51 × 31 in. The Cleveland Museum of Art. Leonard Hanna, Jr. Bequest.
CMA 61.418.

*Frontispiece*
*The Battle Rages*, detail from the Bayeux Tapestry, eleventh century. Wool embroidery on linen,
depth approx. 20 in., entire length 231 ft. Ville de Bayeux, France.
Photo: By special permission of the City of Bayeux.

# Series Contents

# Book 2
# Contents

PART III

# The World Beyond the West *143*

## MUSIC LISTENING SELECTIONS

## MAPS

# Preface

"It's the most curious thing I ever saw in all my life!" exclaimed Lewis Carroll's Alice in Wonderland, as she watched the Cheshire Cat slowly disappear, leaving only the outline of a broad smile. "I've often seen a cat without a grin, but a grin without a cat!" A student who encounters an ancient Greek epic, a Yoruba mask, or a Mozart opera—lacking any context for these works—might be equally baffled. It may be helpful, therefore, to begin by explaining how the artifacts (the "grin") of the humanistic tradition relate to the larger and more elusive phenomenon (the "cat") of human culture.

## The Humanistic Tradition and the Humanities

In its broadest sense, the term *humanistic tradition* refers to humankind's cultural legacy—the sum total of the significant ideas and achievements handed down from generation to generation. This tradition is the product of responses to conditions that have confronted all people throughout history. Since the beginnings of life on earth, human beings have tried to ensure their own survival by achieving harmony with nature. They have attempted to come to terms with the inevitable realities of disease and death. They have endeavored to establish ways of living collectively and communally. And they have persisted in the desire to understand themselves and their place in the universe. In response to these ever-present and universal challenges—*survival, communality,* and *self-knowledge*—human beings have created and transmitted the tools of science and technology, social and cultural institutions, religious and philosophic systems, and various forms of personal expression, the sum total of which we call culture.

Even the most ambitious survey cannot assess all manifestations of the humanistic tradition. This book therefore focuses on the creative legacy referred to collectively as *the humanities*: literature, philosophy, history (in its literary dimension), architecture, the visual arts (including photography and film), music, and dance. Selected examples from each of these disciplines constitute our *primary sources*. Primary sources (that is, works original to the age that produced them) provide firsthand evidence of human inventiveness and ingenuity. The primary sources in this text have been chosen on the basis of their authority, their beauty, and their enduring value. They are, simply stated, the great works of their time and, in some cases, of all time. Universal in their appeal, they have been transmitted from generation to generation. Such works are, as well, the landmark examples of a specific time and place: They offer insight into the ideas and values of the society in which they were produced. The drawings of Leonardo da Vinci, for example, reveal a passionate determination to understand the operations and functions of nature. And while Leonardo's talents far exceeded those of the average individual of his time, his achievements may be viewed as a mirror of the robust curiosity that characterized his time and place—the age of the Renaissance in Italy. *The Humanistic Tradition* surveys such landmark works, but joins "the grin" to "the cat" by examining them within their political, economic, and social contexts.

*The Humanistic Tradition* explores a living legacy. History confirms that the humanities are integral forms of a given culture's values, ambitions, and beliefs. Poetry, painting, philosophy, and music are not, generally speaking, products of unstructured leisure or indulgent individuality; rather, they are tangible expressions of the human quest for the good (one might even say the "complete") life. Throughout history, these forms of expression have served the domains of the sacred, the ceremonial, and the communal. And even in the waning days of the twentieth century, as many time-honored traditions have come under assault, the arts retain their power to awaken our imagination in the quest for survival, communality, and self-knowledge.

## The Scope of the Humanistic Tradition

The humanistic tradition is not the exclusive achievement of any one geographic region, race, or class of human beings. For that reason, this text assumes a global and multicultural rather than exclusively Western perspective. At the same time, Western contributions are emphasized, first, because the audience for these books is predominantly Western, but also because in recent centuries the West has exercised a dominant influence on the course and substance of global history. Clearly, the humanistic tradition belongs to all of humankind, and the best way to understand the Western contribution to that tradition is to examine it in the arena of world culture.

As a survey, *The Humanistic Tradition* cannot provide an exhaustive analysis of our creative legacy. The critical reader will discover many gaps. Some aspects of culture that receive extended examination in traditional Western humanities surveys have been pared down to make room for the too often neglected contributions of

Islam, Africa, and Asia. This book is necessarily selective—it omits many major figures and treats others only briefly. Primary sources are arranged, for the most part, chronologically, but they are presented as manifestations of *the informing ideas of the age* in which they were produced. The intent is to examine the evidence of the humanistic tradition thematically and topically, rather than to compile a series of mini-histories of the individual arts.

## Studying the Humanistic Tradition

To study the creative record is to engage in a dialogue with the past, one that brings us face to face with the values of our ancestors, and, ultimately, with our own. This dialogue is (or should be) a source of personal revelation and delight; like Alice in Wonderland, our strange, new encounters will be enriched according to the degree of curiosity and patience we bring to them. Just as lasting friendships with special people are cultivated by extended familiarity, so our appreciation of a painting, a play, or a symphony depends on close attention and repeated contact. There are no shortcuts to the study of the humanistic tradition, but there are some techniques that may be helpful. It should be useful, for instance, to approach each primary source from the triple perspective of its *text*, its *context*, and its *subtext*.

*The Text*: The *text* of any primary source refers to its *medium* (that is, what it is made of), its *form* (its outward shape), and its *content* (the subject it describes). All literature, for example, whether intended to be spoken or read, depends on the medium of words—the American poet Robert Frost once defined literature as "performance in words." Literary form varies according to the manner in which words are arranged. So poetry, which shares with music and dance rhythmic organization, may be distinguished from prose, which normally lacks regular rhythmic pattern. The main purpose of prose is to convey information, to narrate, and to describe; poetry, by its freedom from conventional patterns of grammar, provides unique opportunities for the expression of intense emotions. Philosophy (the search for truth through reasoned analysis) and history (the record of the past) make use of prose to analyze and communicate ideas and information. In literature, as in most kinds of expression, content and form are usually interrelated. The subject matter or the form of a literary work determines its *genre*. For instance, a long narrative poem recounting the adventures of a hero constitutes an *epic*, while a formal, dignified speech in praise of a person or thing constitutes a *eulogy*.

The visual arts—painting, sculpture, architecture, and photography—employ a wide variety of media, such as wood, clay, colored pigments, marble, granite, steel, and (more recently) plastic, neon, film, and computers.

The form or outward shape of a work of art depends on the manner in which the artist manipulates the formal elements of color, line, texture, and space. Unlike words, these formal elements lack denotative meaning. The artist may manipulate form to describe and interpret the visible world (as in such genres as portraiture and landscape painting); to generate fantastic and imaginative kinds of imagery; or to create imagery that is nonrepresentational—without identifiable subject matter. In general, however, the visual arts are spatial, that is, they operate and are apprehended in space.

The medium of music is sound. Like literature, music is durational: It unfolds over the period of time in which it occurs. The formal elements of music are melody, rhythm, harmony, and tone color—elements that also characterize the oral life of literature. As with the visual arts, the formal elements of music are without symbolic content, but while literature, painting, and sculpture may imitate or describe nature, music is almost always nonrepresentational—it rarely has meaning beyond the sound itself. For that reason, music is the most difficult of the arts to describe in words. It is also (in the view of some) the most affective of the arts. Dance, the artform that makes the human body itself a medium of expression, resembles music in that it is temporal and performance-oriented. Like music, dance exploits rhythm as a formal tool, but, like painting and sculpture, it unfolds in space as well as time.

In analyzing the text of a work of literature, art, or music, we ask how its formal elements contribute to its meaning and affective power. We examine the ways in which the artist manipulates medium and form to achieve a characteristic manner of execution and expression that we call *style*. And we try to determine the extent to which a style reflects the personal vision of the artist and the larger vision of his or her time and place. Comparing the styles of various artworks from a single era, we may discover that they share certain defining features and characteristics. Similarities (both formal and stylistic) between, for instance, golden age Greek temples and Greek tragedies, between Chinese lyric poems and landscape paintings, and between postmodern fiction and pop sculpture, prompt us to seek the unifying moral and aesthetic values of the cultures in which they were produced.

*The Context*: We use the word *context* to describe the historical and cultural environment. To determine the context, we ask: In what time and place did the artifact originate? How did it function within the society in which it was created? Was the purpose of the piece decorative, didactic, magical, propagandistic? Did it serve the religious or political needs of the community? Sometimes our answers to these questions are mere guesses. Nevertheless, understanding the function of an artifact often serves to clarify the nature of its form (and vice versa). For instance, much of the literature produced prior to the fifteenth century was spoken or sung rather than read; for that reason, such literature tends to feature repetition and rhyme, devices that facilitate memorization. We can assume that literary works embellished with frequent repetitions, such as the *Epic of Gilgamesh* and the Hebrew Bible, were products of an oral tradition. Determining the original function of an artwork also permits us to assess its significance in its own time and place: The paintings on the walls of Paleolithic caves, which are among the most compelling animal illustrations in the history of world art, are not "artworks" in the modern sense of the term but, rather, magical signs that accompanied hunting rituals, the performance of which was essential to the survival of the community. Understanding the relationship between text and context is one of the principal concerns of any inquiry into the humanistic tradition.

*The Subtext*: The *subtext* of the literary or artistic object refers to its secondary and implied meanings. The subtext embraces the emotional or intellectual messages embedded in, or implied by, a work of art. The epic poems of the ancient Greeks, for instance, which glorify prowess and physical courage in battle, suggest that such virtues are exclusively male. The state portraits of the seventeenth-century French ruler Louis XIV carry the subtext of unassailable and absolute power. In our own century, Andy Warhol's serial adaptations of soup cans and Coca-Cola bottles offer wry commentary on the supermarket mentality of postmodern American culture. Identifying the implicit message of an artwork helps us to determine the values and customs of the age in which it was produced and to assess those values against others.

## Beyond *The Humanistic Tradition*

This book offers only small, enticing samples from an enormous cultural buffet. To dine more fully, students are encouraged to go beyond the sampling presented at this table; and for the most sumptuous feasting, nothing can substitute for first-hand experience. Students, therefore, should make every effort to supplement this book with visits to art museums and galleries, concert halls, theaters, and libraries. *The Humanistic Tradition* is designed for students who may or may not be able to read music, but who surely are able to cultivate an appreciation of music in performance. The clefs that appear in the text refer to the forty-five Music Listening Selections found on two accompanying cassettes, available from the publishers. Lists of suggestions for further reading are included at the end of each chapter, while a selected general bibliography of humanities resources appears at the end of each book.

## The Third Edition

On the threshold of the new millennium, this third edition of *The Humanistic Tradition* brings increased attention to the theme of global cross-cultural encounter and, in particular, to the interaction of the West with the cultures of Islam, East Asia, and Africa. In this connection, a full chapter has been devoted to the Islamic World, and the chapter on ancient Rome has been expanded to provide parallels between the cultures of the Roman Empire and Han China. Chapter 1 now includes a carefully chosen selection of creation myths. There are new readings from *Beowulf*, Christine de Pisan, Murasaki Shikibu, Ibn Battuta, Hernán Cortés, Jonathan Swift, Mary Shelley, and Alice Walker. Excerpts from the *Iliad* (in chapter 4) appear in the 1990 English translation by Robert Fagles. Sufi poetry, the transatlantic slave trade, Japanese theater, and contemporary computer art add new perspectives to this, the latest version of the text.

The third edition also features two new study aids, both of which are designed to facilitate an appreciation of the arts in relation to their time and place: *Science and Technology Boxes*, which appear throughout the chapters, list key scientific and technological developments that have directly or indirectly affected the history of culture. *Locator Maps* (keyed to the map that appears on p. xii) assist readers in linking specific cultural events with the geographic region in which they occurred. This edition also expands on the number of color illustrations and large color maps, renumbers the Readings by book, and updates the Suggestions for Reading and Selected General Bibliography. Finally, in the transcription of the Chinese language, the older Wade-Giles system has been replaced by the more modern Hanyu Pinyin.

## A Note to Instructors

The key to successful classroom use of *The Humanistic Tradition* is *selectivity*. Although students may be assigned to read whole chapters that focus on a topic or theme, as well as complete works that supplement the abridged readings, the classroom should be the stage for a selective treatment of a single example or a set of examples. The organization of this textbook is designed to emphasize themes that cut across geographic boundaries—themes whose universal significance prompts students to evaluate and compare rather than simply memorize and repeat lists of names and places. In an effort to assist readers in achieving global cultural literacy, every effort has been made to resist isolating (or "ghettoizing") individual cultures and to avoid the inevitable biases we bring to our evaluation of relatively unfamiliar cultures.

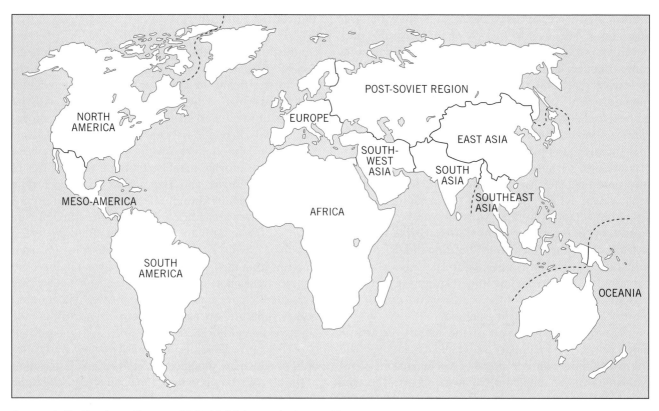

Keymap Indicating Areas Shown as White Highlights on the Locator Maps.

## Acknowledgments

Writing *The Humanistic Tradition* has been an exercise in humility. Without the assistance of learned friends and colleagues, assembling a book of this breadth would have been an impossible task. James H. Dormon read all parts of the manuscript and made extensive and substantive editorial suggestions; as his colleague, best friend, and wife, I am most deeply indebted to him. I owe thanks to the following faculty members of the University of Southwestern Louisiana: for literature, Allen David Barry, Darrell Bourque, C. Harry Bruder, John W. Fiero, Emilio F. Garcia, Doris Meriwether, and Patricia K. Rickels; for history, Ora-Wes S. Cady, John Moore, Bradley Pollack, and Thomas D. Schoonover; for philosophy, Steve Giambrone and Robert T. Kirkpatrick; for geography, Tim Reilly; for the sciences, Mark Konikoff and John R. Meriwether; and for music, James Burke and Robert F. Schmalz.

The following readers and viewers generously shared their insights in matters of content and style: Michael K. Aakhus (University of Southern Indiana), Vaughan B. Baker (University of Southwestern Louisiana), Katherine Charlton (Mt. San Antonio Community College), Bessie Chronaki (Central Piedmont Community College), Debora A. Drehen (Florida Community College—Jacksonville), Paula Drewek (Macomb Community College), William C. Gentry (Henderson State University), Kenneth Ganza (Colby College), Ellen Hofmann (Highline Community College), Burton Raffel (University of Southwestern Louisiana), Frank La Rosa (San Diego City College), George Rogers (Stonehill College), Douglas P. Sjoquist (Lansing Community College), Howard V. Starks (Southeastern Oklahoma State University), Ann Wakefield (Academy of the Sacred Heart—Grand Coteau), Sylvia White (Florida Community College—Jacksonville), and Audrey Wilson (Florida State University).

In the preparation of the third edition, I have benefited from the suggestions and comments generously offered by numerous readers, only some of whom are listed below. Rodney D. Boyd (Collin County Community College), Arnold Bradford (Northern Virginia Community College), Patricia L. Brace (Southwest State University), Orville V. Clark (University of Wisconsin—Green Bay), Carolyn Copeland (Bethune Cookman), Susan Cornett (St. Petersburg Junior College—Tarpon Center), Anthony M. Coyne (University of North Carolina), Kenneth Ganza (Colby College), Margaret Hasselman (Virginia Polytechnic Institute and State University), Victor Hébert (Fayetteville State University), Ellen Hofmann (Highline Community College), Enid Housty (Hampton University), Mabel Khawaja (Hampton University), James W. Mock (University of

Central Oklahoma), Lewis Parkhill (East Central University), Joseph G. Rahme (University of Michigan—Flint), David Simmons (Brevard Community College), J. Paul De Vierville (St. Phillip's College), Bertha L. Wise (Oklahoma City Community College), and Jon Young (Fayetteville State University). I am grateful to Julia Girouard, who provided research assistance for the

third edition, and to Timothy Reilly, who generously assisted in the preparation of the Locator Maps.

The burden of preparing the third edition has been lightened by the assistance of M. J. Kelly, Developmental Editor, and by the editorial vigilance of Ursula Payne and Richard Mason at Calmann & King.

### SUPPLEMENTS FOR THE INSTRUCTOR AND THE STUDENT

A number of useful supplements are available to instructors and students using *The Humanistic Tradition*. Please contact your sales representative or call 1-800-338-3987 to obtain these resources, or to ask for further details.

#### Audiocassettes
Two ninety-minute audiocassettes containing a total of forty-five musical selections have been designed exclusively for use with *The Humanistic Tradition*. Cassette One corresponds to the music listening selections discussed in books 1–3 and Cassette Two contains the music in books 4–6. Each selection on the cassettes is discussed in the text and includes a voice introduction for easier location. Instructors may obtain copies of the cassettes for classroom use by calling 1-800-338-3987. Individual cassettes may be purchased separately; however, upon the request of instructors who place book orders, Cassette One or Two can be packaged with any of the six texts, so that students may use the musical examples *along with* the text.

#### Slide Sets
A set of fifty book-specific slides is available to qualified adopters of *The Humanistic Tradition*. These slides have been especially selected to include many of the less well-known images in the books, and will be a useful complement to your present slide resources. A larger set of two hundred book-specific slides is available for purchase from Sandak, Inc. For more information, contact your McGraw–Hill representative.

#### Instructor's Resource Manual
The Instructor's Resource Manual is designed to assist instructors as they plan and prepare for classes. Course outlines and sample syllabuses for both semester and quarter systems are included. The chapter summaries emphasize key themes and topics that give focus to the primary source readings. The study questions for each chapter may be removed and copied as handouts for student discussion or written assignments. A Test Item File follows each chapter along with a correlation list that directs instructors to the appropriate music examples, slides, transparencies, and software sections of the other supplements. A list of suggested videotapes, recordings, videodiscs, CD-ROMs, and their suppliers is included.

#### MicroTest III
The questions in the Test Item File are available on MicroTest III, a powerful but easy-to-use test generating program. MicroTest is available for DOS, Windows, and Macintosh

personal computers. With MicroTest, an instructor can easily select the questions from the Test Item File and print a test and answer key. You can customize questions, headings, and instructions and add or import questions of your own.

#### Humanities Transparencies
A set of seventy-one acetate transparencies is available with *The Humanistic Tradition*. These show examples of art concepts, architectural styles, art media, maps, musical notation, musical styles, and musical elements.

#### *Culture 3.0* CD-ROM
*Culture 3.0* CD-ROM is a unique Macintosh reference tool that emphasizes the interaction of varied disciplines. It contains 40 historical maps, 120 signature melodies, 50,000 hypertext links, and 170 essays on topics ranging from Greek gods and goddesses to the Cold War. Thirty-two CultureGrids are arranged chronologically from the biblical era to the twentieth century, organizing people, places, and events by country, discipline, and generation. (*Culture 2.0* is also available in a seven-disk set for Mac and IBM.)

#### Student Study Guides, Volumes 1 and 2
Written by Gloria K. Fiero, two new Student Study Guides are now available to help students gain a better understanding of subjects found in *The Humanistic Tradition*. Volume 1 accompanies books 1–3 and Volume 2 accompanies books 4–6. Each chapter contains: a Chapter Objective; a Chapter Outline; Key Terms, Names, and Dates; Vocabulary Building; Multiple Choice Questions; and Essay Questions. Many chapters also contain a Visual/Spatial Exercise and Bonus Material. At the end of each Part, Synthesis material helps students draw together ideas from a set of chapters.

#### *The Art Historian* CD-ROM, Volumes 1 and 2
This flexible two-volume series on dual platform (Mac and Windows) CD-ROMs is designed to supplement introductory level art history education. Volume 1 covers ancient and medieval art, and Volume 2 covers Renaissance to modern art. The images included on the CD were gathered from over three hundred museums, galleries, and private collections throughout the world, and the text and test questions were written by current scholars from universities across the United States. With *The Art Historian*, students may listen to multimedia presentations, review full-color high-resolution images, and test their knowledge with flashcards and essay questions. *The Art Historian* is flexible, allowing students to take notes, compare two images on the screen at the same time, and create personalized collections of images for study and review. With *The Art Historian*, we place the power of multimedia *and* art at your fingertips.

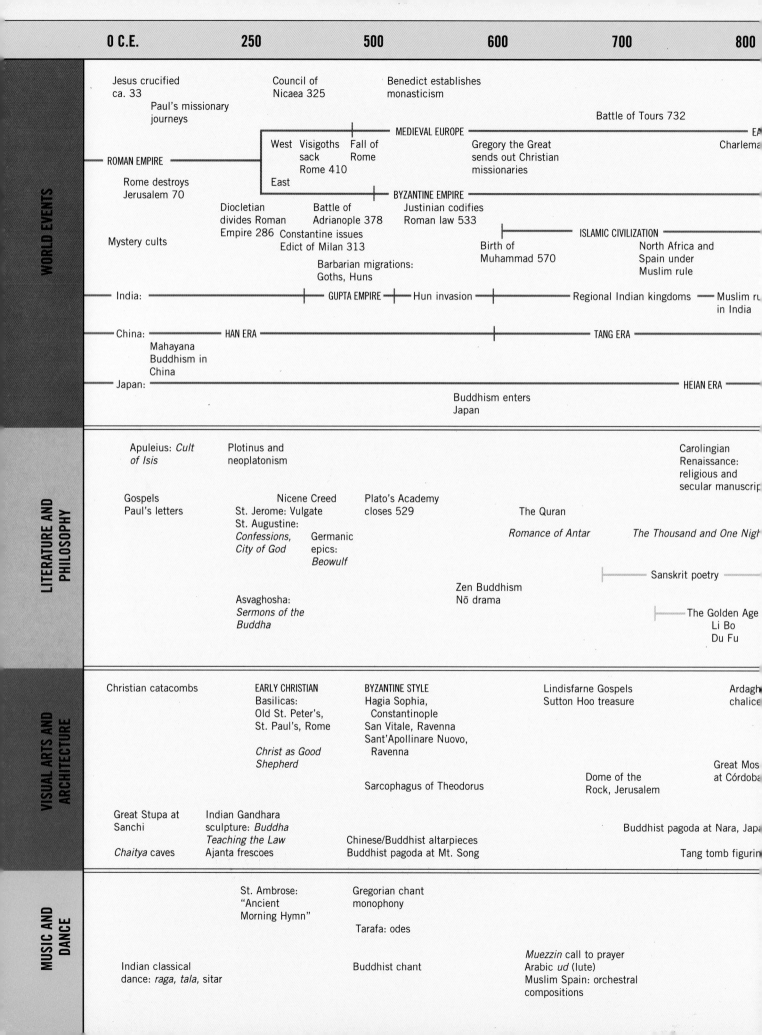

Timeline

| 0 C.E. | 250 | 500 | 600 | 700 | 800 |

**WORLD EVENTS**

Jesus crucified ca. 33
Paul's missionary journeys
Council of Nicaea 325
Benedict establishes monasticism
Battle of Tours 732

MEDIEVAL EUROPE
EA[...]
Charlema[...]

West · Visigoths sack Rome 410 · Fall of Rome
Gregory the Great sends out Christian missionaries

ROMAN EMPIRE

East

Rome destroys Jerusalem 70

BYZANTINE EMPIRE

Diocletian divides Roman Empire 286
Battle of Adrianople 378
Justinian codifies Roman law 533

Mystery cults
Constantine issues Edict of Milan 313

ISLAMIC CIVILIZATION

Birth of Muhammad 570
North Africa and Spain under Muslim rule

Barbarian migrations: Goths, Huns

India: ——— GUPTA EMPIRE ——— Hun invasion ——— Regional Indian kingdoms —— Muslim ru[...] in India

China: ——— HAN ERA ——————————————— TANG ERA ———

Mahayana Buddhism in China

Japan: ———————————————————————— HEIAN ERA —

Buddhism enters Japan

**LITERATURE AND PHILOSOPHY**

Apuleius: *Cult of Isis*
Plotinus and neoplatonism
Carolingian Renaissance: religious and secular manuscrip[...]

Gospels
Paul's letters
Nicene Creed
St. Jerome: Vulgate
St. Augustine: *Confessions, City of God*
Germanic epics: *Beowulf*
Plato's Academy closes 529
The Quran
*Romance of Antar*
*The Thousand and One Nigh[...]*

Sanskrit poetry

Asvaghosha: *Sermons of the Buddha*
Zen Buddhism
Nō drama
The Golden Age
Li Bo
Du Fu

**VISUAL ARTS AND ARCHITECTURE**

Christian catacombs
EARLY CHRISTIAN Basilicas: Old St. Peter's, St. Paul's, Rome
BYZANTINE STYLE Hagia Sophia, Constantinople
San Vitale, Ravenna
Sant'Apollinare Nuovo, Ravenna
Lindisfarne Gospels
Sutton Hoo treasure
Ardagh chalice

*Christ as Good Shepherd*

Great Mos[...] at Córdoba

Sarcophagus of Theodorus
Dome of the Rock, Jerusalem

Great Stupa at Sanchi
Indian Gandhara sculpture: *Buddha Teaching the Law*
Buddhist pagoda at Nara, Japa[...]

*Chaitya* caves
Ajanta frescoes
Chinese/Buddhist altarpieces
Buddhist pagoda at Mt. Song
Tang tomb figurin[...]

**MUSIC AND DANCE**

St. Ambrose: "Ancient Morning Hymn"
Gregorian chant monophony

Tarafa: odes

Muezzin call to prayer
Arabic *ud* (lute)
Muslim Spain: orchestral compositions

Indian classical dance: *raga, tala,* sitar
Buddhist chant

| 900 | 1000 | 1100 | 1200 | 1300 | 1400 |
|---|---|---|---|---|---|

Viking invasions — Norman Conquest of England 1066 — First universities founded in Europe

Rise of towns and guilds — Philip IV ruler of France

•DLE AGES — ands his empire — HIGH MIDDLE AGES

Split between the Roman Catholic and the Greek Orthodox Church — Christian Crusades 1094–1204 — Establishment of Franciscan order — Medieval papacy at its height — Boniface VIII: *Unam Sanctam* 1302

run-al-Rashid ands the basid Empire — Baghdad becomes important center — Mongols conquer Baghdad 1258

Delhi sultanate

lock printing nvented — SONG ERA — Movable type invented — Introduction of paper currency — Marco Polo reaches China ca. 1275

HEIAN ERA — Rise of the *samurai* — KAMAKURA SHOGUNATE

Lindau Gospels — MEDIEVAL SCHOLASTICISM

*Song of Roland* transcribed — Abelard: *Sic et Non* — *Troubadour* and *trouvère* lyrics — Aquinas: *Summa Theologica*

Medieval romance — Chrétien de Troyes: *Lancelot* — Dante: *Divine Comedy*

Avicenna: *Canon of Medicine* — Ibn Zaydun: "Two Fragments" — Ibn Abra: "The Beauty-Spot" — Mystery and miracle plays — Morality play: *Everyman*

World's earliest printed book: *Diamond Sutra* — Sufi poetry: "Empty the Glass of Your Desire," "The Man of God," "The One True Light"

hinese poetry Bo Zhu-yi — Japanese novels, short stories: Murasaki: *Tale of Genji, Diary* — Vidyakara: *Treasury of Well-Turned Verse* — Song Dynasty: painted album leaves and scrolls — Chinese novels, short stories, popular theater: Luo Guanzhong: *Three Kingdoms*

Carolingian Abbey Church St.-Gall — Chapel at Aachen — ROMANESQUE STYLE — Pilgrimage church: St.-Sernin — Gislebertus at Autun Cathedral — Norman architecture: Dover Castle — Bayeux Tapestry — GOTHIC STYLE — St.-Denis Abbey Church — Chartres Cathedral — Notre Dame of Paris — Notre Dame of Amiens — Ste. Chapelle, Paris — Cimabue: *Madonna Enthroned* — Martini: *Annunciation*

China's first manual on architecture — Court of the Lions, Alhambra

Chinese landscape painting: Li Cheng: *A Solitary Temple* — Chinese porcelains — Hindu temple: Kandariya Mahadeo — Chola bronzes: *Shiva, Lord of the Dance* — Buddhist deity in wood: *Kichijoten* — *Samurai* armor — Takanobu: *Minamoto no Yoritomo* — Jokei: *Kongorikishi* — Nō mask: *Ko-omote*

Antiphons, tropes, sequences — Organum/early polyphony — *The Play of Herod* — Jongleurs: *chansons de geste* — Guido of Arezzo: musical notation — Bernart de Ventadour: *troubadour* songs — Leonin: *Magnus Liber Organi* — Pérotin: 3- and 4-part polyphony — *Estampie*

al-Isfahani: *Great Book of Songs* — Motets — *Dies irae*

Chinese opera and court music

# PART

# I

# THE SHAPING OF THE MIDDLE AGES

Scholars once described the thousand-year period between the fall of Rome and the age of the European Renaissance as a "dark" age whose cultural achievements fell far short of those of ancient Greece and Rome. Our present understanding of the Middle Ages suggests otherwise. As the following chapters indicate, this was one of the most creative periods in the history of Western culture. During the Early Middle Ages, that is, the first seven centuries of the first millennium of the common era, a transition from classical to Christian culture took place in the West. Elsewhere in the world, the same period witnessed the vitalizing effects of two world religions: Buddhism and Islam. So powerful were these religious faiths—Christianity, Buddhism, and Islam—that by the year 1000, the Eastern hemisphere could be described as being divided among them (Map **8.1**).

From the perspective of world history, the transition to the Middle Ages encompassed several significant developments: the decline of classical civilization and the rise of the Christian West; the diffusion of Germanic tribal peoples into the lands of the Roman Empire; the golden age of Byzantine civilization; the spread of Buddhism from India to China; and, finally, the birth and expansion of Islam in Southwest Asia and beyond.

Chapter 8, "A Flowering of Faith," examines the climate of religious renewal that resulted in the rise of Christianity in the West and the spread of Buddhism in the East, and compares the spiritual messages of these world faiths. Chapter 9, "The Language of Faith," surveys the establishment of early Christianity in the Roman West and in Byzantium, traces the transition from classical to Christian modes of expression, and, finally, explores the Buddhist language of faith as evidenced in the art, architecture, and music of India and China. Chapter 10, "The Islamic World: Religion and Culture," examines the rich cultural heritage of Islam—a religion practiced today by more than a billion people—uncovering the unique contributions of Muslim artists and scholars and evaluating Islam's role as geographic intermediary between East and West.

(opposite) Interior of the nave of Saint Paul's Outside the Walls, Rome (after reconstruction), begun 386 C.E. © Canali Photobank, Capriolo (BS) Italy.

# 8
# A Flowering of Faith: Christianity and Buddhism

Shortly after the reign of the Roman Emperor Octavian, in the province of Judea (the Roman name for Palestine), an obscure Jewish preacher named Joshua (in Greek, *Jesus*) brought forth a message that became the basis for a new world religion: Christianity. Christianity came to provide an alternative to the secular, rational values associated with classical culture in the West. The pursuit of reason and earthly wisdom gave way to the promise of messianic deliverance and eternal life.

As Christianity began to win converts within the Roman Empire, a somewhat older set of religious teachings was spreading in the East. The message of Siddhartha Gautama, the fifth-century-B.C.E.* founder of Buddhism,

swept through Asia. By the third century B.C.E., Buddhism had become India's state religion, and by the first century C.E., it was the principal religious faith of Han China. The similarities and differences between Buddhism and Christianity offer valuable insights into the spiritual communities of the East and West. While no in-depth analysis of either religion can be offered here, a brief look at the formative stages of these two world faiths provides some understanding of their significance within the humanistic tradition.

*Dates are designated as B.C.E., "Before the Christian (or common) era," or C.E., "Christian (or common) era."

**Map 8.1** Distribution of Major Religious Faiths, ca. 1000 C.E.

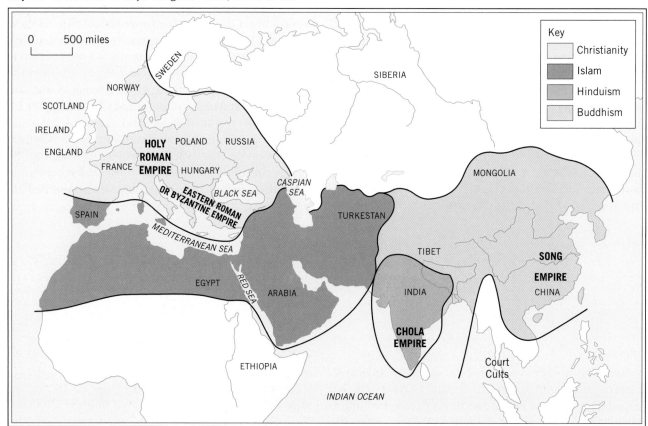

# The Background to Christianity

## Roman Religion and Religious Philosophies

Roman religion, like Roman culture itself, was a blend of native and borrowed traditions. Ancient pagan religious rituals marked seasonal change and celebrated seedtime and harvest. Augury, the interpretation of omens (a practice borrowed from the Etruscans), was important to Roman religious life as a means of predicting future events. The typically eclectic Romans welcomed the gods of non-Roman peoples and honored them along with the greater and lesser Roman gods. They embraced the Greek gods, who assumed Latin names (see Table, chapter 4). Many of the gods protected household and state: Vesta, for instance, guarded the hearth fire, and Mars, god of war, ministered to soldiers. Tolerance for non-Roman cults and creeds contributed to the lack of religious uniformity in the Empire, as well as to wide speculation concerning the possibility of life after death. While Romans might have pictured a shadowy underworld in which the souls of the dead survived (similar to the Greek Hades and the Hebrew Sheol), Roman religion offered neither retribution in the afterlife nor the clear promise of eternal life.

Rome hosted a wide variety of religious beliefs and practices, along with a number of quasi-religious Hellenistic philosophies (see chapter 6). Of these, Stoicism and neoplatonism were the most influential. Stoicism's ethical view of life and its emphasis on equality among human beings offered an idealized alternative to a social order marked by wide gaps between rich and poor, and between citizens and slaves. Neoplatonism, a school of philosophy (developed in Alexandria) that took as inspiration some of the principal ideas in the writings of Plato and his followers, anticipated a mystical union between the individual soul and "the One" or Ultimate Being—comparable with Plato's Form of Goodness. According to Plotinus, a third-century-C.E. Egyptian-born neoplatonist, union with the One could be achieved only by the soul's ascent through a series of levels or degrees of spiritual purification. Neoplatonism's view of the soul as eternal and divine, and its perception of the universe as layered in ascending degrees of perfection, would have a shaping influence on early Christian thought.

Following the decline of the Roman Republic and in the wake of increased contacts with Egypt and Southwest Asia, Rome absorbed a number of uniquely Eastern traditions. Roman emperors came to be regarded as theocratic monarchs and assumed titles such as *dominus* ("lord") and *deus* ("god"). By the second century, Rome enjoyed a full-blown imperial cult that honored the living emperor as semidivine and deified him after his death. At the same time, widespread social, political, and economic unrest fed a rising distrust of reason and a growing impulse toward mysticism. Among the prevailing religious ideas were those associated with the name Zoroaster. This shadowy Persian prophet (who may have lived any time between 1100 and 600 B.C.E.) taught that life was a cosmic battle between the opposing forces of light and darkness. All human beings took part in this struggle by freely choosing between good and evil, the consequence of which determined their eternal fate. According to Zoroastrian doctrine, a Last Judgment (similar to the Egyptian final reckoning; see chapter 2) would consign the wicked to everlasting darkness and the good to *pairidaeza*, the abode of beauty and light (from which the English word "Paradise" derives). As such ideas filtered westward, many began to hope for rewards in the hereafter, rather than in their earthly lives. The mystery cults of the Eastern Mediterranean, and, ultimately, Christianity, would respond to these needs.

## The Mystery Cults

In Greece, Egypt, and many parts of Southwest Asia, there had long flourished numerous religious cults whose appeal was less intellectual than that of neoplatonism and far more personal than that of the prevailing Greco-Roman religious philosophies. The promise of personal immortality was the central feature of these cults, called "mystery cults" because their initiation rituals were secret (in Greek, *mysterios*). The cults of Isis in Egypt, Cybele in Phrygia, Dionysus in Greece, and Mithra in Persia, to name but four, had a heritage dating back to Neolithic times. As we have seen in earlier chapters, ancient agricultural societies celebrated seasonal change by means of symbolic performances of the birth, death, and rebirth of gods and goddesses associated with the regeneration of crops. The mystery cults perpetuated these practices. Their initiates participated in symbolic acts of spiritual death and rebirth, including ritual baptism and a communal meal at which they might partake of the flesh or blood of the deity.

The cult of Isis originated in the Egyptian myth of the descent of the goddess Isis into the underworld to find and resurrect her mate Osiris (see chapter 2). Followers of this cult identified Isis as Earth Mother and Queen of Heaven and looked to her to ensure their own salvation (Figure 8.1). Initiation into the cult included formal processions, a ritual meal, purification of the body, and a ten-day period of fasting that culminated in the ecstatic vision of the goddess herself. During the second century C.E., in a Latin novel entitled *The Golden Ass*, or *Metamorphoses*, the Roman writer Lucius Apuleius described the initiation rites of the cult of Isis. At the close of the solemn rites, according to Apuleius, the initiate fell prostrate before the image of the Queen of Heaven and recited the prayer that is reproduced in part in the passage that follows. The ecstatic tone of this prayer—a startling departure from the measured, rational cast of most Greco-Roman literature—reflects the mood of religious longing that characterized the late classical era.

### READING 2.1

## From Apuleius' *Initiation into the Cult of Isis*

"O holy and eternal savior of mankind, you who ever          1
bountifully nurture mortals, you apply the sweet affection
of a mother to the misfortunes of the wretched. Neither a
day nor a night nor even a tiny moment passes empty of
your blessings: you protect men on sea and land, and you
drive away the storm-winds of life and stretch forth your
rescuing hand, with which you unwind the threads of the
Fates even when they are inextricably twisted, you calm
the storms of Fortune, and you repress harmful motions
of the stars. The spirits above revere you, the spirits     10
below pay you homage. You rotate the earth, light the
sun, rule the universe, and tread Tartarus[1] beneath your
heel. The stars obey you, the seasons return at your will,
deities rejoice in you, and the elements are your slaves.
At your nod breezes breathe, clouds give nourishment,
seeds sprout, and seedlings grow. Your majesty awes the
birds traveling the sky, the beasts wandering upon the
mountains, the snakes lurking in the ground, and the
monsters that swim in the deep. But my talent is too
feeble to speak your praises and my inheritance too       20
meager to bring you sacrifices. The fullness of my voice is
inadequate to express what I feel about your majesty; a
thousand mouths and as many tongues would not be
enough, nor even an endless flow of inexhaustible
speech. I shall therefore take care to do the only thing
that a devout but poor man can: I shall store your divine
countenance and sacred godhead in the secret places of
my heart, forever guarding it and picturing it to myself. . . ."

———————◆———————

While the worship of Isis, Dionysus, and Cybele was peculiar to the Mediterranean, the most popular of the many Southwest Asian mystery cults—the cult of Mithra—centered in Persia. Associated with the sun and with the forces of Light and Goodness in ancient Persian religion, the man-god Mithra was believed to have released the forces of cosmic life and energy by slaughtering the Bull of Fertility. Mithra's followers, who sought regeneration and personal attachment to this hero-god, celebrated his birth on December 25, that is, just after the sun's "rebirth" at the winter solstice. Mithraism, which excluded the participation of women, involved strict initiation rites, periods of fasting, ritual

---

[1]In Greek mythology, a part of the underworld where the wicked are punished.

**Figure 8.1** *Isis and Horus Enthroned*, Middle Egyptian, fourth century C.E. Limestone, height 35 in. Staatliche Museen, Berlin.

baptism, and a communal meal of bread and wine. The favorite religion of Roman soldiers, who readily identified with Mithra's physical prowess and heroic self-discipline, Mithraism spread throughout Europe and North Africa, where archeologists have discovered numerous Mithraic chapels. Indeed, for the first two centuries of the common era, Mithraism was the chief rival of Christianity. The similarities between Mithraism and Christianity—a man-god hero, ritual baptism, a communal meal, and the promise of deliverance from evil—suggest that some of the basic features of Christianity already existed in the religious history of the Roman world prior to the time of Jesus. It is no surprise that many educated Romans considered Christianity to be an imitation of Mithraism.

Although the mystery cults often involved costly and demanding rituals, they were successful in attracting devotees. The Romans readily accommodated the exotic gods and goddesses of these cults as long as their worship did not challenge the authority of the Roman imperial cult or threaten the security of the Roman state.

## The Jewish Background

Judaism, the oldest living religion in the Western world, differed from the other religions and religious cults of this period in its strongly ethical bias, its commitment to monotheism, and its exclusivity—that is, its emphasis on a special relationship (or covenant) between God and the Chosen People, the Jews themselves. During Hellenistic times, a Greek translation of Hebrew Scriptures appeared: Called the *Septuagint* ("Seventy"), as it was reputed to have been translated by seventy or seventy-two scholars in a period of seventy-two days, this edition is the first known translation of a sacred book into another language.

The main religion of Judea (which had become a Roman province in 63 B.C.E.), Judaism forbade the worship of the Roman emperor and the gods of the Roman state. Hence the Roman presence in Jerusalem caused mutual animosity and perpetual discord, conditions that would culminate in the Roman destruction of the city in 70 C.E.* (see chapter 7). During the first century B.C.E., however, unrest in Judea was complicated by disunity of opinion and biblical interpretation. Even as a special group of **rabbis** (Jewish teachers) met in 90 C.E. to draw up the authoritative list of thirty-six books that would constitute the canonic Hebrew Bible,** there was no uniform Jewish doctrine describing the afterlife or the age to come. Indeed, the leading groups of rabbis disagreed over such matters as the question of life after death and the nature of the **Messiah** ("Anointed One") anticipated by some of the Hebrew prophets. The Sadducees, a learned sect of Jewish aristocrats who advocated cultural and religious solidarity among the Jews, envisioned the Messiah as a temporal leader who would consolidate Jewish ideals and lead the Jews to political freedom. They denied that the soul survived the death of the body. The Pharisees, the more influential group of Jewish teachers and the principal interpreters of Hebrew law, believed in the advent of a messianic redeemer who, like a shepherd looking after his flock, would lead the righteous to salvation (Figure 8.2). In their view, the human soul was imperishable and the wicked would suffer eternal punishment.

In addition to the Sadducees and the Pharisees, there existed in Judea a minor religious sect called the Essenes, whose members lived in monastic communities near the Dead Sea. The Essenes renounced worldly goods and practiced **asceticism**—strict self-denial and self-discipline. The Essenes believed in the immortality of the soul and its ultimate release and liberation from the body. They anticipated the coming of a teacher of truth who would appear at the end of time. The Dead Sea Scrolls—found in caves near Essene ruins—include some of the oldest extant fragments of the Hebrew Bible along with scriptures that forecast a final apocalyptic age. In Judea, where all of these groups along with scores of self-proclaimed miracle workers and preachers competed for an audience, the climate of intense religious expectation was altogether receptive to the appearance of a charismatic leader.

## The Message of Jesus

That charismatic leader proved to be a young Jewish rabbi from the city of Nazareth. Since Jesus of Nazareth (0–33 C.E.) is not mentioned in non-Christian literature until almost the end of the first century C.E., the historical Jesus is an elusive figure. Our most important sources of information concerning Jesus are the Christian Gospels (literally, "good news"). The oldest, dating from at least forty years after Jesus' death, provides the earliest biographical evidence of the life of Jesus. Yet, since the authors of the Gospels—the evangelists Matthew, Mark, Luke, and John—gave most of their attention to the last months of Jesus' life, these biblical books are not biographies in the true sense of the word. Perhaps because Jesus' followers anticipated his imminent return, they made no effort to keep a careful historical record of their master's life.

Recorded in Greek, the Gospels describe the life and miracles of an eloquent and inspiring teacher. Like all great teachers, Jesus was concerned with ethical matters. His message, cast in simple and direct language and in parables that carried moral lessons, was essentially pacifistic and antimaterialistic. He warned of the perils of riches and the temptations of the temporal world. Jesus' insistence upon the evils of material wealth represented a radically new direction in ancient culture. Despite such exceptions as the Essenes, the neoplatonists, and the Stoics, the classical world was fundamentally materialistic and secular. Jesus preached the renunciation of material goods ("do not lay up for yourselves treasures on earth") not merely as a means of freeing the soul from temporal enslavement, but as a preparation for eternal life.

With a reformer's zeal, Jesus criticized the Judaism of his day, especially its emphasis on strict observance of ritual. He embraced the spirit (rather than the letter) of Hebrew law and proclaimed the primacy of faith over ritual. Asked which of the laws were primary, Jesus cited love of God and love of one's neighbor (Matthew 22:34–40). He pictured God as stern but merciful, loving and protective, rather than chastising (recall Job's Yahweh; see chapter 2) or remote and inaccessible (as with the deities of the mystery cults). Finally, and most importantly, Jesus preached the cultivation of compassion, righteousness, and trust in God, the rewards for which would be reaped in the "kingdom of heaven." For all its simplicity and directness, however, the message of Jesus prescribed an almost impossibly altruistic ideal—an ideal of unconditional love linked to an equally lofty imperative: "You must . . . be perfect, just as your heavenly

---

*Hereafter, unless otherwise designated, all dates refer to the Christian (or common) era.
**Following ancient Hebrew tradition, these were grouped into three divisions: the Law (the first five books of instruction, called the *Torah*), the Prophets, and the Writings—that is, wisdom literature (see chapters 2, 3).

**Figure 8.2** *The Good Shepherd*, ca. 425–450 C.E. Mosaic. Mausoleum of Galla Placidia, Ravenna, Italy. Giraudon, Paris.

Father is perfect" (Matthew 5:48). The Sermon on the Mount, as recorded by the apostle Matthew, is probably the most representative of Jesus' sermons. Here Jesus sets forth the basic injunctions of an uncompromising ethic to which moral intention is more important than outward behavior: Love your neighbor; accept persecution with humility; pass no judgment on others; and treat others as you would have them treat you.

## READING 2.2
## From the Gospel of Matthew

### "Sermon on the Mount"

#### Chapter 5: The Beatitudes

¹Seeing the crowds, he went onto the mountain. And when he was seated his disciples came to him. ²Then he began to speak. This is what he taught them:
   ³How blessed are the poor in spirit:
   the kingdom of Heaven is theirs.
   ⁴Blessed are *the gentle*:
   *they shall have the earth as inheritance.*
   ⁵Blessed are those who mourn:
   they shall be comforted.
   ⁶Blessed are those who hunger and thirst for uprightness:
   they shall have their fill.
   ⁷Blessed are the merciful:
   they shall have mercy shown them.
   ⁸Blessed are the pure in heart:
   they shall see God.
   ⁹Blessed are the peacemakers:
   they shall be recognised as children of God.
   ¹⁰Blessed are those who are persecuted in the cause of uprightness:
   the kingdom of Heaven is theirs.
¹¹"Blessed are you when people abuse you and persecute you and speak all kinds of calumny against you falsely on my account. ¹²Rejoice and be glad, for your reward will be great in heaven; this is how they persecuted the prophets before you.

#### Salt for the earth and light for the world

¹³"You are salt for the earth. But if salt loses its taste, what can make it salty again? It is good for nothing, and can only be thrown out to be trampled under people's feet.

   ¹⁴"You are light for the world. A city built on a hill-top cannot be hidden. ¹⁵No one lights a lamp to put it under a tub; they put it on the lamp-stand where it shines for everyone in the house. ¹⁶In the same way your light must shine in people's sight, so that, seeing your good works, they may give praise to your Father in heaven.

#### The fulfilment of the Law

¹⁷"Do not imagine that I have come to abolish the Law or the Prophets. I have come not to abolish but to complete them. ¹⁸In truth I tell you, till heaven and earth disappear, not one dot, not one little stroke, is to disappear from the Law until all its purpose is achieved. ¹⁹Therefore, anyone who infringes even

one of the least of these commandments and teaches others to do the same will be considered the least in the kingdom of Heaven; but the person who keeps them and teaches them will be considered great in the kingdom of Heaven.

### The new standard higher than the old

²⁰"For I tell you, if your uprightness does not surpass that of the scribes and Pharisees, you will never get into the kingdom of Heaven.

²¹"You have heard how it was said to our ancestors, *You shall not kill*; and if anyone does kill he must answer for it before the court. ²²But I say this to you, anyone who is angry with a brother will answer for it before the court; anyone who calls a brother 'Fool' will answer for it before the Sanhedrin; and anyone who calls him 'Traitor' will answer for it in hell fire. ²³So then, if you are bringing your offering to the altar and there remember that your brother has something against you, ²⁴leave your offering there before the altar, go and be reconciled with your brother first, and then come back and present your offering. ²⁵Come to terms with your opponent in good time while you are still on the way to the court with him, or he may hand you over to the judge and the judge to the officer, and you will be thrown into prison. ²⁶In truth I tell you, you will not get out till you have paid the last penny.

²⁷"You have heard how it was said, *You shall not commit adultery*. ²⁸But I say this to you, if a man looks at a woman lustfully, he has already committed adultery with her in his heart. ²⁹If your right eye should be your downfall, tear it out and throw it away; for it will do you less harm to lose one part of yourself than to have your whole body thrown into hell. ³⁰And if your right hand should be your downfall, cut it off and throw it away; for it will do you less harm to lose one part of yourself than to have your whole body go to hell.

³¹"It has also been said, *Anyone who divorces his wife must give her a writ of dismissal*. ³²But I say this to you, everyone who divorces his wife, except for the case of an illicit marriage, makes her an adulteress; and anyone who marries a divorced woman commits adultery.

³³"Again, you have heard how it was said to our ancestors, *You must not break your oath, but must fulfil your oaths to the Lord*. ³⁴But I say this to you, do not swear at all, either by *heaven*, since that is *God's throne*; ³⁵or by *earth*, since that is *his footstool*; or by Jerusalem, since that is *the city of the great King*. ³⁶Do not swear by your own head either, since you cannot turn a single hair white or black. ³⁷All you need say is 'Yes' if you mean yes, 'No' if you mean no; anything more than this comes from the Evil One.

³⁸"You have heard how it was said: *Eye for eye and tooth for tooth*. ³⁹But I say this to you: offer no resistance to the wicked. On the contrary, if anyone hits you on the right cheek, offer him the other as well; ⁴⁰if someone wishes to go to law with you to get your tunic, let him have your cloak as well. ⁴¹And if anyone requires you to go one mile, go two miles with him. ⁴²Give to anyone who asks you, and if anyone wants to borrow, do not turn away.

⁴³"You have heard how it was said, *You will love your neighbor* and hate your enemy. ⁴⁴But I say this to you, love your enemies and pray for those who persecute you; ⁴⁵so that you may be children of your Father in heaven, for he causes his sun to rise on the bad as well as the good, and sends down rain to fall on the upright and the wicked alike. ⁴⁶For if you love those who love you, what reward will you get? Do not even the tax collectors do as much? ⁴⁷And if you save your greetings for your brothers, are you doing anything exceptional? ⁴⁸Do not even the gentiles do as much? You must therefore be perfect, just as your heavenly Father is perfect."

### Chapter 6: Almsgiving in secret

¹"Be careful not to parade your uprightness in public to attract attention; otherwise you will lose all reward from your Father in heaven. ²So when you give alms, do not have it trumpeted before you; this is what the hypocrites do in the synagogues and in the streets to win human admiration. In truth I tell you, they have had their reward. ³But when you give alms, your left hand must not know what your right is doing; ⁴your almsgiving must be secret, and your Father who sees all that is done in secret will reward you.

### Prayer in secret

⁵"And when you pray, do not imitate the hypocrites; they love to say their prayers standing up in the synagogues and at the street corners for people to see them. In truth I tell you, they have had their reward. ⁶But when you pray, *go to your private room*, shut yourself in, and so pray to your Father who is in that secret place, and your Father who sees all that is done in secret will reward you.

### How to pray. The Lord's Prayer

⁷"In your prayers do not babble as the gentiles do, for they think that by using many words they will make themselves heard. ⁸Do not be like them; your Father knows what you need before you ask him. ⁹So you should pray like this:

> Our Father in heaven,
>   may your name be held holy,
> ¹⁰your kingdom come,
>   your will be done,
>   on earth as in heaven.
> ¹¹Give us today our daily bread.
> ¹²And forgive us our debts,
>   as we have forgiven those who are in debt to us.
> ¹³And do not put us to the test,
>   but save us from the Evil One.

¹⁴"Yes, if you forgive others their failings, your heavenly Father will forgive you yours; ¹⁵but if you do not forgive others, your Father will not forgive your failings either.

### Fasting in secret

¹⁶"When you are fasting, do not put on a gloomy look as the hypocrites do: they go about looking unsightly to let people know they are fasting. In truth I tell you, they have had their reward. ¹⁷But when you fast, put scent on your head and wash your face, ¹⁸so that no one will know you are fasting except your Father who sees all that is done in secret; and your Father who sees all that is done in secret will reward you.

### True treasures

¹⁹"Do not store up treasures for yourselves on earth, where moth and woodworm destroy them and thieves can break in and steal. ²⁰But store up treasures for yourselves in heaven, where neither moth nor woodworm destroys them and thieves cannot break in and steal. ²¹For wherever your treasure is, there will your heart be too."

### Chapter 7: Do not judge

[1]"Do not judge, and you will not be judged; [2]because the judgements you give are the judgements you will get, and the standard you use will be the standard used for you. [3]Why do you observe the splinter in your brother's eye and never notice the great log in your own? [4]And how dare you say to your brother, 'Let me take that splinter out of your eye,' when, look, there is a great log in your own? [5]Hypocrite! Take the log out of your own eye first, and then you will see clearly enough to take the splinter out of your brother's eye.

### Do not profane sacred things

[6]"Do not give dogs what is holy; and do not throw your pearls in front of pigs, or they may trample them and then turn on you and tear you to pieces.

### Effective prayer

[7]"Ask, and it will be given to you; search, and you will find; knock, and the door will be opened to you. [8]Everyone who asks receives; everyone who searches finds; everyone who knocks will have the door opened. [9]Is there anyone among you who would hand his son a stone when he asked for bread? [10]Or would hand him a snake when he asked for a fish? [11]If you, then, evil as you are, know how to give your children what is good, how much more will your Father in heaven give good things to those who ask him!

### The golden rule

[12]"So always treat others as you would like them to treat you; that is the Law and the Prophets.

### The two ways

[13]"Enter by the narrow gate, since the road that leads to destruction is wide and spacious, and many take it; [14]but it is a narrow gate and a hard road that leads to life, and only a few find it."

———————◆———————

# The Teachings of Paul

Jesus' urgent and prophetic words, along with the stories of his miraculous acts, spread like wildfire throughout Judea; but his message won few converts from among the Jewish population. Both the Pharisees and the Sadducees opposed Jesus and accused him of violating Jewish law. While the learned community of Judea rejected Jesus as the biblical Messiah, the Romans condemned him as a subversive and a threat to imperial stability. By the authority of the Roman governor, Pontius Pilate, Jesus was put to death by crucifixion (Figure 8.3), the punishment that the Romans dispensed to thieves and traitors.

Despite the missionary activities of the apostles, a dedicated group of Jesus' followers, only a small percentage of the population of the Roman Empire—scholarly estimates range from ten to fifteen percent—became Christians in the first hundred years after Jesus' death. And those who did convert came mainly from communities where Jewish tradition was not strong.

However, through the efforts of the best-known of the apostles, Paul (d. 65), the message of Jesus gained widespread appeal. A Jewish tentmaker from Tarsus in Asia Minor, Paul had been schooled in both Greek and Hebrew. Though he probably never met Jesus, he became a passionate convert to the teachings of the preacher from Nazareth. Paul is generally believed to have written ten to fourteen of the twenty-seven books of the Christian Scriptures or "New Testament." Paul's most important contributions lie in his having universalized and systematically explained Jesus' message. While Jesus preached only to the Jews, Paul spread the message of Jesus in the non-Jewish communities of Greece, Asia Minor, and Rome, thus earning the title "Apostle to the Gentiles." Preaching among non-Jews, Paul stressed the universal elements in Jesus' teachings, especially salvation by faith. Paul also clarified the meaning of Jesus' life on earth and his role as the Son of God. Calling Jesus the Christ (*Christos*, Greek for "Messiah"), he described Jesus as a sacrifice for human sin, which had entered the world through Adam and Eve's defiance of God in the Garden of Eden. Finally, Paul interpreted the death of Jesus as an act of atonement that "acquitted" humankind from the condemnation merited by original sin. Thus Paul laid the basis for the exaltation of Jesus as the New Adam.

These concepts, which indelibly separated Christianity from both its parent faith, Judaism, and from the classical belief in the innate goodness and freedom of human nature, were set forth in Paul's Epistle to the Church in Rome, parts of which follow. Written ten years before his death, the epistle imparts a message of faith laden with a view of humankind as condemned by "the law of sin and death." Paul anticipated, however, that those who were "baptized in Christ" would "live a new life." Emphasizing the promise of eternal life, Paul thus interpreted the mission of Jesus in terms that were basic to the mystery cults: the death and resurrection of a savior god. However, Paul's focus on moral renewal and redemption from sin would set Christianity apart from the mystery religions. So important was Paul's contribution to the foundations of the new faith that he has been called "the co-founder of Christianity."

## READING 2.3
### From Paul's Epistle to the Church in Rome

#### Chapter 1: Thanksgiving and prayer

[8]First I give thanks to my God through Jesus Christ for all of you because your faith is talked of all over the world. [9]God, whom I serve with my spirit in preaching the gospel of his Son, is my witness that I continually mention you in my prayers, [10]asking always that by some means I may at long last be enabled to visit you, if it is God's will. [11]For I am longing to see you so that I can convey to you some spiritual gift that will be a

**Figure 8.3** *Crucifixion*, west doors of Santa Sabina, Rome, ca. 430 C.E. Wood, 11 × 15¾ in. © Hirmer Fotoarchiv, Munich.

lasting strength, [12]or rather that we may be strengthened together through our mutual faith, yours and mine. [13]I want you to be quite certain too, brothers, that I have often planned to visit you—though up to the present I have always been prevented—in the hope that I might work as fruitfully among you as I have among the gentiles elsewhere. [14]I have an obligation to Greeks as well as barbarians, to the educated as well as the ignorant, [15]and hence the eagerness on my part to preach the gospel to you in Rome too.

### Chapter 2: The Jews are not exempt from the retribution of God

[1]So no matter who you are, if you pass judgement you have no excuse. It is yourself that you condemn when you judge others, since you behave in the same way as those you are condemning. [2]We are well aware that people who behave like that are justly condemned by God. [3]But you—when you judge those who behave like this while you are doing the same yourself—do you think you will escape God's condemnation? [4]Or are you not disregarding his abundant goodness, tolerance and patience, failing to realise that this generosity of God is meant to bring you to repentance? [5]Your stubborn refusal to repent is only storing up retribution for yourself on that Day of retribution when God's just verdicts will be made known. [6]*He will repay everyone as their deeds deserve.* [7]For those

who aimed for glory and honour and immortality by persevering in doing good, there will be eternal life; [8]but for those who out of jealousy have taken for their guide not truth but injustice, there will be the fury of retribution. [9]Trouble and distress will come to every human being who does evil— Jews first, but Greeks as well; [10]glory and honour and peace will come to everyone who does good—Jews first, but Greeks as well. [11]*There is no favouritism with God.*

### Chapter 5: Faith guarantees salvation

[1]So then, now that we have been justified by faith, we are at peace with God through our Lord Jesus Christ; [2]it is through him, by faith, that we have been admitted into God's favour in which we are living, and look forward exultantly to God's glory. [3]Not only that; let us exult, too, in our hardships, understanding that hardship develops perseverance, [4]and perseverance develops a tested character, something that gives us hope, [5]and a hope which will not let us down, because the love of God has been poured into our hearts by the Holy Spirit which has been given to us. [6]When we were still helpless, at the appointed time, Christ died for the godless. [7]You could hardly find anyone ready to die even for someone upright; though it is just possible that, for a really good person, someone might undertake to die. [8]So it is proof of God's own love for us, that

Christ died for us while we were still sinners. [9]How much more can we be sure, therefore, that, now that we have been justified by his death, we shall be saved through him from the retribution of God. [10]For if, while we were enemies, we were reconciled to God through the death of his Son, how much more can we be sure that, being now reconciled, we shall be saved by his life. [11]What is more, we are filled with exultant trust in God, through our Lord Jesus Christ, through whom we have already gained our reconciliation.

### Adam and Jesus Christ

[12]Well then; it was through one man that sin *came into the world*, and through sin death, and thus death has spread through the whole human race because everyone has sinned. [13]Sin already existed in the world before there was any law, even though sin is not reckoned when there is no law. [14]Nonetheless death reigned over all from Adam to Moses, even over those whose sin was not the breaking of a commandment, as Adam's was. He prefigured the One who was to come. . . .

[15]There is no comparison between the free gift and the offence. If death came to many through the offence of one man, how much greater an effect the grace of God has had, coming to so many and so plentifully as the free gift through the one man Jesus Christ! [16]Again, there is no comparison between the gift and the offence of one man. One single offence brought condemnation, but now, after many offences, have come the free gift and so acquittal! [17]It was by one man's offence that death came to reign over all, but how much greater the reign in life of those who receive the fullness of grace and the gift of saving justice, through the one man, Jesus Christ. [18]One man's offence brought condemnation on all humanity; and one man's good act has brought justification and life to all humanity. [19]Just as by one man's disobedience many were made sinners, so by one man's obedience are many to be made upright. [20]When law came on the scene, it was to multiply the offences. But however much sin increased, grace was always greater; [21]so that as sin's reign brought death, so grace was to rule through saving justice that leads to eternal life through Jesus Christ our Lord.

### Chapter 6: Baptism

[1]What should we say then? Should we remain in sin so that grace may be given the more fully? [2]Out of the question! We have died to sin; how could we go on living in it? [3]You cannot have forgotten that all of us, when we were baptised into Christ Jesus, were baptised into his death. [4]So by our baptism into his death we were buried with him, so that as Christ was raised from the dead by the Father's glorious power, we too should begin living a new life. [5]If we have been joined to him by dying a death like his, so we shall be by a resurrection like his; [6]realising that our former self was crucified with him, so that the self which belonged to sin should be destroyed and we should be freed from the slavery of sin. [7]Someone who has died, of course, no longer has to answer for sin.

[8]But we believe that, if we died with Christ, then we shall live with him too. [9]We know that Christ has been raised from the dead and will never die again. Death has no power over him any more. [10]For by dying, he is dead to sin once and for all, and now the life that he lives is life with God. [11]In the same way, you must see yourselves as being dead to sin but alive for God in Christ Jesus.

### Chapter 8: The life of the spirit

[1]Thus, condemnation will never come to those who are in Christ Jesus, [2]because the law of the Spirit which gives life in Christ Jesus has set you free from the law of sin and death. [3]What the Law could not do because of the weakness of human nature, God did, sending his own Son in the same human nature as any sinner to be a sacrifice for sin, and condemning sin in that human nature. [4]This was so that the Law's requirements might be fully satisfied in us as we direct our lives not by our natural inclinations but by the Spirit. [5]Those who are living by their natural inclinations have their minds on the things human nature desires; those who live in the Spirit have their minds on spiritual things. [6]And human nature has nothing to look forward to but death, while the Spirit looks forward to life and peace, [7]because the outlook of disordered human nature is opposed to God, since it does not submit to God's Law, and indeed it cannot, [8]and those who live by their natural inclinations can never be pleasing to God. . . .

———————◆———————

# The Spread of Christianity

A variety of historical factors contributed to the slow but growing reception to Christianity within the Roman Empire. The decline of the Roman Republic had left in its wake large gaps between the rich and the poor. Octavian's efforts to restore the old Roman values of duty and civic pride failed to offset increasing impersonalism and bureaucratic corruption. Furthermore, as early as the second century B.C.E., Germanic tribes had been migrating into the West and assaulting Rome's borders (see chapter 10). Repeatedly, these nomadic people put Rome on the defensive and added to the prevailing sense of insecurity. Amidst widespread oppression and grinding poverty, Christianity promised redemption from sins, personal immortality, and a life to come from which material adversities were absent. The message of Jesus was easy to understand, free of cumbersome regulations (characteristic of Judaism) and costly rituals (characteristic of the mystery cults), and, in contrast to Mithraism, it was accessible to all—male and female, rich and poor, freeman and slave. The unique feature of the new faith, however, was its historical credibility, that is, the fact that Jesus—unlike the elusive gods of the mystery cults or the remote Yahweh—had actually lived among men and women and had practiced the morality he preached.

Nevertheless, at the outset the new religion failed to win official approval. While both Roman religion and the mystery cults were receptive to many gods, Christianity—like Judaism—professed monotheism. Christians not only refused to worship the emperor as divine but also denied the existence of the Roman gods. Even more threatening to the state was the fact that Christians refused to serve in the Roman army. While the Romans dealt with the Jews by destroying Jerusalem, how might they annihilate a people whose kingdom was in heaven? During the first century, Christian converts were expelled from the city of Rome, but during the late third century—a time of famine, plague, and war—Christians who refused to make sacrifices to the Roman gods of state suffered horrific forms of persecution: They were tortured, burned, beheaded, or thrown to wild beasts in the public amphitheaters. Christian martyrs astonished Roman audiences by going to their deaths joyously proclaiming their anticipation of a better life in the hereafter.

In 313, public persecutions came to an end, as the emperor Constantine issued the Edict of Milan. The Edict, which proclaimed religious toleration in the West, not only liberated Christians from physical and political oppression, but encouraged the development of Christianity as a legitimate faith. Christian leaders were free to establish a uniform doctrine of belief, an administrative hierarchy, the rituals of worship, and a symbolic vocabulary for religious expression (see chapter 9). By the end of the fourth century, the minor religious sect called Christianity had become the official religion of the Roman Empire.

## Buddhism and the Message of the Buddha

The reasons why similar world-historical developments occur at approximately the same time within two remotely related cultures is a mystery that historians have never solved. One of the most interesting such parallels is that between the spread of Buddhism in the East and the emergence of Christianity in the West, both of which occurred during the first century of the Christian era. Siddhartha Gautama, known as the Buddha ("Enlightened One"), lived in India some three to five centuries before Jesus—scholars still disagree as to whether his life spanned the years 560–480 or 440–360 B.C.E. Born into a princely Hindu family, Siddhartha was well-educated and protected from the experience of pain and suffering. At the age of nineteen, he married his cousin and fathered a son. As he matured, however, he began to realize that the lives of most people were far from pleasant. His discovery of the three "truths" of existence—sickness, old age, and death—led the twenty-nine-year-old Siddhartha to renounce his wealth, abandon his wife and child, and begin the quest for inner illumination. With shaven head, yellow robe, and begging bowl, he followed the way of the Hindu ascetic. After six years, however, he concluded that the life of self-denial was futile. Turning inward, Siddhartha

**Figure 8.4** *Seated Buddha*, from the Gandharan region of Northwest Pakistan, ca. 200 C.E. Gray schist, 51 × 31 in. The Cleveland Museum of Art. Leonard Hanna, Jr. Bequest. CMA 61.418.

sat beneath a Bo (fig) tree (Figure **8.4**) and began the work of meditation that would bring him to enlightenment—the omniscient consciousness of reality. Meditation had led Siddhartha to the full perception that the cause of human sufferings was desire, that is, attachment to material things and ignorance and, hence, illusion. For the next forty years—he died at the age of eighty—Siddhartha preached a message of humility and compassion, the pursuit of which might lead his followers to *nirvana*, the ultimate release from illusion and from the Wheel of Rebirth.

The Buddha's message was simple: Any individual might reach *nirvana* by avoiding all extremes in accordance with the Eightfold Path: right views, right intention, right speech, right action, right livelihood, right effort, right mindfulness, and right concentration. The Buddhist's reward was not—as with Christianity—the achievement of personal immortality but, rather, escape from reincarnation (the rebirth of the soul in another bodily form) and, thus, enlightened release from the endless cycle of death and rebirth. To extinguish the Self and its desire was the ultimate salvation. The Buddha restated the Hindu rejection of material wealth and annihilation of worldly desires. But in contrast to the caste-oriented Hinduism of his time, he held that enlightenment might be achieved by all people, regardless of gender or caste (see chapter 3). Opposing the existing forms of religious worship and renouncing reliance on the popular gods of the Vedas (see chapter 2), the Buddha urged his followers to work out their own salvation. Their spiritual journey would take them on the Middle Path, which consists of the Four Noble Truths: Pain is universal, desire causes pain, ceasing to desire relieves pain, and (finally) the practice of the Eightfold Path leads to release from pain. Notably, the second and third Truths call to mind the precepts of the Stoics, while the Middle Path has its Hellenic counterpart in Aristotle's Golden Mean.

Like Jesus, the Buddha was an eloquent teacher whose concerns were profoundly ethical. Just as Jesus criticized Judaism's heavy emphasis on ritual, so Siddhartha attacked the existing forms of Hindu worship, including animal sacrifice and the authority of the Vedas. In this sense, both religions—Christianity and Buddhism—were products of the reformation of older world faiths: Judaism and Hinduism. Soon after his enlightenment, Siddhartha assembled a group of disciples, five of whom founded the first Buddhist monastic order. As with Jesus, Siddhartha's life came to be surrounded by miraculous tales, which, along with his sermons, were preserved and recorded by his followers. For instance, legend has it that Siddhartha was born miraculously from the right side of his mother, Queen Maya, and at that very moment the tree she touched in the royal garden burst into bloom.

The Buddha himself wrote nothing, but his disciples memorized his teachings and set them down during the first century B.C.E. in three main books, the *Pitakas* or "Baskets of the Law." These works, written in Pali and Sanskrit, were divided into instructional chapters known as *sutras* (Sanskrit for "thread"). The most famous of the Buddha's sermons is one that he preached to his disciples at the Deer Park in Benares (in Northeast India). The *Sermon at Benares*, part of which is reproduced here, urges the abandonment of behavioral extremes and the pursuit of the Eightfold Path of right conduct. In its emphasis on faith over good works and on the renunciation of worldly pleasures, the *Sermon at Benares* has much in common with Jesus' Sermon on the Mount. Comparable also to Jesus' teachings (see Matthew 5:11, for instance) is the Buddha's regard for loving kindness that "commends the return of good for evil"—a concept central to the *Sermon on Abuse*.

## READING 2.4
## From the Buddha's *Sermon at Benares*

"There are two extremes, O bhikkhus,[1] which the man     1
who has given up the world ought not to follow—the habitual practice, on the one hand, of self-indulgence which is unworthy, vain and fit only for the worldly-minded—and the habitual practice, on the other hand, of self-mortification, which is painful, useless and unprofitable.

"Neither abstinence from fish or flesh, nor going naked, nor shaving the head, nor wearing matted hair, nor dressing in a rough garment, nor covering oneself with dirt, nor sacrificing to Agni,[2] will cleanse a man who     10
is not free from delusions.

"Reading the Vedas, making offerings to priests, or sacrifices to the gods, self-mortification by heat or cold, and many such penances performed for the sake of immortality, these do not cleanse the man who is not free from delusions.

"Anger, drunkenness, obstinacy, bigotry, deception, envy, self-praise, disparaging others, superciliousness and evil intentions constitute uncleanness; not verily the eating of flesh.     20

"A middle path, O bhikkhus, avoiding the two extremes, had been discovered by the Tathāgata[3]—a path which opens the eyes, and bestows understanding, which leads to peace of mind, to the higher wisdom, to full enlightenment, to Nirvāna!

"What is that middle path, O bhikkhus, avoiding these two extremes, discovered by the Tathāgata—that path which opens the eyes, and bestows understanding, which leads to peace of mind, to the higher wisdom, to full enlightenment, to Nirvāna?     30

"Let me teach you, O bhikkhus, the middle path, which keeps aloof from both extremes. By suffering, the emaciated devotee produces confusion and sickly thoughts in his mind. Mortification is not conducive even to worldly knowledge; how much less to a triumph over the senses!

"He who fills his lamp with water will not dispel the darkness, and he who tries to light a fire with rotten wood will fail. And how can any one be free from self by leading a wretched life, if he does not succeed in quenching the fires of lust, if he still hankers after either worldly or     40
heavenly pleasures. But he in whom self has become extinct is free from lust; he will desire neither worldly nor heavenly pleasures, and the satisfaction of his natural wants will not defile him. However, let him be moderate, let him eat and drink according to the needs of the body.

"Sensuality is enervating; the self-indulgent man is a slave to his passions, and pleasure-seeking is degrading and vulgar.

"But to satisfy the necessities of life is not evil. To keep the body in good health is a duty, for otherwise we     50
shall not be able to trim the lamp of wisdom, and keep our mind strong and clear. Water surrounds the lotus-flower, but does not wet its petals.

"This is the middle path, O bhikkhus, that keeps aloof from both extremes."

And the Blessed One spoke kindly to his disciples, pitying them for their errors, and pointing out the

---

[1]Disciples.     [2]The Vedic god of fire, associated with sun and lightning.
[3]"The successor to his predecessors in office," another name for the Buddha.

uselessness of their endeavors, and the ice of ill-will that chilled their hearts melted away under the gentle warmth of the Master's persuasion. 60

Now the Blessed One set the wheel of the most excellent law[4] rolling, and he began to preach to the five bhikkhus, opening to them the gate of immortality, and showing them the bliss of Nirvāna.

The Buddha said:

"The spokes of the wheel are the rules of pure conduct: justice is the uniformity of their length; wisdom is the tire; modesty and thoughtfulness are the hub in which the immovable axle of truth is fixed.

"He who recognizes the existence of suffering, its 70 cause, its remedy, and its cessation has fathomed the four noble truths. He will walk in the right path.

"Right views will be the torch to light his way. Right aspirations will be his guide. Right speech will be his dwelling-place on the road. His gait will be straight, for it is right behavior. His refreshments will be the right way of earning his livelihood. Right efforts will be his steps: right thoughts his breath; and right contemplation will give him the peace that follows in his footprints.

"Now, this, O bhikkhus, is the noble truth concerning 80 suffering:

"Birth is attended with pain, decay is painful, disease is painful, death is painful. Union with the unpleasant is painful, painful is separation from the pleasant; and any craving that is unsatisfied, that too is painful. In brief, bodily conditions which spring from attachment are painful.

"This, then, O bhikkhus, is the noble truth concerning suffering.

"Now this, O bhikkhus, is the noble truth concerning the origin of suffering: 90

"Verily, it is that craving which causes the renewal of existence, accompanied by sensual delight, seeking satisfaction now here, now there, the craving for the gratification of the passions, the craving for a future life, and the craving for happiness in this life.

"This, then, O bhikkhus, is the noble truth concerning the origin of suffering.

"Now this, O bhikkhus, is the noble truth concerning the destruction of suffering:

"Verily, it is the destruction, in which no passion 100 remains, of this very thirst; it is the laying aside of, the being free from, the dwelling no longer upon this thirst.

"This, then, O bhikkhus, is the noble truth concerning the destruction of suffering.

"Now this, O bhikkhus, is the noble truth concerning the way which leads to the destruction of sorrow. Verily! it is this noble eightfold path; that is to say:

"Right views; right aspirations; right speech; right behavior; right livelihood; right effort; right thoughts; and right contemplation. 110

"This, then, O bhikkhus, is the noble truth concerning the destruction of sorrow.

"By the practice of loving kindness I have attained liberation of heart, and thus I am assured that I shall never return in renewed births. I have even now attained Nirvāna."

And when the Blessed One had thus set the royal chariot wheel of truth rolling onward, a rapture thrilled through the universes. . . .

[4]The Wheel of the Law, or *Dharma*.

## From the Buddha's *Sermon on Abuse*

And the Blessed One observed the ways of society and 1 noticed how much misery came from malignity and foolish offenses done only to gratify vanity and self-seeking pride.

And the Buddha said: "If a man foolishly does me wrong, I will return to him the protection of my ungrudging love; the more evil comes from him, the more good shall go from me; the fragrance of goodness always comes to me, and the harmful air of evil goes to him."

A foolish man learning that the Buddha observed the principle of great love which commends the return of 10 good for evil, came and abused him. The Buddha was silent, pitying his folly.

When the man had finished his abuse, the Buddha asked him, saying: "Son, if a man declined to accept a present made to him, to whom would it belong?" And he answered: "In that case it would belong to the man who offered it."

"My son," said the Buddha, "thou has railed at me, but I decline to accept thy abuse, and request thee to keep it thyself. Will it not be a source of misery to thee? 20 As the echo belongs to the sound, and the shadow to the substance, so misery will overtake the evil-doer without fail."

The abuser made no reply, and the Buddha continued:

"A wicked man who reproaches a virtuous one is like one who looks up and spits at heaven; the spittle soils not the heaven, but comes back and defiles his own person.

"The slanderer is like one who flings dust at another when the wind is contrary; the dust does but return on him who threw it. The virtuous man cannot be hurt and 30 the misery that the other would inflict comes back on himself."

The abuser went away ashamed, but he came again and took refuge in the Buddha, the Dharma,[1] and the Sangha[2]. . . .

———————◆———————

# *The Spread of Buddhism*

During the third century B.C.E. the emperor Asoka (273–232 B.C.E.) made Buddhism the state religion of India. Asoka's active role in spreading Buddhism anticipated Constantine's labors on behalf of Christianity; but Asoka went even further: He sent Buddhist missionaries as far West as Greece and Southeast into Ceylon (present-day Sri Lanka). In spite of Asoka's efforts to give the world a unified faith, the Buddha's teachings generated varying interpretations and numerous factions. By the first century C.E., there were as many as five hundred major and minor Buddhist sects in India alone. In general, however, two principal divisions of Buddhism emerged: Hinayana Buddhism and Mahayana Buddhism. Hinayana Buddhism, which emphasizes the personal pursuit of *nirvana*, remains close to the original teachings of the Buddha. Mahayana Buddhism, on the other hand, elevated the Buddha to the level of a divine

[1]The law of Righteousness; the Wheel of the Law.
[2]An assemblage of those who vow to pursue the Buddhist life.

**Figure 8.5** *Standing Bodhisattva*, from the Gandharan region of Northwest Pakistan, late second century C.E. Gray schist, height approx. 3 ft. Courtesy, Museum of Fine Arts, Boston. Helen and Alice Colburn Fund.

being and added a large body of new teachings and legends. Whereas the Buddha had urged his followers to work out their own salvation, Mahayana Buddhists taught that the Buddha was the path to salvation, indeed, that he was a divinity who had come to earth in the form of a man to assist humankind. Other gods, such as the gods of Hinduism, were incarnations of the Buddha, who himself had appeared in different bodily forms in his previous lives. Moreover, Mahayana Buddhists held that there were many compassionate beings, both before and after the Buddha, who had postponed reaching *nirvana* in order to help suffering humankind. These "Buddhas-to-be," known as *bodhisattvas*, were the heroes of Buddhism; and much like the Christian saints, they became objects of many popular Buddhist cults. The favorite Chinese female *bodhisattva*, Guanyin—originally pictured in Indian art as a mustached male (Figure 8.5)—was widely regarded as a goddess of mercy and worshiped much in the way that Roman Catholics and Orthodox Christians honor the Virgin Mary. For all the similarities between Christianity and Buddhism, however, one profound difference persists: The concept of human sinfulness, evident in the writings of Paul, is absent from Buddhist thought and belief.

Despite Asoka's vigorous leadership, the Buddha's teachings never gained widespread popularity in India. The strength of the established Hindu tradition in India (like that of Judaism in Judea) and the resistance of the Brahmin caste to Buddhist egalitarianism ultimately hindered the success of Buddhism, and by the seventh century Buddhism was absorbed into Hinduism. In China, however, where Mahayana Buddhism became popular, the faith gained a considerable following. Here, as in many other parts of Asia, the Buddha was regarded not simply as a teacher or reformer, but as a savior whose intercession on one's behalf would free the faithful from physical suffering. Indeed, Chinese Buddhism developed the concept of Heaven in place of the more abstract idea of *nirvana*. Buddhism's tolerance for other religions enhanced its popularity and its universal appeal. Mahayana, the "Great Vehicle" of Buddhism, brought a message of hope and salvation to millions of people in China, Korea, Japan, and Vietnam, while the more austere Hinayana or "Little Vehicle" of Buddhism became the major faith in Ceylon (Sri Lanka), Burma (Myanmar), Thailand, and Cambodia.

Buddhism entered China during the first century C.E., and rose to prominence during the last turbulent decades of the Han Era. Although comparisons reduce subtle differences to facile analogy, certain similarities between the Roman and Han empires are irrefutable (see chapter 7). As in Rome, the late Han Era confronted increasing conflicts between wealthy landowners (who deemed themselves exempt from taxation) and impoverished and dissatisfied peasants. The repeated attacks by Mongol tribes along the northern borders of the Han Empire, like those of the Germanic tribes along the frontiers of the Roman Empire, aggravated the prevailing internal disorders and fostered a sense of insecurity. And just as classical humanism gave way to mysticism in the West, the strongly humanistic Confucianism in China felt the challenge of more intuitive forms of religious speculation. During the first century C.E., the Buddha's sermons were translated into Chinese, and over the following centuries, Buddhism was popularized in China by the writings of the Indian poet Asvaghosha (d. 150?). Asvaghosha's Sanskrit descriptions of the life of the Buddha, which became available in Chinese in the year 420, would become the literary medium for Mahayana Buddhism.

In China, Confucianism and Daoism were easily reconciled with Buddhism, which assumed many different forms. Buddhist "paradise sects" closely resembling the mystery cults of Southwest Asia promised their adherents rebirth in an idyllic, heavenly realm called "the Pure Land of the West." Still another Buddhist sect, strongly influenced by Daoism, emphasized the role of meditation and visionary insight in reaching *nirvana*. Known in China as Chan ("meditation") and in Japan as Zen, this sect held that enlightenment could not be attained by rational means but, rather, through intense concentration that led to a spontaneous awakening of the mind. Among the tools of Zen masters were such mind-sharpening riddles as: "You know the sound of two hands clapping; what, then, is the sound of one hand clapping?" The Zen monk's attention to such queries forced him to move beyond reason. Legend has it that heavily caffeinated tea was introduced from India to China and Japan as an aid to prolonging meditation.

## SUMMARY

The world into which Jesus was born was ripe for religious revitalization. Roman religion focused on nature deities and civic gods who provided little in the way of personal spiritual comfort. The mystery cults promised rebirth and resurrection to devotees of fertility gods and goddesses. The province of Judea, beset by religious and political factionalism, sought apocalyptic deliverance from the Roman yoke. The message preached by Jesus demanded an abiding faith in God, compassion for one's fellow human beings, and the renunciation of material wealth. In an age when people were required to serve the state, Jesus asked that they serve God. The apostle Paul universalized Jesus' message by preaching among non-Jews. He explained Jesus' death as atonement for sin and anticipated eternal life for the followers of the *Christos*.

The religion that had begun with the teachings of Siddhartha Gautama in India swept through East Asia in the very centuries that Christianity emerged in the West. Although rooted in different traditions, the two world faiths had much in common, especially in the message of compassion, humility, and right conduct preached by their founders. Christianity and Buddhism had only limited impact in the lands in which their founders were born, but both religions gained popularity in empires that flourished at the same time: Christianity in the Roman world-state, and Buddhism under the late Han dynasty in China. With Pauline Christianity, as with Mahayana Buddhism, the belief in a savior god, the promise of salvation for all human beings, and uncompromising moral goodness provided spiritual alternatives to the prevailing materialism of imperial Rome and Han China. On the soil of these great but declining empires were cast the seeds of two world-historical religions that are still followed by millions of people today.

### GLOSSARY

**asceticism** strict self-denial and self-discipline

**bodhisattva** (Sanskrit, "one whose essence is enlightenment") a being who has postponed his or her own entry into *nirvana* in order to assist others in reaching that goal; worshiped as a deity in Mahayana Buddhism

**Messiah** Anointed One, or Savior; in Greek, *Christos*

**rabbi** a Jewish teacher and master, trained in the Jewish law

**sutra** (Sanskrit, "thread") an instructional chapter or discourse in any of the sacred books of Buddhism

### SUGGESTIONS FOR READING

Baldwin, Summerfield. *The Organization of Medieval Christianity.* Gloucester, Mass.: Peter Smith, 1962.
Brown, Peter. *The World of Late Antiquity, A.D. 150–750.* New York: Norton, 1989.
Crosson, John Dominic. *Jesus: A Revolutionary Biography.* New York: Harper, 1993.
Ferguson, Everett. *Backgrounds of Early Christianity.* Grand Rapids, Mich.: Eerdmans, 1987.
Goodenough, E. R. *The Church in the Roman Empire.* New York: Holt, 1931.
Humphreys, Christmas. *Buddhism.* London: Cassell, 1962.
Meeks, W. A. *The First Urban Christians: The Social World of the Apostle Paul.* New Haven: Yale University Press, 1982.
Ross, Nancy W. *Three Ways of Asian Wisdom.* New York: Simon and Schuster, 1966.
Strong, John S. *The Experience of Buddhism: Sources and Interpretations.* Belmont, Calif.: Wadsworth, 1995.
Walsh, Michael. *The Triumph of the Meek: Why Christianity Succeeded.* New York: Harper, 1986.
Wilson, A. N. *Jesus.* New York: Norton, 1992.

# 9
# The Language of Faith: Symbolism and the Arts

Christianity began its rise to world significance amidst an empire beset by increasing domestic difficulties and the assaults of barbarian nomads (see chapter 11). The last great Roman emperors, Diocletian (245–316) and Constantine (ca. 274–337), made valiant efforts to restructure the Empire and reverse military and economic decline. Resolved to govern Rome's sprawling territories more efficiently, Diocletian divided the Empire into western and eastern halves and appointed a coemperor to share the burden of administration and defense. After Diocletian retired, Constantine levied new taxes and made unsuccessful efforts to revive a money economy. By means of the Edict of Milan (313), which proclaimed toleration of all religions (including the fledgling Christianity), Constantine tried to heal Rome's internal divisions. Having failed to breathe new life into the waning Empire, however, in 330 he moved the seat of power from the beleaguered city of Rome to the Eastern capital of the Empire, Byzantium, which he renamed Constantinople.

While the Roman Empire languished in the West, the East Roman or Byzantine Empire—the economic heart of the Roman world—prospered. Located at the crossroads of Europe and Asia, Constantinople was the hub of a vital trade network and the heir to the cultural traditions of Greece, Rome, and Asia. Byzantine emperors formed a firm alliance with Church leaders and worked to create an empire that flourished until the mid-fifteenth century. The Slavic regions of Eastern Europe (including Russia) converted to Orthodox Christianity during the ninth and tenth centuries, thus sharing the spiritual life of the city that Constantine had designated the "New Rome."

As Christians in Rome and Byzantium worked to formulate an effective language of faith, Buddhists in India, China, and Southeast Asia were developing their own vocabulary of religious expression. Buddhism inspired a glorious outpouring of art, architecture, and music that—like early Christian art in the West—nourished the spiritual needs of millions of people throughout the East.

## The Christian Identity

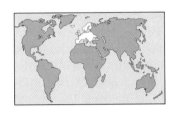

Between the fourth and sixth centuries, Christianity grew from a small, dynamic sect into a full-fledged religion; and its ministerial agent, the Roman Catholic Church, came to replace the Roman Empire as the dominant authority in the West. The history of these developments sheds light on the formation of the Christian identity.

In the first centuries after the death of Jesus, there was little unity of belief and practice among those who called themselves Christians. But after the legalization of the faith in 313, the followers of Jesus moved toward fixing Church hierarchy, **dogma** (prescribed doctrine), and **liturgy** (the rituals for public worship). From Rome, Church leaders in the West borrowed the Latin language, the Roman legal system (which would become the basis for Church, or **canon, law**), and Roman methods of architectural construction. The Church retained Diocletian's administrative divisions, appointing archbishops to oversee the provinces, bishops in the dioceses, and priests in the parishes. As Rome had been the hub of the Western Empire, so it became the administrative center of the new faith, especially as the bishop of Rome rose to prominence within the Church hierarchy. When Church leaders in Constantinople and Antioch contested the administrative primacy of Rome, the bishop of Rome, Leo the Great (ca. 390–461), advanced the "Petrine Doctrine," claiming that Roman pontiffs inherited their position as the successors to Peter, the First Apostle and the principal evangelist of Rome. As Roman emperors had held supreme authority over the state, so Roman Catholic popes—the temporal representatives of Christ—would govern Western Christendom. The new spiritual order in the West was thus patterned after imperial Rome.

While it was essential to the success of the new faith to create a functional administrative hierarchy, it was equally important to formulate a uniform doctrine of belief. As Christianity spread, the story of Jesus and the meaning of his message provoked various kinds of inquiry. Was Jesus human or divine? What was the status of Jesus in relation to God? Such fundamental questions drew conflicting answers. To resolve them, Church officials would convene to hammer out a systematic explanation of the life, death, and resurrection of Jesus. The first **ecumenical** (worldwide) council of churchmen was called by the emperor Constantine. It met at Nicaea (present-day Iznik) in 325 C.E. At the Council of Nicaea, a consensus of opinion among Church representatives laid the basis for Christian dogma. It was resolved—to the objection of some dissenting Eastern churchmen—that Jesus was of one substance (or essence) with God the Father. The council issued a statement of Christian belief known as the Nicene Creed. A version of the Nicene Creed issued in 381 and still used by Eastern Orthodox Christians is reproduced below. It pledges commitment to a variety of miraculous phenomena, including virgin birth, the resurrection of the dead, and a mystical Trinity comprising Jesus, God the Father, and the Holy Spirit. The principal formula of Christian belief, it stands as the turning point between classical rationalism and Christian mysticism. In place of reason and the evidence of the senses, it advances faith and the intuition of truths that transcend ordinary understanding. As such, it anticipates the shift from a homocentric classical worldview to the God-centered medieval worldview.

## READING 2.5
## The Nicene Creed

We believe in one God the Father All-Sovereign, maker    1
of heaven and earth, and of all things visible and invisible;
And in one Lord Jesus Christ, the only-begotten Son of
God, Begotten of the Father before all the ages, Light of
Light, true God of true God, begotten not made, of one
substance with the Father, through whom all things were
made; who for us men and for our salvation came down
from the heavens, and was made flesh of the Holy Spirit
and the Virgin Mary, and became man, and was crucified
for us under Pontius Pilate, and suffered and was buried,    10
and rose again on the third day according to the Scriptures,
and ascended into the heavens, and sitteth on the right
hand of the Father, and cometh again with glory to judge
living and dead, of whose kingdom there shall be no end:
And in the Holy Spirit, the Lord and the Life-giver, that
proceedeth from the Father, who with Father and Son is
worshipped together and glorified together, who spake
through the prophets:
In one holy Catholic and Apostolic Church:
We acknowledge one baptism unto remission of sins.    20
We look for a resurrection of the dead, and the life of the
age to come.

———————◆———————

## Christian Monasticism

Early Christians looked upon life on earth as a period of probation and preparation for the hereafter. What better way to avoid worldly temptation and preserve Christian ideals than to separate oneself from the secular world? Even before the coming of Christ, communal asceticism was a way of life among, for instance, the Essenes in the West and Buddhist monks in Asia. The earliest Christian monastics (the word comes from the Greek *monas*, meaning "alone") lived in the deserts of Egypt. Fasting, poverty, and celibacy were the essential features of the ascetic lifestyle instituted by the Greek bishop Saint Basil (329–379) and still followed by monastics of the Eastern Church.

In the West, the impulse to withdraw from the affairs of the world became more intense as the last remnants of classical civilization disappeared. In 529, the same year that Plato's Academy closed its doors in Athens, the first Western monastic community was founded at Monte Cassino in Southern Italy. Named after its founder, Benedict of Nursia (ca. 480–543), the Benedictine rule required that its members take vows of poverty (the renunciation of all material possessions), chastity (abstention from sexual activity), and obedience to the governing **abbot**, or father of the monastic community. Benedictine monks followed a routine of work that freed them from dependence on the secular world, balanced by at least two hours of religious study and the daily recitation of the Divine Office, a cycle of prayers that marked eight devotional intervals in the twenty-four-hour period. The Benedictine motto, *mens sana in corpore sano* ("a sound mind in a sound body"), expresses the standard of moderation that characterized Benedictine monasticism.

Monastics and church fathers alike generally regarded women as the daughters of Eve, inherently sinful and dangerous as objects of sexual temptation. The Church prohibited women from holding positions of Church authority and from receiving ordination as **secular clerics** (that is, priests); however, women were not excluded from joining the **regular clergy** (that is, those who follow the rule or *regula* of a monastic order). In Egypt, some twenty thousand women—twice the number of men—lived in monastic communities as nuns. In the West, aristocratic women often turned their homes into Benedictine nunneries, where they provided religious education for women of all classes. Although such women maintained monastic communities on equal terms with men, the perception of women as weak, self-indulgent, and intrinsically inferior to men prevailed among churchmen throughout the Middle Ages.

From the fifth century on, members of the regular clergy played an increasingly important role in Western intellectual history. As Greek and Roman sources of education dried up and fewer men and women learned to read and write, the task of preserving the history and literature of the past fell to the last bastions of literacy: the monasteries. Benedictine monks and nuns hand-copied and illustrated Christian as well as classical manuscripts, and stored them in their libraries. Over the centuries, Benedictine monasteries sponsored programs of education (usually available only to the upper classes), contributed to the development of sacred music and art, and produced a continuous stream of missionaries, scholars, and Church reformers.

## The Latin Church Fathers

In the formation of Christian dogma and liturgy in the West, the most important figures were four Latin scholars who lived between the fourth and sixth centuries: Jerome, Ambrose, Gregory, and Augustine. Saint Jerome (ca. 342–420), a Christian educated in Rome, translated into Latin both the Hebrew Bible, which Christians referred to as the "Old Testament," and the Greek books of the "New Testament." This mammoth task resulted in the Vulgate, a Latin edition of Scripture that became the official Bible of the Roman Catholic Church. Although Jerome considered pagan culture a distraction from the spiritual life, he admired the writers of classical antiquity and did not hesitate to plunder the spoils of classicism—and Hebraism—to build the edifice of a new faith.

Like Jerome, Ambrose (339–397) fused Hebrew, Greek, and Southwest Asian traditions in formulating Christian doctrine and liturgy. A Roman aristocrat who became bishop of Milan, Ambrose wrote some of the earliest Christian hymns for congregational use. Influenced by eastern Mediterranean chants and Hebrew psalms, Ambrose's hymns are characterized by a lyrical simplicity that made them models of religious expression. In the hymn that follows, divine light is the unifying theme. The reference to God as the "Light of light" distinctly recalls the cult of Mithras, as well as Plato's analogy between the Good and the Sun. Culminating in a burst of praise for the triune God, the hymn conveys a mood of buoyant optimism similar to that evoked in the Egyptian "Hymn to the Aten" (see chapter 2).

## READING 2.6

### Saint Ambrose's "Ancient Morning Hymn"

O Splendor of God's glory bright,          1
O Thou who bringest light from light,
O Light of light, light's living spring,
O Day, all days illumining!

O Thou true Sun, on us Thy glance          5
Let fall in royal radiance;
The Spirit's sanctifying beam
Upon our earthly senses stream.

The Father, too, our prayers implore,
Father of glory evermore,          10
The Father of all grace and might,
To banish sin from our delight.

To guide whate'er we nobly do,
With love all envy to subdue,
To make ill-fortune turn to fair,          15
And give us grace our wrongs to bear.

Rejoicing may this day go hence;
Like virgin dawn our innocence,
Like fiery noon our faith appear,
Nor know the gloom of twilight drear.          20

Morn in her rosy car is borne:
Let him come forth, our perfect morn,
The Word in God the Father one,
The Father perfect in the Son.

All laud to God the Father be;          25
All praise, eternal Son, to Thee;
All glory, as is ever meet,
To God the holy Paraclete.[1]

————————◆————————

The contribution of the Roman aristocrat Gregory the Great (540–604) was vital to the development of early Church government. Elected to the papacy in 590, Gregory established the administrative machinery by which all subsequent popes would govern the Church of Rome. A born organizer, Gregory sent missionaries to convert England to Christianity; he extended the temporal authority of the Roman Church throughout Western Europe; and with equal efficiency, he organized the liturgical music of the early Church (see p. 32).

The most profound and influential of all the Latin church fathers was Augustine of Hippo (354–430). A native of Roman Africa and an intellectual who came under the spell of both Plotinus and Paul, Augustine converted to Christianity at the age of thirty-three. His treatises on the nature of the soul, free will, and the meaning of evil made him the greatest philosopher of Christian antiquity. Before his conversion to Christianity, Augustine had enjoyed a sensual and turbulent youth, marked by womanizing, gambling, and fathering an illegitimate child. Augustine's lifelong conflict between his love of worldly pleasures, dominated by what he called his "lower self," and his love of God, exercised by the "higher part of our nature," is the focus of his fascinating and self-scrutinizing autobiography known as the *Confessions*. Here, Augustine makes a fundamental distinction between physical and spiritual satisfaction, arguing that "no bodily pleasure, however great it might be . . . [is] worthy of comparison, or even of mention, beside the happiness of the life of the saints." The dualistic model of the human being as the locus of warring elements—the "unclean body" and the "purified

_____
[1] Holy Spirit.

soul"—drew heavily on the neoplatonist duality of Matter and Spirit and the Pauline promise that the sin of Adam might be cleansed by the sacrifice of Jesus.

In the extract below from his *Confessions*, Augustine identifies the three everyday temptations that endanger his soul: the lust of the flesh, the lust of the eyes, and the ambition of the world.

## READING 2.7

# From Saint Augustine's *Confessions*

Certainly you command me to restrain myself from the *lust of the flesh, the lust of the eyes, and the ambition of the world*. You commanded me to abstain from sleeping with a mistress, and with regard to marriage you advised me to take a better course than the one that was permitted me. And since you gave me the power, it was done, even before I became a dispenser of your Sacrament. But there still live in that memory of mine, of which I have spoken so much, images of the things which my habit has fixed there. These images come into my thoughts, and, though when I am awake they are strengthless, in sleep they not only cause pleasure but go so far as to obtain assent and something very like reality. These images, though real, have such an effect on my soul, in my flesh, that false visions in my sleep obtain from me what true visions cannot when I am awake. Surely, Lord my God, I am myself when I am asleep? And yet there is a very great difference between myself and myself in that moment of time when I pass from being awake to being asleep or come back again from sleep to wakefulness. Where then is my reason which, when I am awake, resists such suggestions and remains unshaken if the realities themselves were presented to it? Do reason's eyes close with the eyes of the body? Does reason go to sleep when the bodily senses sleep? If so, how does it happen that even in our sleep we do often resist and, remembering our purpose and most chastely abiding by it, give no assent to enticements of this kind? Nevertheless, there is a great difference, because, when it happens otherwise, we return on waking to a peace of conscience and, by the very remoteness of our state now and then, discover that it was not we who did something which was, to our regret, somehow or other done in us.

Almighty God, surely your hand is powerful enough to cure all the sickness in my soul and, with a more abundant measure of your grace, to quench even the lustful impulses of my sleep. Lord, you will increase your gifts in me more and more, so that my soul, disentangled from the birdlime of concupiscence,[1] may follow me to you; so that it may not be in revolt against itself and may not, even in dreams, succumb to or even give the slightest assent to those degrading corruptions which by means of sensual images actually disturb and pollute the flesh. . . .

I must now mention another form of temptation which is in many ways more dangerous. Apart from the concupiscence of the flesh which is present in the delight we take in all the pleasures of the senses (and the slaves of it perish as they put themselves far from you), there is also present in the soul, by means of these same bodily senses, a kind of empty longing and curiosity which aims not at taking pleasure in the flesh but at acquiring experience through the flesh, and this empty curiosity is dignified by the names of learning and science. Since this is in the appetite for knowing, and since the eyes are the chief of our senses for acquiring knowledge, it is called in the divine language *the lust of the eyes*. For "to see" is used properly of the eyes; but we also use this word of the other senses when we are employing them for the purpose of gaining knowledge. We do not say: "Hear how it flashes" or "Smell how bright it is" or "Taste how it shines" or "Feel how it gleams"; in all these cases we use the verb "to see." But we not only say: "See how it shines," a thing which can only be perceived by the eyes; we also say "See how it sounds," "See how it smells," "See how it tastes," "See how hard it is." Therefore, the general experience of the senses is, as was said before, called "the lust of the eyes," because seeing, which belongs properly to the eyes, is used by analogy of the other senses too when they are attempting to discover any kind of knowledge.

In this it is easy to see how pleasure and curiosity have different objects in their use of the senses. Pleasure goes after what is beautiful to us, sweet to hear, to smell, to taste, to touch; but curiosity, for the sake of experiment, may go after the exact opposites of these, not in order to suffer discomfort, but simply because of the lust to find out and to know. What pleasure can there be in looking at a mangled corpse, which must excite our horror? Yet if there is one near, people flock to see it, so as to grow sad and pale at the sight. They are actually frightened of seeing it in their sleep, as though anyone had forced them to see it when they were awake or as if they had been induced to look at it because it had the reputation of being a beautiful thing to see. The same is true of the other senses. There is no need to go to the length of producing examples. Because of this disease of curiosity monsters and anything out of the ordinary are put on show in our theaters. From the same motive men proceed to investigate the workings of nature which is beyond our ken—things which it does no good to know and which men only want to know for the sake of knowing. So too, and with this same end of perverted science, people make enquiries by means of magic. Even in religion we find the same thing: God is tempted when signs and portents are demanded and are not desired for any salutary purpose, but simply for the experience of seeing them. . . .

We are tempted, Lord, by these temptations every day; without intermission we are tempted. The tongue of man is the furnace in which we are tried every day. Here too you command us to be continent. Give what you command, and command what you will. You know how on this matter my heart groans to you and my eyes stream tears. For I cannot easily discover how far I have become cleaner from this disease, and I much fear my hidden sins which are visible to your eyes, though not to mine. For in other kinds of temptation I have at least some means of finding out about myself; but in this kind it is almost impossible. With regard to the pleasures of the flesh and the unnecessary curiosity for knowledge I can see how far I have advanced in the ability to control my mind simply by observing myself when I am without these things, either from choice or when they are not available. For I can then ask myself how much

1
10
20
30
40
50
60
70
80
90
100
110

[1]Strong desire, especially sexual desire.

or how little I mind not having them. So too with regard to riches, which are desired for the satisfaction of one or two or all of those three concupiscences; if one is not able to be quite sure in one's own mind whether or not one despises them when one has them, it is possible to get rid of them so as to put oneself to the test. But how can we arrange things so as to be without praise and make the same experiment with regard to it? Are we to live a bad life, to live in such a wicked and abandoned way that everyone who knows us will detest us? Nothing could be madder    120
than such a suggestion as that. On the contrary, if praise both goes with and ought to go with a good life and good works, we should no more part with it than with the good life itself. Yet unless a thing is not there I cannot tell whether it is difficult or easy for me to be without it. . . .

———————————◆———————————

A living witness to the decline of the Roman Empire, Augustine defended his faith against pagan charges that Christianity was responsible for Rome's downfall. In his multivolume work *The City of God*, he distinguishes between the earthly city of humankind and the heavenly city that is the eternal dwelling place of the Christian soul. Augustine's earthly abode, a place where "wise men live according to man," represents the classical world prior to the coming of Jesus. By contrast, the heavenly city, the spiritual realm where human beings live according to divine precepts, is the destiny of those who embrace the "New Dispensation" of Christ.

Augustine's influence in shaping Christian dogma cannot be overestimated. His rationalization of evil as the perversion of the good created by God, and his defense of "just war"—that is, war as reprisal for the abuse of morality—testify to the analytic subtlety of his mind. His description of history as divinely ordered and directed toward a predestined end became fundamental to the Christian philosophy of history. Finally, his dualistic (and essentially neoplatonic) model of reality—matter and spirit, body and soul, earth and heaven, Satan and God, state and Church—governed Western thought for centuries to come. The conception of the visible world (matter) as an imperfect reflection of the divine order (spirit) determined the allegorical character of medieval literature. According to this model, matter was the matrix in which God's message was hidden. In Scripture, as well as in every natural and created thing, God's invisible order might be discovered. For Augustine, the Hebrew Bible was a symbolic guide to Christian belief, and history itself was a cloaked message of divine revelation.

The extract from *The City of God* illustrates Augustine's dual perception of reality and suggests its importance to the tradition of Christian allegory. Augustine's description of Noah's ark as symbolic of the City of God, the Church, and the body of Christ exemplifies the way in which a single image might assume various meanings within the language of Christian faith.

## READING 2.8

# From Saint Augustine's
# *City of God Against the Pagans*

*On the character of the two cities, the earthly and the heavenly.*

The two cities then were created by two kinds of love: the    1
earthly city by a love of self carried even to the point of contempt for God, the heavenly city by a love of God carried even to the point of contempt for self. Consequently, the earthly city glories in itself while the other glories in the Lord.[1] For the former seeks glory from men, but the latter finds its greatest glory in God, the witness of our conscience. The earthly city lifts up its head in its own glory; the heavenly city says to its God: "My glory and the lifter of my head."[2] In the one, the lust for dominion has    10
dominion over its princes as well as over the nations that it subdues; in the other, both those put in charge and those placed under them serve one another in love, the former by their counsel, the latter by their obedience. The earthly city loves its own strength as revealed in its men of power; the heavenly city says to its God: "I will love thee, O Lord, my strength."[3]

Thus in the earthly city its wise men who live according to man have pursued the goods either of the body or of their own mind or of both together; or if any of them were able to    20
know God, "they did not honor him as God or give thanks to him, but they became futile in their thinking and their senseless minds were darkened; claiming to be wise," that is, exalting themselves in their own wisdom under the dominion of pride, "they became fools, and exchanged the glory of the immortal God for images resembling mortal man or birds or beasts or reptiles," for in the adoration of idols of this sort they were either leaders or followers of the populace, "and worshipped and served the creature rather than the creator, who is blessed forever."[4] In the heavenly    30
city, on the other hand, man's only wisdom is the religion that guides him rightly to worship the true God and awaits as its reward in the fellowship of saints, not only human but also angelic, this goal, "that God may be all in all."[5] . . .

*That the ark which Noah was ordered to make symbolizes Christ and the church in every detail.*

Now God, as we know, enjoined the building of an ark upon Noah, a man who was righteous and according to the true testimony of Scripture, perfect in his generation,[6] that is, perfect, not as the citizens of the City of God are to become in that immortal state where they will be made equal with the angels of God, but as they can be during    40
their sojourn here on earth. In this ark he was to be rescued from the devastation of the flood with his family, that is, his wife, sons and daughters-in-law, as well as with the animals that came to him in the ark at God's direction. We doubtless have here a symbolic representation of the City of God sojourning as an alien in this world, that is, of the church which wins salvation by virtue of the wood on which the mediator between God and men, the man Christ Jesus,[7] was suspended.

---

[1]Cf. 2 Corinthians 10:17.    [2]Psalms 3:3.    [3]Psalms 18:1.
[4]Romans 1:21–23, 25.    [5]1 Corinthians 15:28.    [6]Cf. Genesis 6:9.
[7]1 Timothy 2:5.

The very measurements of the ark's length, height and breadth symbolize the human body, in the reality of which it was prophesied that Christ would come to mankind, as, in fact, he did come. For the length of the human body from top to toe is six times its breadth from one side to the other and ten times its thickness measured on a side from back to belly. Thus if you measure a man lying on his back or face down, his length from head to foot is six times his breadth from right to left or from left to right and ten times his elevation from the ground. This is why the ark was made three hundred cubits in length, fifty in breadth and thirty in height. And as for the door that it received on its side, that surely is the wound that was made when the side of the crucified one was pierced by the spear.[8] This is the way by which those who come to him enter, because from this opening flowed the sacraments with which believers are initiated. Moreover, the order that it should be made of squared beams contains an allusion to the foursquare stability of saints' lives, for in whatever direction you turn a squared object, it will stand firm. In similar fashion, everything else mentioned in the construction of this ark symbolizes some aspect of the church. . . .

50

60

70

---

## Symbolism and Early Christian Art

**Iconography**, the study of subject matter and its visual imagery, is essential to an understanding of the transition from classical to Christian art. In early Christian art, the symbolic significance of the representation is often more important than its literal meaning. Indeed, the allegorical mode of thought (evidenced in *The City of God*) that identifies invisible truths beneath the visible surface

[8]Cf. John 19:34.

*alpha* — *omega*

(a)

*chi rho*

(b)  Matthew    Mark    Luke    John

(c)  Latin    Greek

**Figure 9.1**
(a) Christian monograms;
(b) symbols of the four evangelists;
(c) Latin and Greek crosses.

dominates all forms of early medieval expression. Before Christianity was legalized in 313, visual symbols served the practical function of identifying the converts to the faith among themselves. Followers of Jesus adopted the sign of the fish because the Greek word for fish (*ichthys*) is an acrostic combination of the first letters of the Greek words "Jesus Christ, Son of God, Savior." They also used the first and last letters of the Greek alphabet, *alpha* and *omega* (Figure **9.1**), to designate Christ's presence at the beginning and the end of time. Roman converts to Christianity saw in the Latin word for peace, *pax*, a symbolic reference to Christ, since the last and first letters could also be read as *chi* and *rho*, the first two letters in the Greek word *Christos*. Indeed, *pax*

**Figure 9.2** Sarcophagus of Archbishop Theodorus, sixth century C.E. Marble. Sant'Apollinare in Classe, Ravenna, Italy. Alinari, Florence.

was emblazoned on the banner under which the emperor Constantine was said to have defeated his enemies. Such symbols soon found their way into early Christian art.

On a sixth-century **sarcophagus** (stone coffin) of the archbishop Theodorus of Ravenna (Figure 9.2), the *chi* and *rho* and the *alpha* and *omega* have been made into an insignia that resembles both a crucifix (symbolizing Christ as Savior) and a pastoral cross (symbolizing Christ as shepherd). Three laurel wreaths, Roman imperial symbols of triumph, encircle the medallions on the coffin lid. On either side of the central medallion are grapevines designating the wine that represents the blood of Christ. The tiny birds that stand beneath the vines—derived from Greek funerary art—refer to the human soul. Also included in the iconographic program are two popular Southwest Asian symbols of immortality: the peacock or phoenix, a legendary bird that was thought to be reborn from its own ashes, and the rosette, a reference to the "wheel of life." Taken as a whole, the archbishop's coffin is the vehicle of a sacred language signifying Christ's triumph and the Christian promise of resurrection and salvation.

In early Christian art, music, and literature, almost every number and combination of numbers was thought to carry allegorical meaning. The number 3, for example, signified the Trinity, 4 signified the evangelists, 5 symbolized the wounds of Jesus, 12 stood for

**Figure 9.4** *Christ as Good Shepherd*, mid-fourth century C.E. Fresco. Catacombs of Saints Pietro and Marcellino, Rome. Pontificia Commissione per l'Archeologia Cristiana, Rome.

**Figure 9.3** *Orans* (praying figure), ca. 300 C.E. Fresco. Catacombs of Saint Priscilla, Rome. Scala, Florence.

the apostles, and so on. The evangelists were usually represented by four winged creatures: the man for Matthew, the lion for Mark, the ox for Luke, and the eagle for John (see Figure 9.1 and the upper portion of Figure 9.10). Prefigured in the Book of Revelation (4:1–8), each of the four creatures came to be associated with a particular Gospel. The lion, for example, was appropriate to Mark because in his Gospel he emphasized the royal dignity of Christ; the heaven-soaring eagle suited John, who produced the most lofty and mystical of the Gospels.

Some of the earliest evidence of Christian art comes from the **catacombs**, subterranean burial chambers outside the city of Rome. These vast networks of underground galleries and rooms include gravesites whose walls are covered with frescoes illustrating scenes from the Old and New Testaments. Worshipers are shown in the *orans* position—with arms upraised in an attitude of prayer—a gesture priests still use in the performance of the Mass (Figure 9.3). Like the story of Noah's ark, "decoded" by Augustine to reveal its hidden significance, early Christian imagery was multilayered and pregnant with symbolic meaning. For example, the popular figure of Jesus as Good Shepherd, an adaptation of the calf- or lamb-bearing youth of Greco-Roman art (see chapter 6), symbolizes Jesus' role as savior-protector (shepherd) and sacrificial victim (lamb). Featured in catacomb frescoes (Figure **9.4**) and in freestanding sculpture (see Figure **9.6**), the Good Shepherd evokes the early Christian theme of deliverance. But while the message of the catacomb frescoes is one of salvation and deliverance, the style of these paintings resembles that of secular Roman art (see chapter 7): Figures are small but substantial and deftly shaded to suggest three-dimensionality. Setting and specific indications of spatial depth are omitted, however, so that human forms appear to float in ethereal space.

In the centuries following the legalization of Christianity, stories about the life of Jesus came to form two main narrative cycles: The Youth of Christ and The Passion of Christ (Figure **9.5**). Not until the fifth century,

however, when the manner of Jesus' death began to lose its ignoble associations, was Jesus depicted on the Cross. One of the earliest of such scenes is that carved in low relief on the wooden west doors of Santa Sabina in Rome (see Figure 8.3). Christ assumes the *orans* in a rigid and static frontal position that also signifies a crucified body. The tripartite composition of the relief includes the smaller (because less important) figures of the thieves who flanked Jesus at the crucifixion. Despite its narrative content, the image is far from being a representation of the crucifixion of Jesus. Rather, it is a symbolic statement of Christian redemption.

Early Christians had little use for the Roman approach to art as a window on the world. Roman

**Figure 9.5** Iconography of the Life of Jesus.

| THE YOUTH OF JESUS (principal events) | | THE PASSION OF CHRIST (principal events) | |
|---|---|---|---|
| 1 **The Annunciation** | The Archangel Gabriel announces to the Virgin Mary that God has chosen her to bear his son | 1 **The Entry into Jerusalem** | Jesus, riding on a donkey, enters Jerusalem amidst his disciples and receptive crowds |
| 2 **The Visitation** | The pregnant Mary visits her cousin Elizabeth, who is pregnant with the future John the Baptist | 2 **The Last Supper** | At the Passover *seder*, Jesus reveals to his disciples his impending death and instructs them to consume the bread (his body) and the wine (his blood) in remembrance of him |
| 3 **The Nativity** | Jesus is born to Mary in Bethlehem | | |
| 4 **The Annunciation to the Shepherds** | An angel announces the birth of Jesus to humble shepherds, who hasten to Bethlehem | 3 **The Agony in the Garden** | At the Garden of Gethsemane on the Mount of Olives, while the disciples Peter, James, and John sleep, Jesus reconciles his soul to death |
| 5 **The Adoration of the Magi** | Three wise men from the East follow a star to Bethlehem where they present the Christ child with precious gifts (gold, frankincense, and myrrh) | 4 **The Betrayal** | Judas Iscariot, who has been bribed to point Jesus out to his enemies, identifies him by kissing him as he leaves the Garden of Gethsemane |
| 6 **The Presentation in the Temple** | Mary and Joseph present Jesus to the high priest at the Temple in Jerusalem | 5 **Jesus Before Pilate** | Jesus comes before the Roman governor of Judea and is charged with treason; when the crowd demands Jesus be put to death, Pilate washes his hands to signify his innocence of the deed |
| 7 **The Massacre of the Innocents and the Flight to Egypt** | King Herod murders all the newborn of Bethlehem; the Holy Family (Mary, Joseph, and Jesus) flee to Egypt | 6 **The Flagellation** | Jesus is scourged by his captors, the Roman soldiers |
| 8 **The Baptism** | John the Baptist, a preacher in the wilderness of Judea, baptizes Jesus in the Jordan River | 7 **The Mocking of Jesus** | Pilate's soldiers dress Jesus in royal robes and a crown of thorns |
| 9 **The Temptation** | Jesus fasts for forty days and nights in the wilderness; he rejects the worldly wealth offered to him by the Devil | 8 **The Road to Calvary** | Jesus carries the Cross to Golgotha (Calvary), where he is to be executed |
| 10 **The Calling of the Apostles** | Near the Sea of Galilee, Jesus calls the brothers Simon (Peter) and Andrew into his service | 9 **The Crucifixion** | At Golgotha, the body of Jesus is affixed to a cross raised to stand between two crucified thieves |
| 11 **The Raising of Lazarus** | Jesus restores to life Lazarus, the brother of Mary and Martha | 10 **The Descent from the Cross and the Lamentation** | Grief-stricken followers remove the body of Jesus from the Cross; the Virgin, Mary Magdalene, and others grieve over the body |
| 12 **The Transfiguration** | On Mount Tabor in Galilee, among his disciples Peter, James, and John the Evangelist, the radiantly transfigured Jesus is hailed by God as his beloved Son | 11 **The Entombment** | Mary and the followers of Jesus place his body in a nearby tomb |
| | | 12 **The Resurrection** | Three days after his death, Jesus rises from the tomb |

realism, with its scrupulous attention to time, place, and personalities, was ill-suited to convey the timeless message of a universal faith and the miraculous events surrounding the life of a savior god. Moreover, Christian artists inherited the Jewish prohibition against "graven images." As a result, very little freestanding sculpture was produced between the second and eleventh centuries; and that which was produced, such as the fourth-century *Good Shepherd* (Figure 9.6), retains only the rudimentary features—such as the *contrapposto* stance—of high classical statuary (see chapters 6 and 7). On the other hand, devotional objects such as hand-illuminated manuscripts and **diptychs** (two-leaved hinged tablets or panels) designed for private use were produced in great numbers. A sixth-century ivory book cover from Murano, Italy (Figure 9.7), is typical of the early Christian artist's preoccupation with didactic content and surface adornment. Scenes of Jesus' miracles are wedged together in airless compartments surrounding the central image of the enthroned Jesus with Peter and Paul. A royal canopy flanked by **Latin crosses** (see Figure 9.1) crowns the holy space. In the top register, two angels modeled on classical *putti* (winged angelic beings) carry a **Greek cross** encircled by a triumphal wreath, while below, several scenes from the life of Jonah ("reborn" from the belly of the whale) make reference to redemption and resurrection in Christ. Despite its classical borrowings, the piece abandons Greco-Roman realism in favor of symbolic abstraction.

## Early Christian Art and Architecture

The legalization of Christianity made possible the construction of monumental houses for public religious worship. In the West, the early Christian church building was modeled on the Roman basilica. One entered Rome's earliest Christian basilicas, Saint Peter's and Saint Paul's, through an atrium that was surrounded on three sides by a covered walkway or **ambulatory**, and on the fourth side (directly in front of the church entrance) by a vestibule, or **narthex**. The church interior featured a long central hall or **nave**, flanked on either side by two aisles; the upper wall of the nave consisted of the **gallery** and the **clerestory** (Figure 9.8). The gallery was often decorated with mosaics or frescoes, while the clerestory was pierced by windows through which light entered the basilica (Figure 9.9; see also Part Opener, p. xvi).

Toward the east end of the church, lying across the axis of the nave, was a rectangular area called the

**Figure 9.6** *The Good Shepherd*, ca. 300 C.E. Marble, height 3 ft. Vatican Museums, Rome. (The legs are restored.)

**Figure 9.7** Book cover, from Murano, Italy, sixth century C.E. Ivory. Scala/Art Resource, New York.

**transept**. The north and south arms of the transept, which might be extended to form a Latin cross, could provide entrances additional to the main doorway at the west end of the church. Entering through the west portal, one proceeded down the colonnaded nave toward the triumphal arch that framed the **apse**, the semicircular space beyond the transept. In the apse, at an altar that stood on a raised platform, the sacrament of Holy Communion was celebrated. As in ancient Egypt, rituals of resurrection looked to the east, where the sun was "reborn" each day of the year. Likewise, the Christian's journey across the atrium, down the nave, and toward the church altar symbolized the soul's progression from the secular world to the spiritual font of salvation.

Early Christian churches served as places of worship, but they also entombed the bones of Christian martyrs, usually beneath the altar. Hence church buildings were massive shrines, as well as settings for the performance of the liturgy. Their spacious interiors—Old Saint Peter's basilica was approximately 355 feet long and 208 feet wide—accommodated thousands of Christian pilgrims. However, the wood-trussed roofs of these churches made them especially vulnerable to fire. None of the great early Christian basilicas has survived, except in pictorial records as in Figure 9.9.

The Latin cross plan (see Figure 9.1) became the model for medieval churches in the West. The church exterior, which clearly reflected the functional divisions of the interior, was usually left plain and unadorned, while the interior was lavishly decorated with mosaics consisting of tiny pieces of colored glass or marble set in wet cement. The technique had been invented by the Romans, who used it largely to decorate the floors of public or private buildings. In the hands of Byzantine craftsmen, however, mosaics became the ideal means of conveying the transcendental character of the Christian message. The medium encouraged the invention of flat, simplified shapes arranged in radiant color patterns. Small pieces of glass backed with gold leaf added splendor to the total effect. As daylight or candlelight moved across walls embellished with mosaic, it transformed surface designs into sparkling and ethereal apparitions.

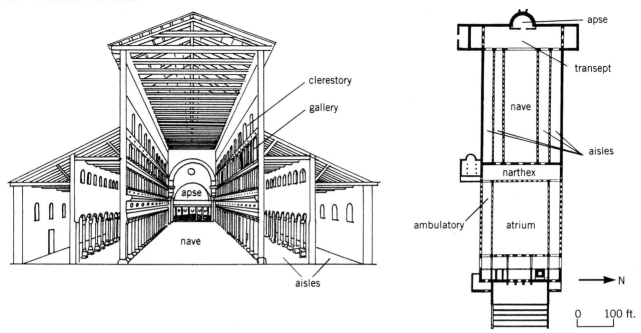

**Figure 9.8** Cross section and floor plan of Old Saint Peter's Basilica, Rome, fourth century C.E. Interior of basilica approx. 208 × 355 ft., height of nave 105 ft.

**Figure 9.9** Interior of Saint Paul's Outside the Walls, Rome, begun 386 C.E. Etching by Giambattista Piranesi, 1749. Photo: Courtesy of Rudy Turk.

In the fifth-century mosaic of *Christ Teaching the Apostles* from the apse of Santa Pudenziana in Rome (Figure **9.10**), the heavenly city unfolds below the hovering image of a magnificent jeweled cross flanked by winged symbols of the four evangelists. The bearded Jesus, conceived as a Roman emperor, rules the world from atop "the throne set in heaven" as described in Revelation 4. Two female figures, personifications of the Old and New Testaments, offer wreaths of victory to Peter and Paul. Looking like an assembly of Roman senators, the apostles receive the Law, symbolized by the open book, and the **benediction** (blessing) of Jesus.

**Figure 9.10** *Christ Teaching the Apostles in the Heavenly Jerusalem*, ca. 401–417 C.E. Mosaic. Apse of Santa Pudenziana, Rome. Scala, Florence.

## Byzantine Art and Architecture

In the churches of Byzantium, the mosaic technique reached its artistic peak. Byzantine church architects favored the Greek cross plan by which all four arms of the structure were of equal length (see Figure 9.1). At the crossing point rose a large and imposing dome. Occasionally, as with the most notable example of Byzantine architecture, Hagia Sophia ("Holy Wisdom"), the longitudinal axis of the Latin cross plan was combined with the Greek cross plan (Figure **9.12**). The crowning architectural glory and principal church of Constantinople, Hagia Sophia (Figures **9.11**, **9.14**) was commissioned in 532 by the East Roman emperor Justinian (482–565). Its massive dome—112 feet in diameter—rises 184 feet above the pavement (40 feet higher than the Pantheon; see chapter 7). Triangular **pendentives** make the transition between the square base of the building and the superstructure (Figure **9.13**). Light filtering through the forty closely set windows at the base of the dome creates the impression that the dome is floating miraculously above the substance of the building. That light, whose symbolic value was as important to Byzantine liturgy as it was to Saint Ambrose's "Ancient Morning Hymn," illuminated the resplendent mosaics and colored marble surfaces that once filled the interior of the church. After the fall of Constantinople to the Turks in 1453, the Muslims transformed Hagia Sophia into a mosque and whitewashed its mosaics (in accordance with the Islamic prohibition against images). Modern Turkish officials, however, have made the building a museum and restored some of the original mosaics.

Hagia Sophia is evidence of the golden age of Byzantine art and architecture that took place under the emperor Justinian. Justinian envisioned Constantinople as the "New Rome." Assuming the throne in 527, he tried unsuccessfully to reunite the two halves of the old Roman Empire (Map **9.1**). Eager to restore the prestige and power of ancient Rome, he comissioned his legal advisers to revise and codify the extensive body of Roman and Church law. The monumental Code of Justinian would have an enormous influence on legal and governmental history in the West, especially after the eleventh century, when it became the basis for the law in most of the European states. Justinian's leadership was equally important to the Byzantine economy. By directing his ambassadors to smuggle silkworm eggs out of China, Justinian initiated the silk industry in the West. A devout Christian, he commissioned an ambitious program of church building both in Constantinople and in Ravenna, the North Italian city that served as his Western imperial outpost before it fell into the hands of the Ostrogoths.

**Figure 9.11** Anthemius of Tralles and Isidorus of Miletus, Hagia Sophia, from the southwest, Constantinople, 532–537 C.E. The body of the original church is now surrounded by later additions, including the minarets built after 1453 under the Ottoman Turks. Dome height 184 ft.; diameter 112 ft. © Hirmer Fotoarchiv, Munich.

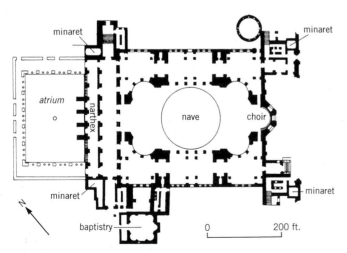

**Figure 9.12** Plan of Hagia Sophia, Constantinople (Istanbul), Turkey.

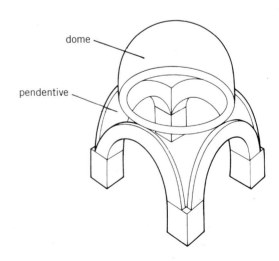

**Figure 9.13** Schematic drawing of the dome of Hagia Sophia, showing pendentives.

**Figure 9.14** (opposite)  Hagia Sophia, Constantinople. E.T. Archive, London.

**Figure 9.15** *Emperor Justinian and His Courtiers*, ca. 547 C.E. Mosaic. San Vitale, Ravenna. Giancarlo Costa, Milan.

The sixth-century octagonal domed church of San Vitale in Ravenna is one of the small gems of Byzantine architecture (Figure 9.16). Its drab exterior hardly prepares one for the radiant and ornate interior, the walls of which are embellished with polychrome marble, carved alabaster columns, and some of the most magnificent mosaics in the history of world art (Figure 9.18). The mosaics on either side of the altar show Justinian and his capable consort Theodora, each carrying offerings to Christ (Figures 9.15, 9.17). The iconography of the Justinian representation illustrates the bond between Church and state that characterized Byzantine history: Justinian is flanked by twelve companions, an allusion to Christ and the apostles. On his right are his soldiers, the defenders of Christ (note the *chi* and *rho* emblazoned on the shield), while on his left are representatives of the clergy, who bear the instruments of the liturgy: the crucifix, the book, and the incense vessel. Crowned by a solar disc or halo—a device often used in Persian and late Roman art to indicate divine status—Justinian personifies the sacred authority of Christ on earth and the unity of temporal and spiritual power. At the same time, he and his empress reenact the ancient role of royal donation, a theme underscored by the illustration of the Three Magi on the hem of Theodora's robe (see Figure 9.17).

The style of the mosaic conveys the solemn formality of the event: Justinian and his courtiers stand

**Figure 9.16** San Vitale, Ravenna, Italy, ca. 526–547 C.E. © Hirmer Fotoarchiv, Munich.

**Figure 9.17** *Empress Theodora and Retinue*, ca. 547 C.E. Mosaic. San Vitale, Ravenna. Giancarlo Costa, Milan.

grave and motionless, as if frozen in ceremonial attention. They are slender, elongated, and rigidly positioned —like the notes of a musical score—against a gold background that works to eliminate spatial depth. Minimally shaded, these "paper cutout" figures with small, flapperlike feet seem to float on the surface of the picture plane, rather than stand anchored in real space. A comparison of this composition with, for instance, any Roman paintings or sculptural reliefs (see chapter 7) underlines the vast differences between the aesthetic aims and purposes of classical and Christian art. Whereas the Romans engaged a realistic narrative style to glorify temporal power, the Christians cultivated an abstract language of line and color to celebrate otherworldly glory.

The sixth-century mosaic of *Jesus Calling the First Apostles, Peter and Andrew* (Figure **9.19**) found in Sant'Apollinare Nuovo in Ravenna—a Christian basilica ornamented by Roman and Byzantine artisans—provides yet another example of the surrender of narrative detail to symbolic abstraction. In the composition, setting is minimal: A gold background shuts out space and provides a supernatural screen against which ritualized action takes place. The figures, stiff and immovable,

seem to lack substance. There is almost no sense of muscle and bone beneath the togas of Christ and the apostles. The enlarged eyes and solemn gestures (reminiscent of Mesopotamian votive sculpture; see chapter 2) impart a powerful sense of otherworldly vision and omniscience.

## The Byzantine Icon

Although religious imagery was essential to the growing influence of Christianity, a fundamental disagreement concerning the role of **icons** (images) in divine worship led to conflict between the Roman Catholic and Greek Orthodox Churches. Most Roman Catholics held that visual representations of God the Father, Jesus, the Virgin, and the saints worked to inspire religious reverence. On the other hand, iconoclasts (those who favored the destruction of icons) held that such images were no better than pagan idols, which were worshiped in and of themselves. During the eighth century, Byzantine iconoclasm resulted in the wholesale destruction of images, while the Iconoclastic Controversy, which remained unresolved until the middle of the ninth century, generated a schism between the Eastern and

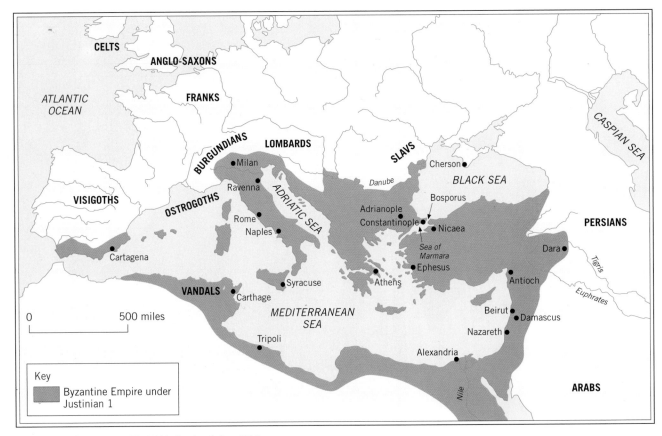

**Map 9.1** The Byzantine World Under Justinian, 565 C.E.

**Figure 9.18** San Vitale, Ravenna. Scala/Art Resource, New York.

**Figure 9.19** *Jesus Calling the First Apostles, Peter and Andrew*, early sixth century C.E. Mosaic. Detail of upper register of north wall, Sant'Apollinare Nuovo, Ravenna. Scala, Florence.

Western Churches. Nevertheless, for over a thousand years, Byzantine monastics produced moving religious portraits that were regarded by the faithful as sacred pictures with supernatural powers. Some were thought to perform miracles. Executed in glowing colors and gold paint on small, portable panels, Byzantine icons usually featured the Virgin and Child (alone or surrounded by saints) staring hypnotically at the worshiper in a formal, stylized manner (Figure **9.20**; compare Figure 9.17). While early representations of the Mother and Child look back to portrayals of Isis and other East Mediterranean mother cult deities (see Figure 8.1), they also prefigure the monumental allegories of the Virgin as the seat or throne of wisdom (see Figures 13.25, 13.30).

Following the conversion of Russia to Orthodox Christianity, Russian artists brought new splendor to the art of the icon, often embellishing the devotional panel with gold leaf and semiprecious jewels, or enhancing the garments of the saint with thin sheets of hammered gold or silver.

## Early Christian Music

Early Christians distrusted the sensuous and emotional powers of music, especially instrumental music. Saint Augustine noted the "dangerous pleasure" of music and confessed that on those occasions when he was more "moved by the singing than by what was sung," he felt that he had "sinned criminally." For such reasons, the Early Church was careful to exclude all forms of

individual expression from liturgical music. Ancient Jewish religious ritual, especially the practice of chanting daily prayers and singing psalms, directly influenced Church music. Hymns of praise such as those produced by Saint Ambrose were sung by the Christian congregation led by a **cantor** (chief solo singer). But the most important music of Christian antiquity, and that which became central to the liturgy of the Church, was the music of the Mass.

The most sacred rite of the Christian liturgy, the Mass celebrated the sacrifice of Christ's body and blood as enacted at the Last Supper. The service culminated in the sacrament of Holy Communion (or Eucharist), by which Christians symbolically shared the body and blood of their Redeemer. In the West, the service called High Mass featured a series of Latin chants known as either plainsong, plainchant, or Gregorian chant[*]—the last because Gregory the Great codified and made uniform the many types of religious chant that existed in early Christian times. The invariable or "ordinary" parts of the Mass, that is, those used throughout the year, included "Kyrie eleison" ("Lord have mercy"), "Gloria" ("Glory to God"), "Credo" (the affirmation of the Nicene Creed), "Sanctus" ("Holy, Holy, Holy"), "Benedictus" ("Blessed is He that cometh in the name of the Lord") and "Agnus Dei" ("Lamb of God"). Eventually, the "Sanctus" and the "Benedictus" appeared as one chant, making a total of five parts to the ordinary of the Mass.

---

[*]See Music Listening Selections at end of chapter.

**Figure 9.20** *Virgin and Child with Saints and Angels*, second half of sixth century C.E. Icon: encaustic on wood, 27 × 18⅞ in. Monastery of Saint Catherine, Mount Sinai, Egypt. Photo: © Ancient Art and Architecture Collection, Middlesex, U.K.

One of the oldest bodies of liturgical song still in everyday use, Gregorian chant stands among the great treasures of Western music. It is—like early Christian hymnody—monophonic, that is, it consists of a single line of melody. Sung *a cappella* (without instrumental accompaniment), the plainsong of the early Christian era was performed by the clergy and by choirs of monks rather than by members of the congregation. Both the Ambrosian hymns and plainsong could be performed in a **responsorial** style, with the chorus answering the voice of the cantor, or **antiphonally**, with parts of the choir or congregation singing alternating verses. In general, the rhythm of the words dictated the rhythm of the music. Plainsong might be **syllabic** (one note to one syllable), or it might involve **melismatic** embellishments

(with many notes to one syllable). Since no method for notating music existed before the ninth century, choristers depended on memory and on **neumes**—marks entered above the words of the text to indicate the rise and fall of the voice. The duration and exact pitch of each note, however, had to be committed to memory.

Lacking fixed meter or climax, the free rhythms of Gregorian chant echoed through early Christian churches, whose cavernous interiors enshrined sound and produced effects that were otherworldly and hypnotic. These qualities, conveyed only to a limited degree by modern recordings, are best appreciated when Gregorian chant is performed in large, acoustically resonant basilicas such as the remodeled Saint Peter's in Rome.

# The Buddhist Identity

Buddhism, as it spread through India and China, followed a very different path from that of Christianity. Whereas the followers of Jesus established an administrative Church hierarchy, prescribed doctrines, and standardized rituals for public worship, the followers of the Buddha remained divided concerning the real meaning of the Buddha's teachings. Under the leadership of Asoka (see chapter 8), councils of Buddhist monks met unsuccessfully to organize the Master's teachings into a uniform, official canon. A large body of folklore and legend came to ornament the history of the Buddha's life along with stories of his previous lives, known as *jakatas* ("birthstories"). The heart of Buddhist scripture, however, is a body of discourses informed by the Master's sermons. There is no Buddhist equivalent of the Nicene Creed, the Mass, or the secular priesthood—in short, no "authority" other than the words of the Buddha. If indeed there is a Buddhist "creed," it calls for adherence to the Law of Righteousness (*Dharma*) and the Eightfold Path. And in its purist (Hinayana) form, it urges Buddhists to work out their own salvation. Among all sects of Buddhism, however, monasteries arose as centers for meditation and instruction. The monastic complex centered on a hall used for teaching and meditation. An adjacent shrine or pagoda might hold relics or ashes of the Buddha.

The Buddhist monk became the model of religious life for a faith that remained aloof from dogma. To this day, religious "services" consist only of the chanting of Buddhist texts (mainly the Buddha's sermons), the recitation of hymns and *mantras* (word and sound formulas), meditation, and confession. Unencumbered by an elaborate liturgy, Buddhism remained grounded in reverence for the Buddha and his teachings. And despite the deification of the Buddha among Mahayana Buddhists and the worship of *bodhisattvas* who might aid humans to achieve *nirvana*, Buddhism never abandoned its profoundly contemplative character.

## Buddhist Art and Architecture in India

When the emperor Asoka made Buddhism the state religion of India in the third century B.C.E. he commissioned the construction of thousands of shrines—over eighty thousand within three years—to house the relics of the Buddha and mark the places at which he had taught. The most typical Buddhist structure was the *stupa*, a beehivelike mound of earth encased by brick or stone, atop which were enshrined relics of the Buddha or his disciples. Derived from the prehistoric burial mound, the *stupa* is a symbolic representation of the

**Figure 9.21** West gateway, the Great Stupa, Sanchi, Central India, Shunga and early Andhra periods, third century B.C.E. early first century C.E. Shrine height 50 ft.; diameter 105 ft. Government of India, Archeological Survey of India.

cosmos, at once the World Mountain, the dwelling-place of the ancient gods, and the sacred womb of the universe. Stone balustrades carved with symbols of the Buddha's teachings and gates marking the four cardinal points of the compass separate this reliquary shrine from the secular world. Circling the *stupa* clockwise, Buddhist pilgrims make the sacred journey that, like the act of meditation, awakens the mind to the rhythms of the universe. If the spiritual journey of the early Christian pilgrim was linear (from narthex to apse or sin to salvation), the Buddhist one was cyclical and cosmic.

Begun in the third century B.C.E., the Great Stupa at Sanchi in Central India was one of Asoka's foremost achievements (Figure **9.21**). Elevated on a 20-foot drum and surrounded by a circular stone railing, the shrine is 105 feet in diameter and rises to a height of 50 feet. It is surmounted by a series of *chatras*, umbrellalike shapes that signify the sacred Bo tree under which the

**Figure 9.22** (above) Interior of carved *chaitya* cave, Karli, India, ca. 50 C.E. Government of India, Archeological Survey of India.

**Figure 9.23** (below) Elevation and ground plan of *chaitya* cave, Karli, ca. 50 C.E.

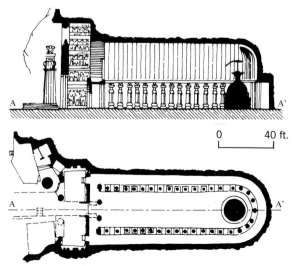

**Figure 9.24** East *torana* (gate), Great Stupa, Sanchi, India, early Andhra period, mid-first century B.C.E. Sandstone, height of gate 34 ft. Photo: A. F. Kersting, London.

Buddha reached *nirvana*. The *chatras* also symbolize the levels of human consciousness through which the soul ascends in seeking enlightenment. Occasionally, *stupas* were enclosed in massive, rock-cut caves and placed at the end of arcaded halls (Figures **9.22**, **9.23**), that resembled early Christian basilicas. Known as *chaitya* halls, these sacred spaces were not sites for ceremonial worship, as with early Christian churches but, rather, womblike sanctuaries for spiritual retreat.

Buddhism's prohibition of idolatry influenced art in that artists avoided portraying the Buddha in human form. Like the early Christians, who devised a body of sacred signs to represent the Christos (see Figure 9.1), Buddhists adopted symbols for the Buddha, such as the fig tree under which he meditated, his footprints, elephants (one of the bodily forms assumed by the Buddha), and, most important, the wheel (signifying both the sun and the Wheel of the Law). These symbols, along with sensuous images of nature deities retained from Vedic tradition, make up the densely ornamented surface of the 34-foot-high *toranas* (stone gateways) that mark the entrances to the Great Stupa at Sanchi (Figure **9.24**). Notably different from the Augustinian antagonism of flesh and spirit evidenced in the *Confessions*, and Christianity's general abhorrence of carnal pleasure, Buddhism (like Hinduism) regarded sexuality and spirituality as variant forms of the single, fundamental cosmic energy. Hence, Buddhist art—in contrast with Christian art—did not condemn the representation of

**Figure 9.25** *Yakshi* (female fertility spirit) bracket figure, east *torana*, Great Stupa, Sanchi. Sandstone, height approx. 5 ft. Photo: Wendy Holden, University of Michigan.

influenced the emergence of a distinctly human Buddha icon inspired by Hellenistic and Roman representations of the god Apollo. Gandharan artists created classically draped and idealized freestanding figures of the Buddha and the *bodhisattvas* (see Figures 8.4, 8.5). They also carved scenes from the life of the Buddha, one of which depicts the Master seated among a group of monks and devotees (Figure 9.26) in a manner that may be compared with benedictional images of Jesus among the apostles (see Figures 9.7, 9.10).

Between the fourth and sixth centuries, under the sway of the Gupta Empire, India experienced a golden age in the arts as well as in the sciences. Gupta rulers commissioned Sanskrit prose and poetry that ranged from adventure stories and plays to sacred and philosophical works. Gupta mathematicians were the first to use a special sign for the numeric zero and Hindu physicans made significant advances in medicine. (As we shall see in chapter 10, the Arabs transmitted many of these innovations to the West.) In the hands of Gupta sculptors, the image of the Buddha assumed its classic form (Figure 9.27): a cross-legged figure, seated in the position of meditation. The Buddha's oval head, framed by an elaborately ornamented halo, features a mounded protuberance (symbolizing spiritual wisdom), elongated earlobes (a reference to Siddhartha's princely origins), and a third "eye"—a symbol of spiritual vision—between the eyebrows (see Figure 8.4). The Buddha's masklike face, with downcast eyes and gentle smile, denotes the state of inner repose. His hands form a *mudra* (symbolic gesture) that indicates the Wheel of the Law, the subject of the Buddha's first sermon (Figure 9.28). Wheels, also symbolic of the Wheel of the Law, are additionally engraved on the palms of his

the nude body. Indeed, Sanchi's voluptuous fertility goddesses, whose globular breasts and tubelike limbs appear to swell with life, seem to celebrate female sexuality (Figure 9.25).

Mahayana Buddhism, however, glorified the Buddha as a savior, and thus the image of the Buddha himself became important in popular worship. Contacts between Northwest India (Gandhara) and the West

**Figure 9.26** *Enlightenment*, detail of frieze showing four scenes from the life of Buddha: *Birth*, *Enlightenment*, *First Preaching*, and *Nirvana*, from the Gandharan region of Northwest Pakistan, Kushan dynasty, late second–early third century C.E. Dark gray-blue slate, height 26⅜ in., width 114⅛ in., thickness 31³⁄₁₆ in. Courtesy of the Freer Gallery of Art, Smithsonian Institution, Washington, D.C. 49.9.

**Figure 9.27** *Teaching Buddha*, from Sarnath, India, Gupta dynasty, fifth century C.E. Sandstone, height 5 ft. 2 in. Archeological Museum, Sarnath.

**Figure 9.29** Palace scene, Cave 17, Ajanta, India. Wall painting. Gupta period, fifth century C.E. Photo: Victor Kennett/Robert Harding Picture Library, London.

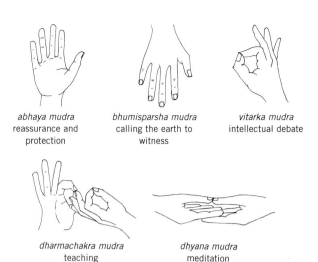

*abhaya mudra*
reassurance and
protection

*bhumisparsha mudra*
calling the earth to
witness

*vitarka mudra*
intellectual debate

*dharmachakra mudra*
teaching

*dhyana mudra*
meditation

**Figure 9.28** *Mudras.*

hands and the soles of his feet. More stylized than their Gandharan predecessors, Gupta figures are typically full-bodied and smoothly modeled with details reduced to decorative linear patterns.

The Gupta period also produced some of the earliest surviving examples of Indian painting. Hundreds of frescoes found on the walls of some thirty rock-cut sanctuaries at Ajanta in Central India show scenes from the lives and incarnations of the Buddha (as told in Mahayana literature), as well as stories from Indian history and legend. In the Ajanta frescoes, musicians, dancers, and lightly clad *bodhisattvas* (Figure **9.29**) rival the sensual elegance of the carved goddesses at Sanchi. The Ajanta frescoes are among the best-preserved and most magnificent of Indian paintings. They rank with the frescoes of the catacombs and the mosaic cycles of Early Christian and Byzantine churches, though in

**Figure 9.30** Pagoda of the Song Yue Temple, Mount Song, Henan, China, 523 C.E.

## Buddhist Art and Architecture in China

Between the first and third centuries, Buddhist missionaries introduced many of the basic conventions of Indian art and architecture into China. The Chinese adopted the *stupa* as a temple-shrine and place of private worship, transforming its moundlike base and umbrellalike structure into a **pagoda**, or multitiered tower with many roofs. These Chinese temple-towers are characterized by sweeping curves and upturned corners similar to those used in ancient watchtowers and multistoried houses (see chapter 7). Favoring timber as the principal building medium, Chinese architects devised complex vaulting systems for the construction of pagodas, of which no early examples have survived.

The earliest Buddhist building in China whose date is known is the twelve-sided brick pagoda on Mount Song in Henan, which served as a shrine for the nearby Buddhist monastery (Figure 9.30). Constructed in the early sixth century, this pagoda has a hollow interior that may once have held a large statue of the Buddha. Pagodas, whether built in brick or painted wood, became popular throughout Southeast Asia and provided a model for all religious shrines—Daoist and Confucian—as well as for Hindu temples in medieval India.

In addition, the Chinese produced rock-cut sanctuaries modeled on the reliquary shrines of India. These contain colossal images of the Buddha and his *bodhisattvas* (Figure 9.31). Carved into the native sandstone, the sharply cut masklike faces and clinging draperies produce animated surface designs. The Chinese preference for abstract patterns and flowing, rhythmic lines also dominates the relief carvings in the limestone rock walls of late fifth- and sixth-century Buddhist caves

subject matter—and especially in their depiction of erotic love—they have no equivalent in the medieval West. They underline the fact that, in Buddhist thought, the divine and the human, the spirit and the body, are considered complementary rather than antagonistic.

**Figure 9.31** *Large Seated Buddha with Standing Bodhisattva*, Cave 20, Yungang, Shanxi, China, Northern Wei dynasty, ca. 460–470 C.E. Stone, height 44 ft. Photo: Paolo Koch/Robert Harding Picture Library, London.

(Figure **9.32**). Once painted with bright colors, the reliefs showing the emperor Xuanwu and his consort bearing ritual gifts to the shrine of the Buddha may be compared with the almost contemporaneous mosaics of Justinian and Theodora in San Vitale, Ravenna (see Figures 9.17, 9.18). Both the Ravenna mosaics and the Longmen reliefs are permanent memorials of rulers in the act of religious devotion. Lacking the ceremonial formality of its Byzantine counterpart, the image of *The Empress as Donor with Attendants* achieves an ornamental elegance that is as typical of Chinese relief sculpture as it is of Chinese calligraphy and painting.

Sixth-century China produced a generous selection of elegant bronze altarpieces. In Figure **9.33** a slender Buddha stands, his right hand in the gesture of reassurance, amidst a group of *bodhisattvas* and monks. His head is framed by a pierced, flame-shaped halo from which winged angelic creatures sprout. The vitality of the design depends on a calligraphic line that twists and flutters as if blown by a gentle breeze. A comparison of this devotional object with the Gupta statue of the *Teaching Buddha* (see Figure 9.27) and with the Christian *Crucifixion* on the west doors of Santa Sabina (see Figure 8.3) or the ivory book cover from Murano (see Figure 9.7) shows how artists—East and West—depended on stylization and abstraction to convey divine truths that surpassed the illusions of ordinary reality.

**Figure 9.32** *The Empress as Donor with Attendants*, from the Binyang cave chapel, Longmen, Henan, China, Northern Wei dynasty, ca. 522 C.E. Fine gray limestone with traces of color, 6 ft. 4 in. × 9 ft. 1 in. The Nelson-Atkins Museum of Art, Kansas City, Missouri. Purchase: Nelson Trust.

**Figure 9.33** Altar with Maitreya Buddha, Northern Wei dynasty, 524 C.E. Gilt bronze, height 30¼ in. The Metropolitan Museum of Art, New York. 38.158.1a–n.

## Buddhist Music in India and China

In its origins and development, the music of India was inseparable from India's religious history. For thousands of years, Hindu priests chanted Vedic hymns (see chapter 2). Like the ancient Greeks, Hindus identified sound and rhythm with the cosmic principle and considered music a powerful curative. Moreover, to the Hindu, music represented the marriage of physical breath and spiritual being, a union of the personal life force (*Atman*) and the Absolute Spirit (*Brahman*).

Scholars did not begin to survey Buddhist music until the early twentieth century. It seems clear, however, that Buddhist religious practices were based in India's ancient musical traditions, specifically those that involved the intoning of sacred Hindu texts. The recitation of *mantras* and the chanting of Sanskrit prayers were central acts of meditation among Buddhist monks, and the performance of such texts assumed a trancelike quality similar to that of Western plainsong. Buddhist chant was monophonic and lacked a fixed beat; but, unlike Western Church music, it was usually accompanied by percussion instruments (such as drums, bells, cymbals, and gongs) that imparted a rich rhythmic texture. Complex drumming techniques were among the most notable of Indian musical contributions.

As in India, Buddhist chant in China and Japan was performed in the monasteries. It featured the intoning of statements and responses interrupted by the sounding of percussion instruments such as bells or drums. As the chant proceeded, the pace of recitation increased, causing an overlapping of voices and instruments that produced a hypnotic web of sound.⸸

Sliding, nasal tones characterized the performance of Chinese music. Such tones were achieved by both the voice and by the instruments peculiar to Chinese culture. China's earliest and most important instrument was the **zither**, a five- or seven-stringed instrument that is generally plucked with a plectrum and the fingertips (see Figure 14.10). Associated with ancient religious and ceremonial music, the zither was quickly adopted by Buddhist monks. The vibrato or hum produced by plucking the strings of the zither is audible long after the instrument is touched, a phenomenon that Buddhists found comparable to the pervasive resonance of chant (and to the human breath seeking union with the One).

## SUMMARY

Between the fourth and sixth centuries, Christianity and Buddhism became world religions, each with its own set of religious symbols and its own identity. The Roman Empire was the vehicle by which Christianity rose to prominence in the West. It provided the early Christian Church with unique forms of administrative and cultural expression. A governing Church hierarchy and periodic Church councils worked to transform Christianity from a minor sect to an institutionalized religion. Four Latin church fathers—Augustine, Jerome, Ambrose, and Gregory—helped to formulate a uniform Christian doctrine and a distinctive liturgy. The writings of Augustine of Hippo, the most important of the Latin church fathers, were crucial to the development of the allegorical tradition. Christian monasticism, established in the West by Saint Benedict, played a large part in preserving and spreading the Christian message.

Christianity provided a mystical alternative to classical rationalism. The Christian promise of personal salvation encouraged intuition and faith as primary modes of experience. In the visual arts, Christianity inspired a turning away from objective representation and the world of the senses. A language of symbolism and allegory came to convey the Christian message of deliverance.

Parallel with the rise of Roman Catholicism in the West, the Eastern Orthodox Church grew powerful in the East Roman or Byzantine Empire. The fifth and sixth centuries were a time of great church construction. Saint Peter's in Rome and Hagia Sophia in Constantinople typify the respective Western and Eastern church styles. During the reign of the Byzantine emperor Justinian, some of the finest mosaics in the history of art were produced in Constantinople and Ravenna. In these mosaics, as in other examples of early Christian art, formal abstraction replaced realism, and symbolism replaced literal representation. Christian churches provided splendid settings for the performance of the Mass, the ceremony celebrating the sacrament of Holy Communion. The principal parts of this ceremony were recited in fluid, monophonic Gregorian chant.

Buddhist art and architecture flourished in India three centuries before the time of Jesus, but Buddhism spread into China and Southeast Asia only after the second century C.E. Unlike Christianity, Buddhism provided no fixed doctrine, no liturgy, and no clerical hierarchy to mediate between human beings and God. Buddhism shared with Christianity a strong monastic component and a reverence for sacred relics. But while early Christian churches became resplendent precincts for the public performance of the Christian liturgy, Buddhist *stupas*, rock-cut temples, and Chinese pagodas were essentially shrines for private worship and devotional meditation. The Mahayana Buddhist emphasis on the role of the Buddha as savior led to the increasing popularity of three-dimensional statues of the Buddha and the *bodhisattvas*, often shown teaching or meditating. Although music did not serve in any sacramental ceremony comparable with the Mass, in both India and China the percussive rhythms of religious chant filled Buddhist monasteries.

While personal salvation was the primary theme of early Christianity, spiritual enlightenment was the focus of Buddhism. Nevertheless, both religions employed the arts to glorify their respective founders and their teachings, and both left legacies that are rich in symbolic meaning and artistic value.

---

⸸See Music Listening Selections (right).

<hr>

### MUSIC LISTENING SELECTIONS

**Cassette I Selection 2** Gregorian chant, "Alleluya, vidimus stellam," codified 590–604.

**Cassette I Selection 3** Buddhist chant, Morning prayers (based on the Lotus Scripture) at Nomanji, Japan, excerpt.

# GLOSSARY

**abbot** (Latin, "father") the superior of an abbey or monastery for men; the female equivalent in a convent of nuns is called an "abbess"

*a cappella* choral singing without instrumental accompaniment

**ambulatory** a covered walkway, outdoors or indoors (see Figures 9.8, 13.7)

**antiphonal** a type of music in which two or more groups of voices or instruments alternate with one another

**apse** the semicircular recess at the east end of a Roman basilica or a Christian church (see Figure 9.8)

**benediction** the invocation of a blessing; in art, indicated by the raised right hand with fore and middle fingers extended

**canon law** the ecclesiastical law that governs the Christian Church

**cantor** the official in Judaism who sings or chants the liturgy; the official in medieval Christianity in charge of music at a cathedral, later a choir leader and soloist for the responsorial singing

**catacomb** a subterranean complex consisting of burial chambers and galleries with recesses for tombs

*chaitya* a sacred space, often applied to arcaded assembly halls that enclose a *stupa*

*chatra* an umbrellalike shape that signifies the sacred tree under which the Buddha reached *nirvana*

**clerestory** (also "clerstory") the upper part of the nave, whose walls contain openings for light (see Figure 9.8)

**diptych** a two-leaved hinged tablet; a two-paneled altarpiece

**dogma** a prescribed body of doctrines concerning faith or morals, formally stated and authoritatively proclaimed by the Church

**ecumenical** worldwide in extent; representing the whole body of churches

**gallery** the area between the clerestory and the nave arcade, usually adorned with mosaics in early Christian churches (see Figure 9.8)

**Greek cross** a cross in which all four arms are of equal length

**icon** (Greek, "likeness") the image of a saint or other religious figure

**iconography** the study of subject matter in art; also the visual imagery that conveys specific concepts and ideas in a work of art

**Latin cross** a cross in which the vertical member is longer than the horizontal member it intersects

**liturgy** the prescribed rituals or body of rites for public worship

**mantra** a mystical formula of invocation or incantation common to Hinduism and Buddhism

**melismatic** with many notes of music to one syllable

*mudra* (Sanskrit, "sign") a symbolic gesture commonly used in Buddhist art

**narthex** a porch or vestibule at the main entrance of a church (see Figure 9.8)

**nave** the central aisle of a church between the altar and the apse, usually demarcated from the side aisles by columns or piers (see Figure 9.8)

**neume** a mark or symbol indicating the direction of the voice in the early notation of Gregorian chant

*orans* a gesture involving the raising of the arms in an attitude of prayer

**pagoda** an East Asian shrine in the shape of a tower, usually with roofs curving upward at the division of each of several stories

**pendentive** a concave piece of masonry that makes the transition between the angle of two walls and the base of the dome above (see Figure 9.13)

*putto* (Italian, "child," plural *putti*) a nude, male child, usually winged; related to the classical Cupid (see chapter 7) and to Greco-Roman images of the angelic *psyche* or soul

**regular clergy** (Latin, *regula*, meaning "rule") those who have taken vows to obey the rules of a monastic order; as opposed to secular clergy (see below)

**responsorial** a type of music in which a single voice answers another voice or a chorus

**sarcophagus** (plural, "sarcophagi") a stone coffin

**secular clergy** those ordained to serve the Christian Church in the world

*stupa* a hemispherical mound that serves as a Buddhist shrine

**syllabic** with one note of music per syllable

*torana* a gateway that marks one of the four cardinal points in the stone fence surrounding a *stupa*

**transept** the part of a basilican-plan church that runs perpendicular to the nave (see Figure 9.8)

**zither** a five- or seven-stringed instrument that is usually plucked with a plectrum and the fingertips; the favorite instrument of ancient China

# SUGGESTIONS FOR READING

Bechert, Heinz, and Richard Gombrich. *The World of Buddhism: Buddhist Monks and Nuns in Society and Culture.* New York: Facts on File, 1984.

Beckwith, John. *Early Christian and Byzantine Art.* New York: Penguin, 1980.

Chadwick, Henry. *Augustine.* New York: Oxford University Press, 1986.

Fisher, Robert E. *Buddhist Art and Architecture.* New York: Thames and Hudson, 1993.

Kitzinger, Ernst. *Byzantine Art in the Making.* Cambridge, Mass.: Harvard University Press, 1977.

Knowles, David. *Christian Monasticism.* New York: McGraw-Hill, 1969.

Lowden, John. *Early Christian and Byzantine Art.* New York: Phaidon, 1997.

Lowrie, Walter. *Art in the Early Church.* New York: Harper, 1965.

Magoulias, H. J. *Byzantine Christianity: Emperor, Church and the West.* Detroit: Wayne State University Press, 1982.

Maguire, Henry. *Art and Eloquence in Byzantium.* Princeton, N.J.: Princeton University Press, 1995.

———. *The Icons of their Bodies: Saints and their Images in Byzantium.* Princeton, N.J.: Princeton University Press, 1996.

Milburn, Robert. *Early Christian Art and Architecture.* Berkeley, Calif.: University of California Press, 1988.

Taylor, H. O. *The Classical Heritage of the Middle Ages.* New York: Harper, 1968.

Weitzmann, Kurt. *Age of Spirituality: Late Antique and Early Christian Art.* New York: Metropolitan Museum of Art, 1979.

# 10

# The Islamic World: Religion and Culture

Islam, the world's youngest major religion, was born among the tribal peoples of the Arabian peninsula. The faith of the followers of Muhammad (ca. 570–632), it became the unifying force in the rise of the first global civilization since the fall of Rome. Islamic civilization was the geographic bridge between Europe and East Asia, as well as the historical link between the classical and early modern eras. But beyond its role as intermediary between the cultures of the East and the medieval West, Islam generated a rich cultural heritage of its own.

Between the eighth and fourteenth centuries, as Islam brought spiritual unity and cultural cohesiveness to people of a wide variety of languages and customs, it sustained an international community that stretched from Spain (in the West) across North Africa and into India (Map 10.1). Just as Christianity absorbed the cultural legacy of the Mediterranean in its reach across the Roman world, so, in its rise, Islam drew on the cultures of Arabia, Southwest Asia, and Persia. Islam's control of the Mediterranean snuffed out the waning Western sea trade and ushered in a period of incubation in Christian Europe. At the same time, Muslim expansion played a key role in defining the geographic borders of Western Europe. During the Middle Ages, Muslim communities in Spain, North Africa, and Southwest Asia cultivated rich traditions in the arts and sciences. Muslim scholars

**Map 10.1** The Expansion of Islam, 622–ca. 750 C.E.

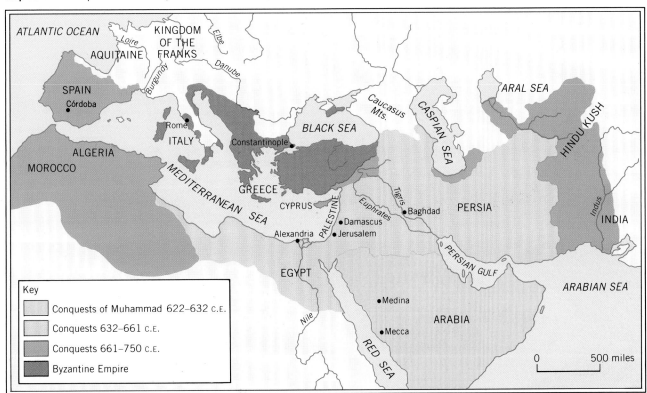

in the cities of Baghdad (in present-day Iraq) and Córdoba (in Andalusia, or Southern Spain) copied Greek manuscripts, creating a rich preserve of classical literature; and Islamic intermediaries carried into the West many of the greatest innovations of Asian culture. These achievements had far-reaching effects on global culture, on the subsequent rise of the European West and, more broadly, on the humanistic tradition.

The religion of Islam is practiced today by some one billion people, more than two-thirds of whom live outside of Southwest Asia. In the United States, home to over six million Muslims, Islam is the fastest growing religion. These facts suggest that, despite a decline in Islamic culture after 1350, Islam remains one of the most powerful religious forces in world history.

# The Religion of Islam

## Muhammad and Islam

Centuries before the time of Christ, nomadic Arabs known as Bedouins lived in the desert peninsula of Arabia east of Egypt. At the mercy of this arid land, they traded along the caravan routes of Southwest Asia. Bedouin Arabs were an animistic, tribal people who worshiped some three hundred different nature deities. Idols of these gods, along with the sacred Black Stone (probably an ancient meteorite), were housed in the *Kaaba*, a cubic,

roofless sanctuary located in the city of Mecca. Until the sixth century C.E., the Arabs remained polytheistic and disunited, but the birth of the prophet Muhammad in 570 in Mecca changed these circumstances dramatically.

Orphaned at the age of six, Muhammad received little formal education. He traveled with his uncle as a camel driver on caravan journeys that brought him into contact with communities of Jews, Christians, and pagans. At the age of twenty-five he married Khadijah, a wealthy widow fifteen years his senior, and assisted in running her flourishing caravan trade. Periods of solitary meditation in the desert, however, led to a transformation in Muhammad's career: According to Muslim teachings, the Angel Gabriel commanded Muhammad to proclaim his role as the prophet of the one and only Allah (the Arab word for God). Now forty-one years old, Muhammad declared himself the final messenger—human, not divine—in a history of religious revelation that had begun with Abraham and continued through Moses and Jesus. Preaching the revealed word of Allah to his followers—called Muslims—Muhammad taught that Allah was identical with the god of the Jews and that of the Christians: Fulfilling the long Judeo-Christian biblical tradition of deliverance, Islam ("submission to God's will") completed God's revelation to all "People of the Book."

Many of Allah's revelations to Muhammad, such as resurrection, the promise of personal immortality, and the concepts of Heaven and Hell, were staples of Christianity, while others, such as an uncompromising monotheism and a set of strict social and ethical commandments, were fundamental to Judaism. Addressed

**Figure 10.1** The *Kaaba*, Mecca, Saudi Arabia. Photo: Mohamed Amin/Robert Harding Picture Library, London.

to all people, however, the message of Islam holds simply: "There is no god but Allah [God], and Muhammad is the Messenger of God." Religious practise rests on the "Five Pillars of Faith": (1) declaration of the central belief, that is, the confession of faith, (2) recitation of prayers five times daily, (3) charitable contribution to the welfare of the Islamic community, (4) fasting from dawn until sunset during the sacred month of Ramadan, in which Muhammad received his divine calling, and (5) making the *hajj* or pilgrimage to the city of Mecca, Muhammad's birthplace. Pilgrims who throng to Mecca make the ritual procession that circles the *Kaaba* (Figure 10.1) seven times (compare Buddhist ritual, as described in chapter 9). Muslims identify the shrine of the Black Stone as the sacred spot where, at God's command, the biblical Abraham had prepared to sacrifice his son Isaac.

Despite Muhammad's effectiveness as a preacher, the polytheistic Meccans were slow to embrace the new faith. After a series of indecisive battles with the Meccan opposition, the Prophet abandoned his native city, emigrating, in 622, to nearby Medina—a journey known as the *hijra* or *hegira* ("migration"). After converting the population of Medina to Islam, he returned to Mecca with a following of ten thousand men, conquering the city and destroying the idols in the *Kaaba*, with the exception of the Black Stone. Thereafter, Muhammad would assume a position of spiritual and political leadership, and his disciples carried his teachings throughout and beyond Arabia. By the time Muhammad died in 632, the whole Arabian peninsula was united in its commitment to Islam. Since the history of successful missionary activity began with Muhammad's *hijra* in 622, his followers designated that date as the first year of the Muslim calendar.

## The Quran

Muhammad himself wrote nothing, but his disciples memorized his teachings and recorded them some ten years after his death. Written in Arabic, the Quran (sometimes transcribed as "Koran"; literally, "recitation") is the Holy Book of Islam (Figure 10.2). The Muslim guide to spiritual and secular life, the Quran consists of 114 chapters (*suras*) that reveal the nature of God and the inevitability of judgment and resurrection. Muslim Scripture offers guidelines for worship and specific moral and social injunctions for everyday conduct. It condemns drinking wine, eating pork, and all forms of gambling. Islam limits **polygyny** (marriage to several women at the same time) to no more than four wives, provided that a man can support and protect all of them. Although the Quran defends the equality of men and women before God (see Sura 4.3–7), it describes men as being "a degree higher than women" (in that they are the providers) and requires women to veil their bodies from public view (see Figure 10.3). Moreover, a husband has unrestricted rights of divorce and can end a marriage by renouncing his wife publicly. Nevertheless, Muhammad's teachings actually raised the status of women by condemning female infanticide, according women property rights, and ensuring their financial support in an age when such protections were not commonly guaranteed.

Muslims consider the Quran the eternal and absolute word of God, and centuries of Muslim leaders have governed according to its precepts. It is sacred poetry, intended to be chanted or recited, not read silently. Committed to memory by devout Muslims, the Quran is considered untranslatable, not only because its contents are deemed holy, but because it is impossible to

**Figure 10.2** Kufic calligraphy from the Quran, from Persia, ninth–tenth centuries C.E. Ink and gold leaf on vellum, 8½ × 21 in. The Nelson-Atkins Museum of Art, Kansas City, Missouri. Purchase: Nelson Trust.

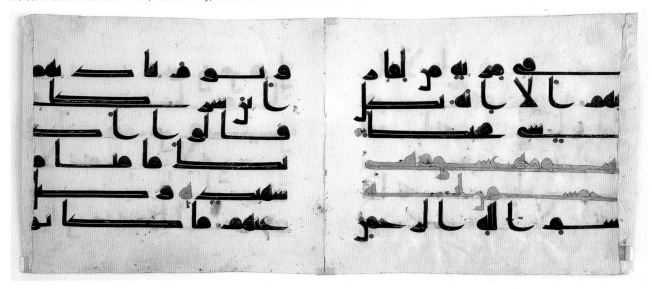

capture in other languages the musical nuances of the original Arabic. Since the main textbook of the Muslim world is written in Arabic, many non-Arab-speaking Muslims over the centuries have felt it necessary to learn that language. Crucial to Arab culture and Islamic civilization, the Quran is also the primary text for the study of the Arabic language.

# READING 2.9

## From the Quran

### Chapter 5 The Food

*In the name of Allah, most benevolent, ever-merciful.*

. . . . . . . . . .

8. O you who believe! Be upright for Allah, bearers of witness with justice, and let not hatred of a people incite you not to act equitably; act equitably, that is nearer to piety, and be careful of (your duty to) Allah; surely Allah is Aware of what you do.

9. Allah has promised to those who believe and do good deeds (that) they shall have forgiveness and a mighty reward.

10. And (as for) those who disbelieve and reject our communications, these are the companions of the flame.[2]

11. O you who believe! remember Allah's favor on you when a people had determined to stretch forth their hands towards you, but He withheld their hands from you, and be careful of (your duty to) Allah; and on Allah let the believers rely.

. . . . . . . . . .

68. Say: O followers of the Book![3] you follow no good till you keep up the [Torah] and the [Gospel] and that which is revealed to you from your Lord; and surely that which has been revealed to you from your Lord shall make many of them increase in inordinacy and unbelief; grieve not therefore for the unbelieving people.

69. Surely those who believe and those who are Jews and the Sebeans[4] and the Christians whoever believes in Allah and the last day and does good—they shall have no fear nor shall they grieve.

70. Certainly We made a covenant with the children of Israel and We sent to them apostles; whenever there came to them an apostle with what that their souls did not desire, some (of them) did they call liars and some they slew.

71. And they thought that there would be no affliction, so they became blind and deaf; then Allah turned to them mercifully, but many of them became blind and deaf; and Allah is well seeing what they do.

72. Certainly they disbelieve who say: Surely Allah, He is the Messiah, son of [Mary];[5] and the Messiah said: O Children of Israel! serve Allah, my Lord and your Lord. Surely whoever

associates (others) with Allah, then Allah has forbidden to him the garden,[6] and his abode is the fire; and there shall be no helpers for the unjust.

73. Certainly they disbelieve who say: Surely Allah is the third (person) of the three; and there is no god but the one God, and if they desist not from what they say, a painful chastisement shall befall those among them who disbelieve.

74. Will they not then turn to Allah and ask His forgiveness? And Allah is Forgiving, Merciful.

75. The Messiah, son of [Mary] is but an apostle; apostles before him have indeed passed away; and his mother was a truthful woman; they both used to eat food. See how We make the communications clear to them, then behold, how they are turned away.

76. Say: Do you serve besides Allah that which does not control for you any harm, or any profit? And Allah—He is the Hearing, the Knowing.

77. Say: O followers of the Book! be not unduly immoderate in your religion, and do not follow the low desires of people who went astray before and led many astray and went astray from the right path.

. . . . . . . . . .

### Chapter 17 The Israelites

*In the name of Allah, most benevolent, ever-merciful.*

. . . . . . . . . .

9. Surely this Quran guides to that which is most upright and gives good news to the believers who do good that they shall have a great reward.

10. And that (as for) those who do not believe in the hereafter, We have prepared for them a painful chastisement.

11. And man prays for evil as he ought to pray for good, and man is ever hasty.

12. And We have made the night and the day two signs, then We have made the sign of the night to pass away and We have made the sign of the day manifest, so that you may seek grace from your Lord, and that you might know the numbering of years and the reckoning; and We have explained everything with distinctness.

13. And We have made every man's actions to cling to his neck, and We will bring forth to him on the resurrection day a book which he will find wide open:

14. Read your book; your own self is sufficient as a reckoner against you this day.

15. Whoever goes aright, for his own soul does he go aright; and whoever goes astray, to its detriment only does he go astray; nor can the bearer of a burden bear the burden of another, nor do We chastise until We raise an apostle.

16. And when We wish to destroy a town, We send Our commandment to the people of it who lead easy lives, but they transgress therein; thus the word proves true against it, so We destroy it with utter destruction.

17. And how many of the generations did We destroy after [Noah] and your Lord is sufficient as Knowing and Seeing with regard to His servants' faults.

18. Whoever desires this present life, We hasten to him therein what We please for whomsoever We desire, then We assign to him the hell; he shall enter it despised, driven away.

19. And whoever desires the hereafter and strives for it as he

---

[1]Muhammad's followers arranged the 114 chapters of the Quran in order of length, from longest to shortest. The shorter chapters are, however, earlier in date.

[2]That is, Hell.

[3]Jews and Christians.

[4]Semitic merchants from the Saba, a kingdom in southern Arabia.

[5]Muslims believe in Jesus' virgin birth, his miraculous powers, and his ascent to Heaven, but not in his resurrection from the dead nor in his divinity.

[6]Heaven, or Paradise.

ought to strive and he is a believer; (as for) these, their striving shall surely be accepted.

20. All do We aid—these as well as those—out of the bounty of your Lord, and the bounty of your Lord is not confined.

21. See how We have made some of them to excel others, and certainly the hereafter is much superior in respect of excellence.

22. Do not associate with Allah any other god, lest you sit down despised, neglected.

23. And your Lord has commanded that you shall not serve (any) but Him, and goodness to your parents. If either or both of them reach old age with you, say not to them (so much as) "Ugh" nor chide them, and speak to them a generous word.

24. And make yourself submissively gentle to them with compassion, and say: O my Lord! have compassion on them, as they brought me up (when I was) little.

25. Your Lord knows best what is in your minds; if you are good, then He is surely Forgiving to those who turn (to Him) frequently.

26. And give to the near of kin his due and (to) the needy and the wayfarer, and do not squander wastefully.

. . . . . . . . . . .

31. And do not kill your children for fear of poverty; We give them sustenance and yourselves (too); surely to kill them is a great wrong.

32. And go not nigh to fornication; surely it is an indecency and an evil way.

33. And do not kill any one whom Allah has forbidden, except for a just cause, and whoever is slain unjustly, We have indeed given to his heir authority, so let him not exceed the just limits in slaying; surely he is aided.

34. And draw not near to the property of the orphan except in a goodly way till he attains his maturity and fulfill the promise; surely (every) promise shall be questioned about.

35. And give full measure when you measure out, and weigh with a true balance; this is fair and better in the end.

36. And follow not that of which you have not the knowledge; surely the hearing and the sight and the heart, all of these, shall be questioned about that.

37. And do not go about in the land exultingly, for you cannot cut through the earth nor reach the mountains in height.

38. All this—the evil of it—is hateful in the sight of your Lord.

39. This is of what your Lord has revealed to you of wisdom, and do not associate any other god with Allah lest you should be thrown into hell, blamed, cast away.

40. What! has then your Lord preferred to give you sons, and (for Himself) taken daughters from among the angels? Most surely you utter a grievous saying.

. . . . . . . . . . .

## Chapter 47 Muhammad

*In the name of Allah, most benevolent, ever-merciful.*

1. (As for) those who disbelieve and turn away from Allah's way, He shall render their works ineffective.

2. And (as for) those who believe and do good, and believe in what has been revealed to Muhammad, and it is the very truth from their Lord, He will remove their evil from them and improve their condition.

3. That is because those who disbelieve follow falsehood, and those who believe follow the truth from their Lord; thus does Allah set forth to men their examples.

4. So when you meet in battle those who disbelieve, then smite the necks until when you have overcome them, then make (them) prisoners, and afterwards either set them free as a favor or let them ransom (themselves) until the war terminates. That (shall be so); and if Allah had pleased He would certainly have exacted what is due from them, but that He may try some of you by means of others; and (as for) those who are slain in the way of Allah, He will by no means allow their deeds to perish.

5. He will guide them and improve their condition.

6. And cause them to enter the garden which He has made known to them.

7. O you who believe! if you help (the cause of) Allah, He will help you and make firm your feet.

8. And (as for) those who disbelieve, for them is destruction, and He has made their deeds ineffective.

9. That is because they hated what Allah revealed, so He rendered their deeds null.

10. Have they not then journeyed in the land and seen how was the end of those before them: Allah brought down destruction upon them, and the unbelievers shall have the like of it.

11. That is because Allah is the Protector of those who believe, and because the unbelievers shall have no protector for them.

. . . . . . . . . . .

## Chapter 76 The Man

*In the name of Allah, most benevolent, ever-merciful.*

1. There surely came over man a period of time when he was a thing not worth mentioning.

2. Surely We have created man from a small life-germ uniting (itself): We mean to try him, so We have made him hearing, seeing.

3. Surely We have shown him the way: he may be thankful or unthankful.

4. Surely We have prepared for the unbelievers chains and shackles and a burning fire.

5. Surely the righteous shall drink of a cup the admixture of which is camphor,[7]

6. A fountain from which the servants of Allah shall drink; they make it to flow a (goodly) flowing forth.

7. They fulfill vows and fear a day the evil of which shall be spreading far and wide.

8. And they give food out of love for Him to the poor and the orphan and the captive:

9. We only feed you for Allah's sake; we desire from you neither reward nor thanks:

10. Surely we fear from our Lord a stern, distressful day.

11. Therefore Allah will guard them from the evil of that day and cause them to meet with ease and happiness;

12. And reward them, because they were patient, with garden and silk [in Paradise],

13. Reclining therein on raised couches, they shall find therein neither (the severe heat of) the sun nor intense cold.

14. And close down upon them (shall be) its shadows, and its fruits shall be made near (to them), being easy to reach.

---

[7]A cool and refreshing aromatic.

15. And there shall be made to go round[8] about them vessels of silver and goblets which are of glass,

16. (Transparent as) glass, made of silver; they have measured them according to a measure.

17. And they shall be made to drink therein a cup the admixture of which shall be ginger,

18. (Of) a fountain therein which is named Salsabil.[9]

19. And round about them shall go youths never altering in age; when you see them you will think them to be scattered pearls.

20. And when you see there, you shall see blessings and a great kingdom.

21. Upon them shall be garments of fine green silk and thick silk interwoven with gold, and they shall be adorned with bracelets of silver, and their Lord shall make them drink a pure drink.

22. Surely this is a reward for you, and your striving shall be recompensed.

23. Surely We Ourselves have revealed the Quran to you, revealing (it) in portions.

24. Therefore wait patiently for the command of your Lord, and obey not from among them a sinner or an ungrateful one.

25. And glorify the name of your Lord morning and evening.

◆

## The Spread of Islam

To the people of the hot and arid Arab desert, the Quran promised a paradise filled with flowing rivers, shade-providing fruit trees, and handsome youths serving cool liquids in silver goblets. But paired with the sensuous pleasures of divine reward were the terrifying punishments of Hell—as hot and dusty as the desert itself—the destination of the wicked and of **infidels** (non-believers). For those who accepted Allah, Islam provided a system of social justice and the guidelines for obedient worship. It offered, as well, a universal ethic that emphasized equality among all members of the Islamic community.

Islam's success in becoming a world faith is a remarkable historical phenomenon, one that is explained in part by the fact that, at the outset, religious, political, and military goals were allied—somewhat as with Christianity after the Edict of Milan. However, other factors were crucial to the success of Islam. The new faith offered rules of conduct that were easy to understand and to follow—a timely alternative, perhaps, to the complexities of Jewish ritual and Christian theology. In contrast with Christianity and Judaism, Islam remained free of dogma and liturgy, and was unencumbered by a priestly hierarchy. Orthodox Muslims venerated no intercessors and regarded the Christian cult of saints as

a form of polytheism. The core Islamic texts, the Quran and the *Hadith* (a compilation of Muhammad's sayings and deeds), provided the all-embracing code of ethical conduct known as the **sharia** ("the path to follow"). Spiritual supervision fell into the hands of prayer leaders (**imams**) and scholars trained in Muslim law (**mullahs**), whose duty it was to interpret the *sharia*.

Islam unified the tribal population of Arabia in a common religious and ethnic bond that propelled Muslims out of their desert confines into East Asia, Africa, and the West. The fledgling religion assumed a sense of historical mission much like that which drove the ancient Romans or the early Christians. In fact, the militant expansion of Islam—like the militant expansion of the Christian West (discussed in chapter 11)—was the evangelical counterpart of unbounded religious zeal. *Jihad*, or fervent religious struggle, describes the nature of Muslim expansion. Usually translated (too narrowly) as "holy war," the word signifies all aspects of the Muslim drive toward moral and religious perfection, including the defense and spread of Islam. Although there are multiple interpretations of this term in Muslim thought and practice, its dual aspect may be understood in Muhammad's distinction between "the lesser *jihad*" (war) and "the greater *jihad*" (self-control, or struggle to contain lust, anger, and other forms of indulgence). It is fair to assume that militant Muslims would have agreed with Augustine that a "just cause" made warfare acceptable in the eyes of God (see chapter 9). Indeed, Christian soldiers looked forward to Paradise if they died fighting for Christ, while Muslims looked for Paradise if they died in the service of Allah.

Generally speaking, early Muslim expansion succeeded not so much by the militant coercion of foreign populations as it did by the economic opportunities Muslims offered conquered people. Unlike Christianity and Buddhism, Islam neither renounced nor condemned material wealth. Converts to Islam were exempt from paying a poll-tax levied on all non-Muslim subjects. Into the towns that would soon become cultural oases, Muslims brought expertise in navigation, trade, and commercial exchange; they fostered favorable associations between Arab merchants and members of the ruling elite (in Africa, for instance) and rewarded converts with access to positions of power and authority. While many subject people embraced Islam out of genuine spiritual conviction, others found clear commercial and social advantages in conversion to the faith of Muhammad.

Muhammad never designated a successor; hence, after his death, bitter controversies arose concerning religious leadership. Rival claims to authority produced major divisions within the faith that still exist today; the **Sunni** (from *sunna*, "the tradition of the Prophet") consider themselves the orthodox of Islam. Representing approximately ninety percent of the modern Muslim

---

[8]That is, passed around.

[9]Literally, "Seek the Way"; the word also means "sweet" and "rapid-flowing".

**Figure 10.3** *The Slave Market at Zabīd, Yemen*, from the *Maqāmāt of al-Harīrī*, 1237. Bibliothèque Nationale, Paris, MS Arabe 5847, fol. 105.

world population, they hold that religious rulers should be chosen by the faithful. By contrast, the Shiites (living primarily in Iran and Iraq today) claim descent through Muhammad's cousin and son-in-law Ali and believe that only his direct descendants should rule. Following Muhammad's death, the **caliphs,** or successors to Muhammad, were appointed by his followers. The first four caliphs, who ruled until 661, assumed political and religious authority, and their success in carrying Islam outside of Arabia (see Map 10.1) resulted in the establishment of a Muslim empire. Damascus fell to Islam in 634, Persia in 636, Jerusalem in 638, and Egypt in 640. Within another seventy years, all of North Africa and Spain also lay under Muslim rule. The Muslim advance upon the West encountered only two significant obstacles: The first was Constantinople, where Byzantine forces equipped with "Greek fire" (an incendiary compound catapulted from ships) deterred repeated Arab attacks. The second was in Southwest France near Tours, where, in 732, Frankish soldiers led by Charles Martel (the grandfather of Charlemagne) turned back the Muslims, barring the progress of Islam into Europe.

Nevertheless, in less than a century, Islam had won more converts than Christianity had gained in its first three hundred years.

Followers of Muhammad may have entered the African continent even before the Prophet's *hijra* in the early seventh century. On the edges of the Sahara Desert and in North Africa, Muslim traders came to dominate commerce in salt, gold, and slaves (Figure 10.3). They soon commanded the trans-Saharan network that linked West Africa to Cairo and continued through Asia via the Silk Road to China (see chapters 7, 14). Islam would quickly become Africa's fastest growing religion, mingling with various aspects of local belief systems as it attracted a following primarily among the ruling elite of the continent's burgeoning kingdoms: in West Africa, Ghana, Mali, and Songhai (see chapter 19). The kings of Mali incorporated Islamic rituals into native African ceremonies; adopted the Arabic language for administrative purposes; hired Muslim scribes and jurists; and underwrote the construction of mosques and universities, the greatest of which was located at Timbuktu. In East Africa, as elsewhere, Swahili rulers who converted to Islam did not actively impose the religion on their subjects, so that only the larger African towns and centers of trade became oases of Islamic culture.

Between 661 and 750, Damascus served as the political center of the Muslim world. However, as Islam spread eastward under the leadership of a new Muslim dynasty—the Abbasids—the capital shifted to Baghdad in Iraq. Here, between the ninth and twelfth centuries, a golden age flourished with the riches of expansive commercial activity feeding an energetic urban population. Arab merchants imported leopards and rubies from India; silk, paper, and porcelain from China; horses and camels from Arabia; topaz and cotton cloth from Egypt. The court of the caliph Harun al-Rashid (ruled 786–809) attracted musicians, dancers, writers, and poets. Harun's sons opened a "house of wisdom" in which scholars prepared Arabic translations of Greek, Persian, Syraic, and Sanskrit manuscripts. In the ninth century, no city in the world could match the breadth of educational instruction or boast a library as large as that of Baghdad. Al-Yaqubi, a late ninth-century visitor to Baghdad, called Iraq "the navel of the earth" and Baghdad "the greatest city, which has no peer in the east or the west of the world in extent, size, prosperity, abundance of water, or health of climate. . . ." He continued:

> To [Baghdad] they come from all countries, far and near, and people from every side have preferred Baghdad to their own homelands. There is no country, the peoples of which have not their own quarter and their own trading and financial arrangements. In it there is gathered that which does not exist in any other city in the world. On its flanks flow two great rivers, the Tigris and the Euphrates, and thus goods and foodstuffs come to it by land and water with the greatest ease, so that every kind of merchandise is completely available, from east and west, from Muslim and non-Muslim lands. Goods are brought from India, Sind [modern Pakistan], China, Tibet, the lands of the Turks, . . . the Ethiopians, and others to such an extent that

[products] are more plentiful in Baghdad than in the countries from which they come. They can be procured so readily and so certainly that it is as if all the good things of the world are sent there, all the treasures of the earth assembled there, and all the blessings of creation perfected there. . . . The people excel in knowledge, understanding, letters, manners, insight, discernment, skill in commerce and crafts, cleverness in every argument, proficiency in every calling, and mastery of every craft. There is none more learned than their scholars, better informed than their traditionists, more cogent than their theologians, more perspicuous than their grammarians, more accurate than their [calligraphers], more skillful than their physicians, more melodious than their singers, more delicate than their craftsmen, more literate than their scribes, more lucid than their logicians, more devoted than their worshipers, more pious than their ascetics, more juridical than their [magistrates], more eloquent than their preachers, more poetic than their poets, and more reckless than their rakes.*

Although this description may reflect the sentiments of an overly enthusiastic tourist, it is accurate to say that, between the eighth and tenth centuries, the cosmopolitan cities of the Muslim world boasted levels of wealth and culture that far exceeded those of Western Christendom. Even after invading Turkish nomads gained control of Baghdad during the eleventh century, the city retained cultural primacy within the civilized world—although Córdoba, with a library of some 400,000 volumes, came to rival Baghdad as a cultural and educational center. The destruction of Baghdad in 1258 at the hands of the Mongols ushered in centuries of slow cultural decline. However, Mongols and Turks, themselves converts to Islam, carried Islamic culture into India and China. In Egypt, an independent Islamic government ruled until the sixteenth century. The Tunisian historian Ibn Khaldun, visiting fourteenth-century Egypt, called Cairo "the mother of the world, the great center of Islam and the mainspring of the sciences and the crafts." Until the mid-fourteenth century, Muslims continued to dominate a system of world trade that stretched from Western Europe to China; thereafter, the glories of medieval Muslim culture waned. The same cannot be said of the religion of Islam: Over the centuries of Islamic expansion, millions of people found Islam responsive to their immediate spiritual needs, and in most of the Asiatic and African regions conquered prior to the late seventh century (see Map 10.1), it still remains the dominant faith. To date, Islam has experienced less change and remains closer to its original form than any other world religion.

| | |
|---|---|
| **765** | the medical hospital constructed at Baghdad becomes a prototype for those built elsewhere |
| **783** | a paper mill (based on a Chinese design) is introduced in Baghdad |
| **820** | publication of *Al-jabr wa l mugābalah*, an Arabic adaptation of Hindu numerals to solve equations (called "algebra" in Europe) |
| **ca. 830** | Geographers at Baghdad's House of Wisdom estimate the earth's circumference by directly measuring one degree of latitude on the earth's surface |
| **850** | the Arabs refine the astrolabe (from Greek prototypes) |
| **950** | al-Farabi publishes a treatise—the *Catalogue of the Sciences*—on applied mathematics |

*Bernard Lewis, ed. and trans., *Islam from the Prophet Muhammad to the Capture of Constantinople.* New York: Oxford University Press, 1987, 69–71.

## Islamic Culture

From its beginnings, Islam held the status of a state-sponsored religion; however, the unique feature of Islamic civilization is its diversity, the product of its assimilation of the many different cultures and peoples it encountered. The principal languages of the Islamic world, for instance, are Arabic, Persian, and Turkish, but dozens of other languages, including Berber, Swahili, Kurdish, Tamil, Malay, and Javanese, are spoken by Muslims. Moreover, as Islam expanded, it absorbed many different styles from the arts of non-Arab cultures. "Islamic," then, is a term used to describe the culture of geographically diverse regions—Arab and non-Arab—dominated by Islam.

### Scholarship in the Islamic World

Following Muhammad's dictum to "seek knowledge," Islam was enthusiastically receptive to the intellectual achievements of other cultures and aggressive in its will to understand the workings of the natural world. At a time when few Westerners could read or write Latin and even fewer could decipher Greek, Arab scholars preserved hundreds of ancient Greek manuscripts, copying and editing them in Arabic translations. Prior to the twelfth century, Muslims absorbed and preserved much of the medical, botanical, and astrological lore of the Hellenized Mediterranean. This fund of scientific and technological knowledge, along with Arabic translations of Aristotle's works in logic and natural philosophy, they ultimately transmitted to the West.

By the twelfth century, Muslim commentaries on Aristotle filtered into the urban centers of Europe, where they stimulated a rebirth of learning and contributed to the rise of Western universities (see chapter 12). Muslim philosophers compared the theories of Aristotle and the neoplatonists with the precepts of Islam, seeking a unity of truth that would become the object of inquiry among Italian Renaissance humanists

**Figure 10.4** *Preparing Medicine from Honey*, from an Arabic manuscript of *Materia Medica* by Dioscorides, thirteenth century. Colors and gilt on paper, 12⅜ × 9 in. The Metropolitan Museum of Art, New York. Cora Timken Burnett Collection of Persian Miniatures and Other Persian Art Objects. Bequest of Cora Timken Burnett, 1956. 57.51.21.

(see chapter 16). Crucial to the advancement of learning was the Muslim transmission of Hindu numbers, which replaced cumbersome Roman numerals with so-called "Arabic numbers" such as those used to paginate this book. Muslims also provided the West with such technological wonders as paper and block printing (after the eighth century) and gunpowder (after the thirteenth century), all of which originated in China (see chapter 14). Muslims thus borrowed and diffused the knowledge of Greek, Chinese, and Indian culture as energetically as they circulated commercial goods.

But the scholars of the Islamic world were not merely copyists; they made original contributions in mathematics, medicine, optics, chemistry, geography, philosophy, and astronomy. In the field of medicine, Islamic physicians wrote treatises on smallpox, measles, and diseases transmitted by animals (such as rabies), on the cauterization of wounds, and on the preparation of medicinal drugs (Figure 10.4). The vast *Canon of Medicine* compiled by the Persian physician and philosopher Ibn Sina (Avicenna, 980–1037) was a systematic repository of medical knowledge in use well into the sixteenth century. Muslim chemists invented the process of distillation and produced a volatile liquid (and forbidden intoxicant) called *alkuhl* (alcohol). At a time when most Europeans knew little of the earth's physical size or shape, geographers in Baghdad estimated with some accuracy the earth's circumference, as well as its shape and curvature. Muslim astronomers made advances in spherical geometry and trigonometry that aided religious observance, which required an accurate lunar calendar and the means of determining the direction of Mecca from any given location. By refining the astrolabe, an ancient instrument for measuring the altitude of heavenly bodies above the horizon (Figure 10.5), Muslims were able to determine the time of day, hence estimate the correct hours for worship.

## Islamic Poetry

In the Islamic literary tradition—a tradition dominated by two highly lyrical languages, Arabic and Persian—poetry played an infinitely more important role than

**Figure 10.5** Abd al-Karim al-Misri, Astrolabe, from Cairo, 1235–1236. Brass, height 15½ in. British Museum, London.

prose. As within the cultures of ancient Greece, Africa, and China, poetry and music were intimately related, and local bards or wandering minstrels were the "keepers" of a popular oral verse tradition (see chapters 4, 19). The Bedouin minstrels of pre-Islamic culture celebrated in song themes of romantic love, tribal warfare, and nomadic life. Bedouin songs, like the Arabic language itself, are rich in rhyme, and a single rhyme often dominates an entire poem. No English translation can capture the musical qualities of Arabic verse, and only some translations succeed in preserving its colorful descriptive imagery. Such is the case with the sixth-century ode by Tarafa in Reading 2.10, which uses vivid similes to convey a memorable portrait of the camel that has captured his heart.

Following the rise of Islam, no literature was prized more highly than the Arabic lyrics that constituted the Quran. However, the pre-Islamic affection for secular verse persisted: The dominant themes in Islamic poetry included laments over injustice, elegies for the departed, and celebrations of the physical delights of nature. Romantic love—both heterosexual and homosexual, and often strongly erotic—was a favorite subject, especially among those who came under the influence of Persian literature. The eighth-century "Romance of Antar," a eulogy in honor of a beautiful and bewitching female, attributed to al-Asmai, reflects the sensual power of the finest Islamic lyrics. The poet's "ailment" of unrequited love, or "lovesickness," was a popular conceit in Arabic verse and one that became central to the code of courtly love in the medieval West. With their frank examination of physical desire and their reverence for female beauty, the poems of al-Asmai (740–828), Ibn Zaydun (1003–1071), and Ibn Abra—

| | | |
|---|---|---|
| **1005** | a comprehensive science library is founded in Cairo |
| **1030** | Ibn al-Haytham (Alhazen) publishes the first major work on optics since Hellenistic times |
| **1035** | publication of Ibn Sina's *Canon of Medicine*, an Arab compilation of Greek and Arab medical principles |
| **1075** | Arab astronomers posit the elliptical orbits of the planets |
| **ca. 1150** | al-Idrisi prepares a geographical survey of the world with maps for climatic sections |

the latter two representative of Moorish* Islam—influenced the various genres of literature in Western Europe. This includes *troubadour* poetry, the medieval romance (see chapter 11), and the sonnets and songs of the Renaissance poet Petrarch (see chapter 16).

## READING 2.10
### Secular Islamic Poems

#### From Tarafa's "Praise for His Camel"

. . . . . . . . . .

Yet I have means to fly from grief, when such pursues me,      1
    on a lean high beast, which paces swiftly by day and
    by night,
A camel sure of foot, firm and thin as the planks of a bier,
    whom I guide surely over the trodden ways, ways         5
    etched in earth as texture is in cloth;
A she-camel, rival of the best, swift as an ostrich. When
    she trots her hind feet fall in the marks of her forefeet
    on the beaten road.

With her white feathery tail she lashes backward and         10
    forward. Sometimes the lash falls on her rider,
    sometimes on her own dried udder, where no milk is,
    flaccid as an old bottle of leather.
Firm and polished are her haunches as two worn jambs of
    a castle gate.                                           15
The bones of her spine are supple and well-attached, and
    her neck rises solidly.

When she raises her long neck it is like the rudder of a
    boat going up the Tigris.
She carries her strong thighs well apart, as a carrier of    20
    water holds apart his buckets.
Red is the hair under her chin. Strong she is of back, long
    of stride; easily she moves her forelegs.

The marks of the girths on her sides are as the marks of
    water-courses over smooth rock.                          25
Sometimes the marks unite and sometimes are distinct,
    like the gores in fine linen, well-cut and stitched.
Her long skull is like an anvil, and where the bones unite
    their edges are sharp as the teeth of a file.
Her cheek is smooth as paper of Syria, and her upper lip    30
    like leather of Yemen, exactly and smoothly cut.
The two polished mirrors of her eyes gleam in the caverns
    of their sockets as water gleams in rocky pools.

Her ears are sharp to hear the low voices of the night, and
    not inattentive to the loud call,                        35
Pricked ears, that show her breeding, like those of a lone
    wild bull in the groves of Haumel.
Her upper lip is divided and her nose pierced. When she
    stretches them along the ground her pace increases.
I touch her with my whip and she quickens her step, even    40
    though it be the time when the mirage shimmers on
    the burning sands.
She walks with graceful gait, as the dancing girl walks,
    showing her master the skirts of her trailing garment.

#### From Al-Asmai's "Romance of Antar"

. . . . . . . . . .

The lovely virgin has struck my heart with the arrow of a    1
    glance, for which there is no cure.
Sometimes she wishes for a feast in the sand-hills, like a
    fawn whose eyes are full of magic.
My disease preys on me; it is in my entrails: I conceal it;  5
    but its very concealment discloses it.
She moves: I should say it was the branch of the tamarisk[1]
    that waves its branches to the southern breeze.
She approaches: I should say her face was truly the sun
    when its luster dazzles the beholders.                  10
She walks away: I should say her face was truly the sun
    when its luster dazzles the beholders.
She gazes: I should say it was the full moon of the night
    when Orion[2] girds it with stars.
She smiles: and the pearls of her teeth sparkle, in which   15
    there is the cure for the sickness of lovers.
She prostrates herself in reverence towards her God;
    and the greatest of men bow down to her beauties.
O Abla! when I most despair, love for thee and all its
    weaknesses are my only hope!                            20

#### Ibn Zaydun's "Two Fragments"
##### I

The world is strange
For lack of you;
Times change their common hue—
The day is black, but very night
With you was shining white.

##### II

Two secrets in the heart of night
We were until the light
Of busybody day
Gave both of us away.

#### Ibn Abra's "The Beauty-Spot"

A mole on Ahmad's cheek
Draws all men's eyes to seek
The love they swear reposes
In a garden there.
That breathing bed of roses
In a Nubian's care.

---◆---

## Sufi Poetry

One of the richest sources of literary inspiration in Islamic history was the movement known as Sufism. As early as the eighth century, some followers of Muhammad began to pursue a meditative, world-renouncing religious life that resembled the spiritual ideals of Christian and Buddhist ascetics and neoplatonic mystics. The Sufi, so-called for the coarse wool (*suf*) garments they wore, were committed to purification of the soul and mystical

---

*The term "Moor" describes a Northwest African Muslim of mixed Arab and Berber descent. The Moors invaded and occupied Spain in the eighth century and maintained a strong presence there until they were expelled from Granada, their last stronghold, in 1492.

[1]A small tree or shrub from the Mediterranean region.
[2]A constellation of bright stars represented by the figure of a hunter with belt and sword.

union with God through meditation, fasting, and prayer. As the movement grew, Sufism placed increasing emphasis on visionary experience and the practice of intensifying physical sensation through music, poetry, and dance. Religious rituals involving whirling dances (associated with Persian sufis, known as "dervishes") functioned to transport the pious to a state of ecstasy. The union of the senses and the spirit sought by the members of this ascetic brotherhood is also evident in Sufi poetry.

Sufi poetry, as represented in the works of the great Persian mystic and poet Jalal al-Din Rumi (1203–1273), draws on the intuitive, nonrational dimensions of the religious experience. In the first of the following three poems, a number of seeming contradictions work to characterize the unique nature of the spiritual master. The body of Sufi instructions outlined in the second poem might be equally appropriate to the Buddhist or the Christian mystic. In the third piece, "The One True Light," Rumi rehearses an ancient parable that illuminates the unity of God: Seeing beyond the dim gropings of the ordinary intellect, the mystic perceives that religions are many, but God is One.

## READING 2.11
## Rumi's Poems

### "The Man of God"

| | |
|---|---|
| The man of God is drunken while sober. | 1 |
| The man of God is full without meat. | |
| The man of God is perplexed and bewildered. | |
| The man of God neither sleeps nor eats. | |
| The man of God is a king clothed in rags. | 5 |
| The man of God is a treasure in the streets. | |
| The man of God is neither of sky nor land. | |
| The man of God is neither of earth nor sea. | |
| The man of God is an ocean without end. | |
| The man of God drops pearls at your feet. | 10 |
| The man of God has a hundred moons at night. | |
| The man of God has a hundred suns' light. | |
| The man of God's knowledge is complete. | |
| The man of God doesn't read with his sight. | |
| The man of God is beyond form and disbelief. | 15 |
| The man of God sees good and bad alike. | |
| The man of God is far beyond non-being. | |
| The man of God is seen riding high. | |
| The man of God is hidden, Shamsuddin. | |
| The man of God you must seek and find. | 20 |

### "Empty the Glass of Your Desire"

| | |
|---|---|
| Join yourself to friends | 1 |
| and know the joy of the soul. | |
| Enter the neighborhood of ruin | |
| with those who drink to the dregs. | |
| | |
| Empty the glass of your desire | 5 |
| so that you won't be disgraced. | |

| | |
|---|---|
| Stop looking for something out there | |
| and begin seeing within. | |
| | |
| Open your arms if you want an embrace. | |
| Break the earthen idols and release the radiance. | 10 |
| Why get involved with a hag like this world? | |
| You know what it will cost. | |
| | |
| And three pitiful meals a day | |
| is all that weapons and violence can earn. | |
| At night when the Beloved comes | 15 |
| will you be nodding on opium? | |
| | |
| If you close your mouth to food, | |
| you can know a sweeter taste. | |
| Our Host is no tyrant. We gather in a circle. | |
| Sit down with us beyond the wheel of time. | 20 |
| | |
| Here is the deal: give one life | |
| and receive a hundred. | |
| Stop growling like dogs, | |
| and know the shepherd's care. | |
| | |
| You keep complaining about others | 25 |
| and all they owe you? | |
| Well, forget about them; | |
| just be in His presence. | |
| | |
| When the earth is this wide, | |
| why are you asleep in a prison? | 30 |
| Think of nothing but the source of thought. | |
| Feed the soul; let the body fast. | |
| | |
| Avoid knotted ideas; | |
| untie yourself in a higher world. | |
| Limit your talk | 35 |
| for the sake of timeless communion. | |
| | |
| Abandon life and the world, | |
| and find the life *of* the world. | |

### "The One True Light"

| | |
|---|---|
| The lamps are different, but the Light is the same: it comes from Beyond. | 1 |
| If thou keep looking at the lamp, thou art lost: for thence arises the appearance of number and plurality. | |
| Fix thy gaze upon the Light, and thou art delivered from the dualism inherent in the finite body. | |
| O thou who art the kernel of Existence, the disagreement between Moslem, Zoroastrian and Jew depends on the standpoint. | |
| | |
| Some Hindus brought an elephant, which they exhibited in a dark shed. | 5 |
| As seeing it with the eye was impossible, every one felt it with the palm of his hand. | |
| The hand of one fell on its trunk: he said, "This animal is like a water-pipe." | |
| Another touched its ear: to him the creature seemed like a fan. | |
| Another handled its leg and described the elephant as having the shape of a pillar. | |
| Another stroked its back. "Truly," said he, "this elephant resembles a throne." | 10 |
| Had each of them held a lighted candle, there would have been no contradiction in their words. | |

------------ ◆ ------------

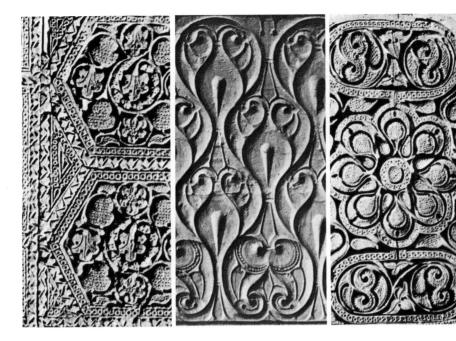

**Figure 10.6** Carved panels, from Samarra, Iraq, ninth century C.E. Stucco. © Editions Citadelles et Mazenod, Paris.

## Islamic Prose Literature

Islam prized poetry over prose, but both forms drew on enduring oral tradition and on the verbal treasures of many regions. Unique to Arabic literature was rhyming prose, which brought a musical quality to everyday speech. One of the most popular forms of prose literary entertainment was a collection of eighth-century animal fables, which instructed as they amused. Another, which narrated the adventures of a rogue or vagabond characters, anticipated by five centuries the picaresque novel in the West (see chapter 24).

The rich diversity of Islamic culture is nowhere better revealed, however, than in the collection of prose tales known as *The Thousand and One Nights*. This literary classic, gradually assembled between the eighth and tenth centuries, brought together in the Arabic tongue various tales from Persian, Arabic, and Indian sources—the earliest is probably the story of Sinbad the Sailor, Merchant of Baghdad. The framework for the whole derives from an Indian fairy tale: Shahrasad (in English, Scheherazade) marries a king who fears female infidelity so greatly that he kills each new wife on the morning after the wedding night. In order to forestall her own death, Scheherazade entertains the king by telling stories, each of which she carefully brings to a climax just before dawn, so that, in order to learn the ending, the king must allow her to live. Scheherazade—or, more exactly, her storytelling—has a humanizing effect upon the king, who, after a thousand nights, comes to prize his clever wife. *The Thousand and One Nights*, which exists in many versions, actually contains only some 250 tales, many of which have become favorites with readers throughout the world: The adventures of Ali Baba, Aladdin, Sinbad, and others are filled with fantasy, exotic characters, and spicy romance. The manner in which each tale loops into the next, linking story to story and parts of each story to each other, resembles the regulating principles of design in Islamic art, which include repetition, infinite extension, and the looping together of motifs to form a meandering, overall pattern (Figure **10.6**).

The story of Prince Behram and the Princess Al-Datma, reproduced below, addresses some of the major themes in Islamic literary culture: the power of female beauty, survival through cunning, and the "battle" of the sexes. It also provides gentle insight into Islamic notions of etiquette and sexual identity. Finally, ingenuity (exercised by both of the major characters in their efforts to achieve what they most desire) becomes a metaphor for Scheherazade herself, whose beauty, wit, and verbal powers prove to be a civilizing force.

### READING 2.12
## From *The Thousand and One Nights*

#### "Prince Behram and the Princess Al-Datma"

There was once a king's daughter called Al-Datma who, in her time, had no equal in beauty and grace. In addition to her lovely looks, she was brilliant and feisty and took great pleasure in ravishing the wits of the male sex. In fact, she used to boast, "There is nobody who can match me in anything." And the fact is that she was most accomplished in horsemanship and martial exercises, and all those things a cavalier should know. 1

Given her qualities, numerous princes sought her hand in marriage, but she rejected them all. Instead, she proclaimed, "No man shall marry me unless he defeats me with his lance and sword in fair battle. He who succeeds I will gladly wed. But if I overcome him, I will take his horse, clothes, and arms and brand his head with the following words: 'This is the freedom of Al-Datma.'" 10

Now the sons of kings flocked to her from every quarter far and near, but she prevailed and put them to shame, stripping them of their arms and branding them

**Figure 10.7** Niche (*mihrab*) showing Islamic calligraphy, from Iran. The Metropolitan Museum of Art, New York. 39.20.

with fire. Soon, a son of the king of Persia named Behram ibn Taji heard about her and journeyed from afar to her father's court. He brought men and horses with him and a great deal of wealth and royal treasures. When he drew near the city, he sent her father a rich present, and the king came out to meet him and bestowed great honors on him. Then the king's son sent a message to him through his vizier and requested his daughter's hand in marriage. However, the king answered, "With regard to my daughter Al-Datma, I have no power over her, for she has sworn by her soul to marry no one but him who defeats her in the listed field." 30

"I journeyed here from my father's court with no other purpose but this," the prince declared. "I came here to woo her and to form an alliance with you."

"Then you shall meet her tomorrow," said the king.

So the next day he sent for his daughter, who got ready for battle by donning her armor of war. Since the people of the kingdom had heard about the coming joust, they flocked from all sides to the field. Soon the princess rode into the lists, armed head to toe with her visor down, and the Persian king's son came out to meet her, 40 equipped in the fairest of fashions. Then they charged at each other and fought a long time, wheeling and sparring, advancing and retreating, and the princess realized that he had more courage and skill than she had ever encountered before. Indeed, she began to fear that he might put her to shame before the bystanders and defeat her. Consequently, she decided to trick him, and raising her visor, she showed her face, which appeared more radiant than the full moon, and when he saw it, he was bewildered by her beauty. His strength failed, and 50 his spirit faltered. When she perceived this moment of weakness, she attacked and knocked him from his saddle. Consequently, he became like a sparrow in the clutches of an eagle. Amazed and confused, he did not know what was happening to him when she took his steed, clothes, and armor. Then, after branding him with fire, she let him go his way.

When he recovered from his stupor, he spent several days without food, drink, or sleep. Indeed, love had gripped his heart. Finally, he decided to send a letter to 60 his father via a messenger, informing him that he could not return home until he had won the princess or died for want of her. When his sire received the letter, he was extremely distressed about his son and wanted to rescue him by sending troops and soldiers. However, his ministers dissuaded him from this action and advised him to be patient. So he prayed to Almighty Allah for guidance.

In the meantime, the prince thought of different ways to attain his goal, and soon he decided to disguise himself as a decrepit old man. So he put a white beard 70 over his own black one and went to the garden where the princess used to walk most of the days. Here he sought out the gardener and said to him, "I'm a stranger from a country far away, and from my youth onward I've been a gardener, and nobody is more skilled than I am in the grafting of trees and cultivating fruit, flowers, and vines."

When the gardener heard this, he was extremely pleased and led him into the garden, where he let him do his work. So the prince began to tend the garden and improved the Persian waterwheels and the irrigation 80 channels. One day, as he was occupied with some work,

he saw some slaves enter the garden leading mules and carrying carpets and vessels, and he asked them what they were doing there.

"The princess wants to spend an enjoyable afternoon here," they answered.

When he heard these words, he rushed to his lodging and fetched some jewels and ornaments he had brought with him from home. After returning to the garden, he sat down and spread some of the valuable items before 90 him while shaking and pretending to be a very old man.

*And Scheherazade noticed that dawn was approaching and stopped telling her story. When the next night arrived, however, she received the king's permission to continue her tale and said,*

In fact, the prince made it seem as if he were extremely decrepit and senile. After an hour or so a company of damsels and eunuchs entered the garden with the princess, who looked just like the radiant moon among the stars. They ran about the garden, plucking 100 fruits and enjoying themselves, until they caught sight of the prince disguised as an old man sitting under one of the trees. The man's hands and feet were trembling from old age, and he had spread a great many precious jewels and regal ornaments before him. Of course, they were astounded by this and asked him what he was doing there with the jewels.

"I want to use these trinkets," he said, "to buy me a wife from among the lot of you."

They all laughed at him and said, "If one of us marries 110 you, what will you do with her?"

"I'll give her one kiss," he replied, "and then divorce her."

"If that's the case," said the princess, "I'll give this damsel to you for your wife."

So he rose, leaned on his staff, staggered toward the damsel, and gave her a kiss. Right after that he gave her the jewels and ornaments, whereupon she rejoiced and they all went on their way laughing at him.

The next day they came again to the garden, and they 120 found him seated in the same place with more jewels and ornaments than before spread before him.

"Oh sheikh," they asked him, "what are you going to do with all this jewelry?"

"I want to wed one of you again," he answered, "just as I did yesterday."

So the princess said, "I'll marry you to this damsel."

And the prince went up to her, kissed her, and gave her the jewels, and they all went their way.

After seeing how generous the old man was to her 130 slave girls, the princess said to herself, "I have more right to these fine things than my slaves, and there's surely no danger involved in this game." So when morning arrived, she went down by herself into the garden dressed as one of her own damsels, and she appeared all alone before the prince and said to him, "Old man, the king's daughter has sent me to you so that you can marry me."

When he looked at her, he knew who she was. So he answered, "With all my heart and love," and he gave her 140 the finest and costliest of jewels and ornaments. Then he rose to kiss her, and since she was not on her guard and thought she had nothing to fear, he grabbed hold of her with his strong hands and threw her down on the ground, where he deprived her of her maidenhead. Then he pulled the beard from his face and said, "Do you recognize me?"

"Who are you?"

"I am Behram, The King of Persia's son," he replied. "I've changed myself and have become a stranger to my people, all for your sake. And I have lavished my treasures for your love."  150

She rose from him in silence and did not say a word to him. Indeed, she was dazed by what had happened and felt that it was best to be silent, especially since she did not want to be shamed. All the while she was thinking to herself, "If I kill myself, it will be senseless, and if I have him put to death, there's nothing that I'd really gain. The best thing for me to do is to elope with him to his own country."

So, after leaving him in the garden, she gathered  160 together her money and treasures and sent him a message informing him what she intended to do and telling him to get ready to depart with his possessions and whatever else he needed. Then they set a rendezvous for their departure.

At the appointed time they mounted racehorses and set out under cover of darkness, and by the next morning they had traveled a great distance. They kept traveling at a fast pace until they drew near his father's capital in Persia, and when his father heard about his son's  170 coming, he rode out to meet him with his troops and was full of joy.

After a few days went by, the king of Persia sent a splendid present to the princess's father along with a letter to the effect that his daughter was with him and requested her wedding outfit. Al-Datma's father greeted the messenger with a happy heart (for he thought he had lost his daughter and had been grieving for her). In response to the king's letter, he summoned the kazi[1] and the witnesses and drew up a marriage contract between  180 his daughter and the prince of Persia. In addition, he bestowed robes of honor on the envoys from the king of Persia and sent his daughter her marriage equipage. After the official wedding took place, Prince Behram lived with her until death came and sundered their union.

*No sooner had Scheherazade concluded her tale than she said, "And yet, oh king, this tale is no more wondrous than the tale of the three apples."*

———————◆———————

## Islamic Art and Architecture

Five times a day, at the call of *muezzins* (criers) usually located atop **minarets** (tall, slender towers; see Figure 9.12), Muslims are summoned to interrupt their activities to kneel and pray facing Mecca. Such prayer is required whether believers are in the heart of the desert or in their homes. The official Muslim place of worship, however, is the **mosque**: a large, columned hall whose square or rectangular shape derives from the simple urban house made of sun-dried bricks. The design of the mosque is not, as with the Early Christian Church,

———————————

[1]Chief justice.

determined by the needs of religious liturgy. Rather, the mosque is first and foremost a place of prayer. Every mosque is oriented toward Mecca, and that direction is marked by a niche (*mihrab*) located in the wall (Figure **10.7**). Occasionally, the niche holds a lamp that symbolizes Allah as the light of heavens and the earth (Sura 24.35). To the right of the *mihrab* is a small, elevated platform (*minbar*) at which the Quran may be read.

The Great Mosque in Córdoba, Spain (Figure **10.8**), begun in 784 and enlarged over a period of three hundred years, is one of the noblest examples of early Islamic architecture. Its interior consists of more than five hundred double-tiered columns that originally supported a wooden roof (Figure 10.9). Horseshoe-shaped arches, consisting of contrasting wedges of white marble and red sandstone, crown a forest of ornamental pillars (Figure **10.10**). In parts of the interior and exterior, **hexafoil** (six-leafed) arches make up a pattern of rhythmic forms on which horseshoe arches may be set in a "piggyback" fashion. Within the spacious interior of the Great Mosque (now a Catholic cathedral), arches seem to "flower" like palm fronds from column "stems." Its unbounded and unfocused ground plan provides a sharp contrast with the design of the Early Christian basilica, which moves the worshiper in a linear fashion from sin to salvation, that is, from portal to altar.

Islam was self-consciously resistant to image-making. Like the Jews, Muslims condemned the worship of pagan idols and considered making likenesses of living creatures an act of pride that "competed" with the Creator God. Hence, in Islamic religious art, there is almost no three-dimensional sculpture, and, with the exception of occasional scenes of the Muslim Paradise, no pictorial representations of the kind found in the cycles of the Youth and Passion of Jesus (see chapter 9). Islamic art also differs from Christian art in its self-conscious avoidance of symbols. But such self-imposed limitations did not prevent Muslims from creating one of the richest bodies of visual ornamentation in the history of world art. The exterior of the Great Mosque at Córdoba, for instance, features a bold horseshoe arch at a portal framed by panels of abstract surface motifs (see Figure 10.8). Some are geometric, while others make use of the **arabesque**, a type of linear ornamentation drawn from plant and flower forms (see Figure 10.6). Such motifs, whether vegetal, floral, or geometric, are repeated in seemingly infinite, rhythmic extension, bound only by the borders of the frame. "Meander and frame"—an expression of the universal theme of variety and unity in nature— is a fundamental principle of the Islamic decorative tradition and (as noted earlier) of Islamic aesthetics. The aesthetic of infinite extension sees Truth as intuitive and all-pervasive in time and space, rather than (as in Western Christian thought) as apocalyptic and self-fulfilling.

**Figure 10.8** (right) Great Mosque, Córdoba, Spain, originally built 784–787 C.E.; additions 832–848, 961, and 987. The Bettmann Archive, New York.

**Figure 10.9** (far right) Plan of the Great Mosque, Córdoba. The additions of 832–848 and 961 are shown, but not the final enlargement of 987.

**Figure 10.10** (below) Columns in the Moorish part of the Great Mosque, Córdoba. White marble and red sandstone. Photo: A. F. Kersting, London.

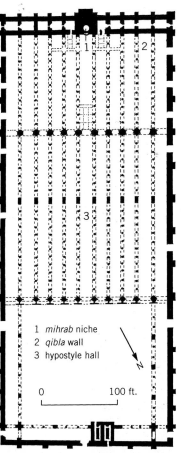

1 *mihrab* niche
2 *qibla* wall
3 hypostyle hall

0          100 ft.

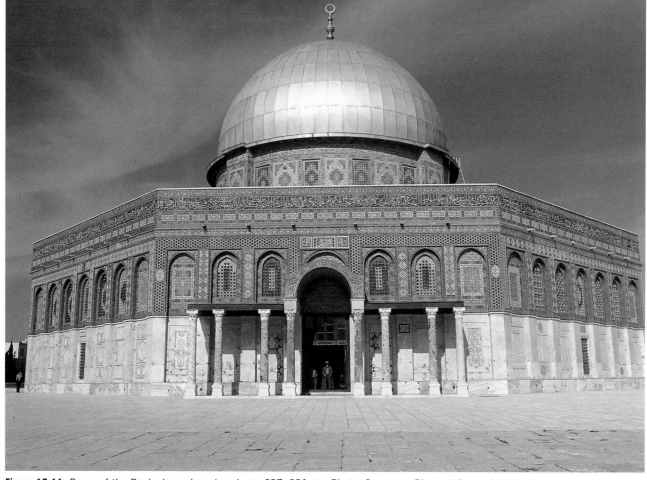

**Figure 10.11** Dome of the Rock, Jerusalem, Israel, ca. 687–691 C.E. Photo: Spectrum Picture Library, London.

In Islamic art, where the written word takes precedence over the human form, calligraphy (that is, beautiful writing) is of primary importance. Since the Quran is considered a "recitation," the written word, the record of revelation, carries a sacramental character. In the lintel above the horseshoe arch on the portal illustrated in Figure 10.8, the Word of Allah is carved in high relief in elegant **Kufic** (the earliest form of Arabic script, originating in the Iraqi town of Kufa). Elsewhere the words of Allah—so central to Muslim faith—play an essential role in embellishment.

Complex surface designs executed in mosaics and polychrome-patterned glazed tiles regularly transformed the exteriors of mosques and palaces into shimmering veils of light and color. Indeed, the bold use of color in monumental buildings is one of the unique achievements of Islamic architects over the centuries (see chapter 23). At the Dome of the Rock (Figure 10.11), the earliest surviving Islamic building, Quranic inscriptions in gold mosaic cubes on a blue ground wind around the spectacular dome. The shrine (now also a mosque) is believed to crown the sacred site of the creation of Adam, the biblical Temple of Solomon, and Muhammad's ascent to Heaven.

A lavish combination of geometric, arabesque, and calligraphic designs usually distinguishes Islamic frescoes, carpets, ivories, manuscripts, textiles, and ceramics but, occasionally, calligraphy alone provides ornamentation. Along the rim of a tenth-century earthenware bowl, for instance, elegant Kufic script imparts Muhammad's injunction: "Planning before work protects one from regret; prosperity and peace" (Figure 10.12). Here, as on the pages of an early **illuminated**

**Figure 10.12** Islamic bowl with inscription. Glazed earthenware, height 7 in., diameter 18 in. The Metropolitan Museum of Art, New York. Rogers Fund, 1965.

**Figure 10.13** Shaykh Muhammad, *A Camel and Keeper Approached by His Conductor*, from Persia, Safavid period, Mashhad school, dated 1556–1557. Full color and gold on paper, 4⁵⁄₁₆ × 5³⁄₁₆ in. Courtesy of the Freer Gallery of Art, Smithsonian Institution, Washington, D.C. 37.21.

**manuscript** of the Quran (see Figure 10.2), fluid calligraphic strokes (with red and yellow dots to indicate vowels) provide the sole "decoration." While figural subjects are avoided in religious art, they abound in secular manuscripts, and especially in those produced after 1200. Tales, poems, chronicles, and fables are freely illustrated with human and animal activities, even as calligraphic and arabesque motifs often frame the central scenes (Figure 10.13; see also Figures 10.3, 10.4).

**Figure 10.14** Court of the Lions, the Alhambra, Granada, Spain, fourteenth century. Photo: Dagli Orti, Paris.

Islamic art and architecture often feature the garden and garden motifs as symbolic of the Muslim Paradise. Like the biblical Garden of Eden and the Babylonian Dilmun (see chapter 2), the paradisic garden (mentioned in the Quran no less than 130 times) is a place of spiritual and physical refreshment. Watered by cool rivers and filled with luscious fruit trees, the Garden of the Afterlife takes its earthly form in Islamic architecture. Luxuriant palaces throughout the Muslim world—real-life settings for the fictional Scheherazade—as well as royal tombs (see chapter 23) normally feature gardens and park pavilions with fountains and water pools. At the oldest well-preserved Islamic palace in the world, the Alhambra in Granada, Spain, rectangular courtyards are cooled by clear, reflecting pools of water and bubbling, central fountains fed by the four "paradisal rivers" (Figure 10.14). This fourteenth-century palace—the stronghold of Muslim culture in the West until 1492—makes use of polychrome **stucco** reliefs, glazed tiles, lacy arabesque designs, and lush gardens simulating Heaven on earth.

## Music in the Islamic World

For the devout Muslim, there was no religious music other than the sound of the chanted Quran and the *muezzin*'s call to prayer. Although Muslims regarded music as a forbidden pleasure and condemned its "killing charm" (as *The Thousand and One Nights* describes it), the therapeutic uses of music were recognized by Arab physicians and its sensual powers tapped by Sufi mystics. During Islam's golden age, secular music flourished in the courts of Córdoba and Baghdad, and, even earlier, Arab song mingled with the music of Persia, Syria, Egypt, and Byzantium.

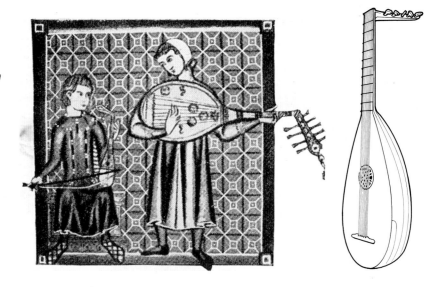

**Figure 10.15** (right) Lute with nine strings. Spanish miniature from the *Cantigas de Santa Maria*, 1221–1289. El Escorial de Santa Maria, MS E-Eb-1-2, f.162.

**Figure 10.16** (far right) Drawing of a lute.

The music of the Islamic world originated in the songs of the desert nomads—songs featuring the solo voice and unmeasured rhythms. (The meter of one type of caravan song, however, is said to resemble the rhythm of the camel's lurching stride.) As in ancient Greece, India, and China, the music of Arabia consisted of a single melodic line, either unaccompanied or with occasional instrumental accompaniment. It was, as well, modal (each mode bearing association with a specific quality of emotion). Two additional characteristics of Arab music (to this day) are its use of microtones (the intervals that lie between the semitones of the Western twelve-note system) and its preference for improvisation (the performer's original, spur-of-the-moment variations on the melody or rhythm of a given piece). Both of these features, which occur in modern jazz, work to give Arab music its unique sound. The melodic line of the Arab song weaves and wanders, looping and repeating themes in a kind of aural arabesque; the voice slides and intones in subtle and hypnotic stretches.§ This vocal pattern, resembling Hebrew, Christian, or Buddhist chant, is not unlike the sound of the *muezzin* calling Muslims to prayer. In its linear ornamentation and in its repetitive rhythmic phrasing, Arab music has much in common with literary and visual forms of Islamic expression.

Instrumental music took second place to the voice everywhere in the Islamic world, except in Persia, where a strong pre-Islamic instrumental tradition flourished. Lyres, flutes, and drums—all light, portable instruments—were used to accompany the songs of Bedouin camel drivers, while bells and tambourines might provide percussion for dancing. By the seventh century, the Arabs developed the lute (in Arabic, *ud*, meaning "wood"), a half-pear-shaped wooden string instrument that was used to accompany vocal performance (Figures **10.15**, **10.16**). The forerunner of the guitar, the lute has a right-angled neck and is played with a small quill. Some time after the eighth century, Muslim musicians in Spain began to compose larger orchestral pieces divided into five or more distinct movements, to be performed by string and wind instruments, percussion, and voices. It is possible that the Western tradition of orchestral music, along with the development of such instruments as oboes, trumpets, viols, and kettledrums, originated among Arab musicians during the centuries of Muslim rule in Spain. Indeed, the renowned ninth-century musician Ziryab (known for his dark complexion as "the Blackbird") traveled from Baghdad to Córdoba to become the founder of the first conservatory of music and patriarch of Spanish musical art. Music composition and theory reached a peak between the ninth and eleventh centuries, when noted Islamic scholars wrote treatises on musical performance and theory. They classified the aesthetic, ethical, and medicinal functions of the modes, recommending specific types of music to relieve specific illnesses. One Arab writer, al-Isfahani (897–967), compiled the *Great Book of Songs*, a twenty-one-volume encyclopedia that remains the most important source of information about Arab music and poetry from its beginnings to the tenth century. The wide range of love songs, many with motifs of complaint and yearning, would have a distinct influence on the secular music of the Western Middle Ages and the Renaissance.

## SUMMARY

In seventh-century Arabia, Islam emerged as the third of the global monotheistic religions. As the teachings of Muhammad, the Prophet of Allah, came to be recorded in the Quran, Muslims throughout Arabia followed the religious, social, and ethical mandates of a vibrant new faith. Islam rapidly expanded beyond the Arabian homeland to establish the most culturally productive civilization since Roman times. Dominating the Mediterranean and much of Southwest Asia, Muslim traders and travelers formed a global community whose

§See Music Listening Selection at end of chapter.

internal cohesiveness was based on a set of common moral and religious values.

Between the eighth and thirteenth centuries, the great centers of Muslim urban life—Baghdad in Iraq, Córdoba in Spain, and Cairo in Egypt—outshone the cities of Western Europe in learning and the arts. Muslims made unique contributions in the realms of poetry and prose, as well as in architecture, the visual arts, and music. The high degree of technical craftsmanship in these forms of expression is matched by a sophisticated taste for complex abstract design. Compositions marked by lyrical repetition and infinite extension are as evident in *The Thousand and One Nights* as in the Great Mosque at Córdoba. Muslim scholars translated into Arabic the valuable corpus of Greek writings, which they transmitted to the West along with the technological and scientific inventions of Asian civilizations. But the scholars of the Islamic world also produced original work in the fields of mathematics, optics, philosophy, geography, and medicine, much of which had profound effects on the course of European culture. As the geographic intermediaries between Asia and Europe, the Muslims created the first truly global culture—a culture united by a single system of belief, but embracing a wide variety of regions, languages, and customs. To this day, Islam, with over one billion adherents, has preserved with little change the teachings of its founder. And, in our own time, Muslim countries and their populations have reassumed positions of worldwide consequence.

## GLOSSARY

**arabesque** a type of ornament featuring plant and flower forms

**caliph** the official successor to Muhammad and theocratic ruler of an Islamic state

*hajj* pilgrimage to Mecca, the fifth Pillar of the Faith in Islam

**hexafoil** having six leaves or arcs

*hijra* (Arabic, "migration" or "flight") Muhammad's journey from Mecca to Medina in the year 622

**illuminated manuscript** a handwritten and ornamented book, parts of which (the script, illustrations, or decorative devices) may be embellished with gold or silver paint or with gold foil, hence "illuminated"

*imam* a Muslim prayer leader

**infidel** a nonbeliever

*jihad* (Arabic, "struggle" [to follow God's will]) the struggle to lead a virtuous life and to further the universal mission of Islam through teaching, preaching, and, when necessary, warfare

*Kaaba* (Arabic, "cube") a religious sanctuary in Mecca; a square temple containing the sacred Black Stone thought to have been delivered to Abraham by the Angel Gabriel

**Kufic** the earliest form of Arabic script; it originated in the Iraqi town of Kufa

*mihrab* a special niche in the wall of a mosque that indicates the direction of Mecca

**minaret** a tall, slender tower usually attached to a mosque and surrounded by a balcony from which the *muezzin* summons Muslims to prayer

*minbar* a stepped pulpit in a mosque

**mosque** the Muslim house of worship

*muezzin* a "crier" who calls the hours of Muslim prayer five times a day

*mullah* a Muslim trained in Islamic law and doctrine

**polygyny** the marriage of one man to several women at the same time

*sharia* the body of Muslim law based on the Quran and the *Hadith*

**stucco** fine plaster or cement used to coat or decorate walls

## SUGGESTIONS FOR READING

Abu-Lughod, Janet L. *Before European Hegemony: The World System* A.D. *1250–1350*. New York: Oxford University Press, 1989.

Blair, Sheila S., and Jonathan M. Bloom. *The Art and Architecture of Islam 1259–1800*. New Haven: Yale University Press, 1994.

Bloom, Jonathan M., and Sheila S. Blair. *Islamic Arts*. New York: Phaidon, 1997.

Brend, Barbara. *Islamic Art*. Cambridge, Mass.: Harvard University Press, 1980.

Christopher, J. B. *The Islamic Tradition*. New York: Harper, 1972.

Hitti, Philip K. *Islam: A Way of Life*. Chicago: Regnery Gateway, 1970.

Hodgson, Marshall. *The Venture of Islam*. 3 vols. Chicago: University of Chicago Press, 1974.

Lewis, Bernard, ed. *Islam from the Prophet Muhammad to the Capture of Constantinople*. New York: Oxford University Press, 1987.

Martin, Richard. *Islam: A Cultural Perspective*. New York: Prentice-Hall, 1982.

Mitchell, George, ed. *Architecture of the Islamic World: Its History and Social Meaning*. New York: William Morrow, 1978.

Otto-Dorn, Katharina. *The Art and Architecture of the Islamic World*. Berkeley, Calif. University of California Press, 1991.

Peters, F. E. *Muhammad and the Origins of Islam*. Ithaca, N.Y.: State University of New York, 1994.

Rice, D. R. *Islamic Art*, rev. ed. New York: Praeger, 1985.

Stanton, Charles M. *Higher Learning in Islam: The Classical Period, 700 A.D. to 1300 A.D.* Langham, Md.: Rowman and Littlefield, 1990.

## MUSIC LISTENING SELECTION

**Cassette I Selection 4** Arabic song from Egypt for solo voice, lute, and flute, "Maqam sika," excerpt.

# PART

# II

# THE MEDIEVAL WEST

The popular picture of the Middle Ages is colored by knights in shining armor, hooded monks, walled castles, and bloody crusades. There is, indeed, much about the medieval world that provides food for fantasy; but, in reality, the era had a powerful impact on the evolution of Western values, beliefs, and practices. The geographic contours of modern European states and the basic political, religious, and linguistic traditions of Western Europe (to which Americans are deeply indebted) took shape during the Middle Ages. The prototypes of nation-states, cities, and universities emerged at this time, and the Roman Catholic Church reached its peak as a powerful political and spiritual institution. The feudal epic, the courtly romance, and the morality play appeared, along with the vernacular languages used in the West today. Medieval artists and artisans produced works of art and architecture that still dazzle modern beholders.

Our examination begins with an appraisal of Germanic culture and the ways in which the tribal invasions of the West affected the identity of the Christian Middle Ages. Chapter 11, "Patterns of Medieval Life," reviews the mingling of Germanic, classical, and Christian cultures that culminated in the court of Charlemagne. The feudal and manorial patterns of early medieval life (ca. 500–1000) are analyzed in relation to those of the High Middle Ages (ca. 1000–1300), a period that witnessed the revival of trade and the emergence of towns. Chapter 12, "Christianity and the Medieval Mind," focuses on the articulation of the Christian promise of life after death in prose and poetry, on the role of the Church in medieval life, and, finally, on the major intellectual movements of the High Middle Ages, including the rise of universities. Chapter 13, "The Medieval Synthesis in the Arts," examines the development of the Romanesque and Gothic styles in art and architecture, the changing character of polyphonic religious music, and the role of symbolism in visual and aural expression. This chapter explores the vitalizing "medieval synthesis" that, by bringing into harmony diverse cultural components, worked to fulfill the spiritual yearnings of an age of faith.

# 11
# Patterns of Medieval Life

In the five centuries following the fall of Rome in 476—a period often called the Dark Ages—Western Europe struggled for order and stability. During this formative era, more aptly termed the Early Middle Ages (ca. 500–1000), three traditions—classical, Christian, and Germanic—became interwoven, ultimately to produce the vigorous new culture of the medieval West. The Germanic tribes that moved upon the West in the first centuries of the Christian era (Map 11.1) contributed to the decline and decentralization of Roman civilization. Ultimately, however, Germanic tribal people and practices blended with those of classical Rome and Western Christianity to forge the basic economic, social, and cultural patterns of medieval life. The system of feudalism came to dominate early medieval society, while in the centuries immediately following the Crusades the revival of trade stimulated the rise of cities and the development of an urban culture.

## The Germanic Tribes

The Germanic peoples were a tribal folk who followed a migratory existence. Dependent on their flocks and herds, they lived in pre-urban village communities throughout Asia and frequently raided and plundered nearby lands for material gain. They settled no territorial state, nor did they produce any monumental architecture or sculpture. As early as the first century B.C.E., the loose confederacy of Germanic tribes began to threaten Roman territories, but it was not until the fourth century C.E. that these tribes, driven westward by the fierce Central Asian nomads known as Huns, pressed into the

**Map 11.1** The Early Christian World and the Barbarian Invasions, ca. 500 C.E.

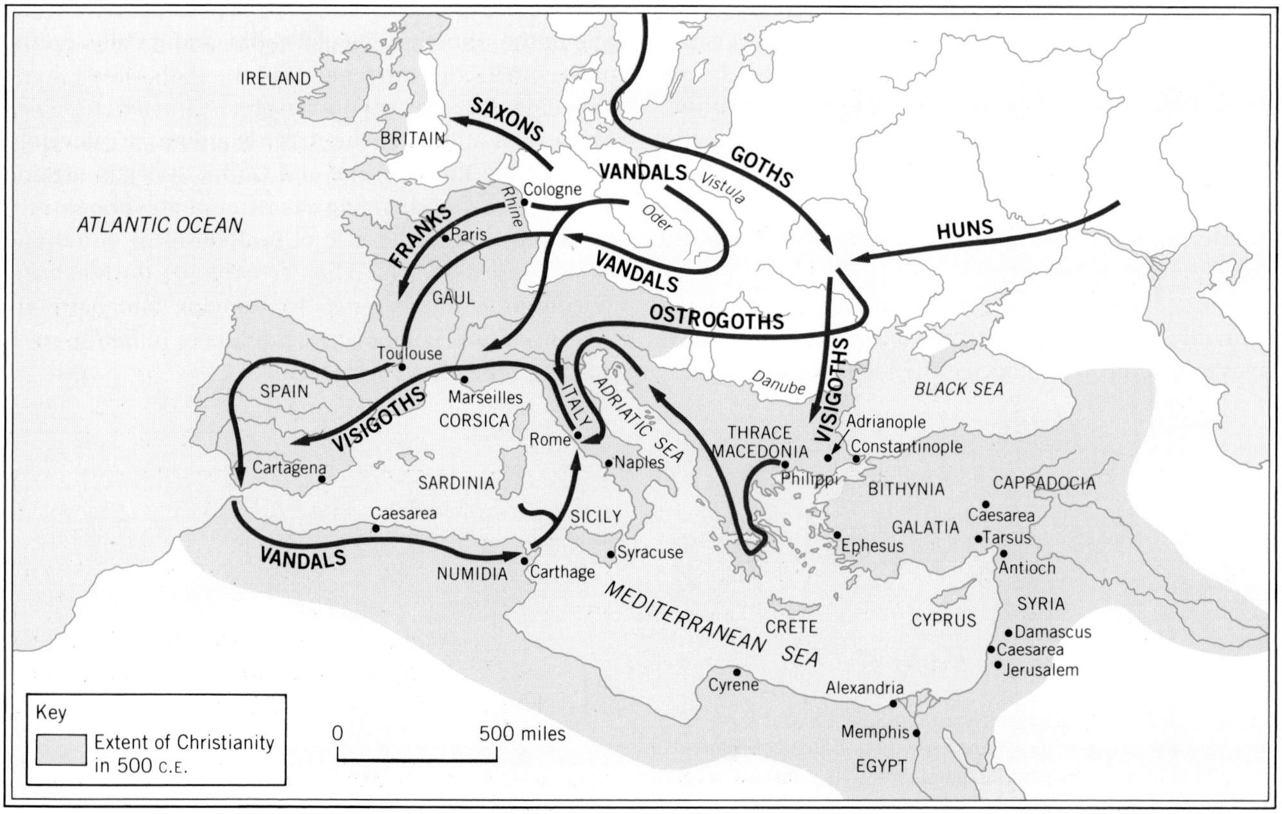

Roman Empire. Lacking the hallmarks of civilization—urban settlements, monumental architecture, and the art of writing—the Germanic tribes struck the Romans as inferiors, as outsiders, hence, as "barbarians." In fact, the Germanic peoples were ethnically distinct from the Huns. East Goths (Ostrogoths), West Goths (Visigoths), Franks, Vandals, Burgundians, Angles, and Saxons—to name only a few—belonged to one and the same (Germanic) language family, dialects of which differed from tribe to tribe. The Ostrogoths occupied the steppe region between the Black and Baltic seas, while the Visigoths settled in territories closer to the Danube River (see Map 11.1). As the tribes pressed westward, however, an uneasy alliance was forged: The Romans allowed the barbarians to settle on the borders of the Empire, in exchange for which Germanic warriors afforded Rome protection against other invaders. Antagonisms between Rome and the West Goths led to a military showdown. At the Battle of Adrianople (130 miles northwest of Constantinople) in 378, the Visigoths defeated the "invincible" Roman army, killing the East Roman Emperor Valens and dispersing his army. Almost immediately thereafter, the Visigoths swept across the Roman border, raiding the cities of the declining West, including Rome itself in 410.

The Battle of Adrianople opened the door to a sequence of barbarian invasions. During the fifth century, the Empire fell prey to the assaults of many Germanic tribes, including the Vandals, whose willful, malicious destruction of Rome in 455 produced the English word "vandalize." In 476, a Germanic commander named Odoacer deposed the reigning Roman emperor in the West, an event that is traditionally taken to mark the official end of the Roman Empire. Although the Germanic tribes leveled the final assaults on an already declining empire, they did not utterly destroy Rome's vast resources, nor did they ignore the culture of the late Roman world. The Ostrogoths embraced Christianity and sponsored literary and architectural enterprises modeled on those of Rome and Byzantium, while the Franks and the Burgundians chose to commit their legal traditions to writing, styling their codes of law on Roman models.

But Germanic culture differed dramatically from that of Rome: In the agrarian and essentially self-sufficient communities of these nomadic peoples, fighting was a way of life and a highly respected skill. Armed with javelins and shields, Germanic warriors fought fiercely on foot and on horseback. Superb

horsemen, the Germanic cavalry would come to borrow from the Mongols spurs and foot stirrups—devices (originating in China) that firmly secured the rider in his saddle and improved his driving force. In addition to introducing to the West superior methods of fighting on horseback, the Germanic tribes imposed their own long-standing traditions on medieval Europe. Every Germanic chieftain retained a band of warriors that followed him into battle, and every warrior anticipated sharing with his chieftain the spoils of victory. At the end of the first century, the Roman historian Tacitus (see chapter 7) wrote an account of the habits and customs of the Germanic peoples. He observes:

> All [men] are bound, to defend their leader . . . and to make even their own actions subservient to his renown. If he dies in the field, he who survives him survives to live in infamy. . . . This is the bond of union, the most sacred obligation. The chief fights for victory; the followers for their chief. . . . The chief must show his liberality, and the follower expects it. He demands, at one time this warlike horse, at another, that victorious lance drenched with the blood of the enemy.*

The bond of **fealty**, or loyalty, between the Germanic warrior and his chieftain and the practice of rewarding the warrior with land or the spoils of battle would become fundamental to the medieval practice of feudalism.

## Germanic Law

Germanic law was not legislated by the state, as in Roman tradition, but was, rather, a collection of customs passed orally from generation to generation. Among the Germanic peoples, tribal chiefs were responsible for governing, but general assemblies met to make important decisions: Fully armed, clan warriors demonstrated their assent to propositions "in a military manner," according to Tacitus—by brandishing their javelins. Since warlike behavior was commonplace, tribal law was severe, uncompromising, and directed toward publicly shaming the guilty. Tacitus records that punishment for an adulterous wife was "instant, and inflicted by the husband. He cuts off the hair of his guilty wife, and having assembled her relations, expels her naked from his house, pursuing her with stripes through the village. To public loss of honor no favor is shown. She may possess beauty, youth and riches; but a husband she can never obtain."

As in most ancient societies—Hammurabi's Babylon, for instance—penalties for crimes varied according to the social standing of the guilty party.

| | |
|---|---|
| **568** | Germanic tribes introduce stirrups (from China) into Europe |
| **600** | a heavy iron plow is used in Northern Europe |
| **770** | iron horseshoes are used widely in Western Europe |

---

*Tacitus: Historical Works*, translated by Arthur Murphey. London: J. M. Dent, 1907, 320–321.

Among the Germanic tribes, however, a person's guilt or innocence might be determined by an ordeal involving fire or water; such trials reflected the faith Germanic peoples placed in the will of nature deities. Some of the names of these gods came to designate days of the week; for instance, the English word "Wednesday" derives from "Woden's day" and "Thursday" from "Thor's day." Similarly, the Germanic dependence on custom had a lasting influence on the development of law, and especially **common law**, in parts of the medieval West.

## Germanic Literature

Germanic traditions, including those of personal valor and heroism associated with a warring culture, are reflected in the epic poems of the Early Middle Ages. The three most famous of these, *Beowulf, The Song of the Nibelungen,* and the *Song of Roland,* were transmitted orally for hundreds of years before they were written down sometime between the tenth and thirteenth centuries. *Beowulf,* which originated among the Anglo-Saxons, was recorded in Old English, the Germanic language spoken in the British Isles between the fifth and eleventh centuries. *The Song of the Nibelungen,* a product of the Burgundian tribes, was recorded in Old German; and the Frankish *Song of Roland,* in Old French. Celebrating the deeds of warrior-heroes, these three epic poems have much in common with the *Iliad,* the *Mahabharata,* and other orally transmitted adventure poems.

The three-thousand-line epic known as *Beowulf* is the first monumental literary composition in a European vernacular language, but its significance as a work of art derives from its lyrical power. In unrhymed Old English verse embellished with numerous two-term metaphors known as **kennings** ("whale-path" for "sea," "ring-giver" for "king"), the poem recounts three major adventures: Beowulf's encounter with the monster Grendel, his destruction of Grendel's hideous and vengeful mother, and (some five decades later) his effort to destroy the fire-breathing dragon which threatens his people. These adventures—the stuff of legend, folk tale, and fantasy—immortalize the mythic origins of the Anglo-Saxons. Composed in the newly Christianized England of the eighth century, the poem was not written down for another two centuries. Only a full reading of *Beowulf* offers an appreciation of its significance as a work of art. However, the passage that follows—from a modern translation by Burton Raffel—offers an idea of the poem's vigorous style and narrative. The excerpt (lines 2510–2601 of the work), which describes Beowulf's assault on the fire-dragon, opens with a "battle-vow" that broadcasts the boastful courage of the epic hero. Those who wish to know the outcome of this gory contest must read further in the poem.

## READING 2.13

## From *Beowulf*

And Beowulf uttered his final boast: 1
  "I've never known fear; as a youth I fought
In endless battles. I am old, now,
But I will fight again, seek fame still,
If the dragon hiding in his tower dares 5
To face me."
           Then he said farewell to his followers,
Each in his turn, for the last time:
  "I'd use no sword, no weapon, if this beast
Could be killed without it, crushed to death
Like Grendel, gripped in my hands and torn 10
Limb from limb. But his breath will be burning
Hot, poison will pour from his tongue.
I feel no shame, with shield and sword
And armor, against this monster: when he comes to me
I mean to stand, not run from his shooting 15
Flames, stand till fate decides
Which of us wins. My heart is firm,
My hands calm: I need no hot
Words. Wait for me close by, my friends.
We shall see, soon, who will survive 20
This bloody battle, stand when the fighting
Is done. No one else could do
What I mean to, here, no man but me
Could hope to defeat this monster. No one
Could try. And this dragon's treasure, his gold 25
And everything hidden in that tower, will be mine
Or war will sweep me to a bitter death!"
  Then Beowulf rose, still brave, still strong,
And with his shield at his side, and a mail shirt on his
     breast,
Strode calmly, confidently, toward the tower, under 30
The rocky cliffs: no coward could have walked there!
And then he who'd endured dozens of desperate
Battles, who'd stood boldly while swords and shields
Clashed, the best of kings, saw
Huge stone arches and felt the heat 35
Of the dragon's breath, flooding down
Through the hidden entrance, too hot for anyone
To stand, a streaming current of fire
And smoke that blocked all passage. And the Geats'[1]
Lord and leader, angry, lowered 40
His sword and roared out a battle cry,
A call so loud and clear that it reached through
The hoary rock, hung in the dragon's
Ear. The beast rose, angry,
Knowing a man had come—and then nothing 45
But war could have followed. Its breath came first,
A steaming cloud pouring from the stone,
Then the earth itself shook. Beowulf
Swung his shield into place, held it
In front of him, facing the entrance. The dragon 50
Coiled and uncoiled, its heart urging it
Into battle. Beowulf's ancient sword
Was waiting, unsheathed, his sharp and gleaming
Blade. The beast came closer; both of them
Were ready, each set on slaughter. The Geats' 55
Great prince stood firm, unmoving, prepared

---

[1]The Scandinavian tribe led by Beowulf.

**Figure 11.1** Hinged shoulder clasps, from Sutton Hoo, Suffolk, U.K., first half of seventh century C.E. *Cloisonné* enamel and filigree, length 5 in. British Museum, London. Bridgeman/Art Resource, New York.

Behind his high shield, waiting in his shining
Armor. The monster came quickly toward him,
Pouring out fire and smoke, hurrying
To its fate. Flames beat at the iron                                   60
Shield, and for a time it held, protected
Beowulf as he'd planned; then it began to melt,
And for the first time in his life that famous prince
Fought with fate against him, with glory
Denied him. He knew it, but he raised his sword          65
And struck at the dragon's scaly hide.
The ancient blade broke, bit into
The monster's skin, drew blood, but cracked
And failed him before it went deep enough, helped him
Less than he needed. The dragon leaped                       70
With pain, thrashed and beat at him, spouting
Murderous flames, spreading them everywhere.
And the Geats' ring-giver did not boast of glorious
Victories in other wars: his weapon
Had failed him, deserted him, now when he needed it    75
Most, that excellent sword. Edgetho's
Famous son stared at death,
Unwilling to leave this world, to exchange it
For a dwelling in some distant place—a journey
Into darkness that all men must make, as death            80
Ends their few brief hours on earth.
    Quickly, the dragon came at him, encouraged
As Beowulf fell back; its breath flared,
And he suffered, wrapped around in swirling
Flames—a king, before, but now                                   85
A beaten warrior. None of his comrades
Came to him, helped him, his brave and noble
Followers; they ran for their lives, fled
Deep in a wood. And only one of them
Remained, stood there, miserable, remembering,          90
As a good man must, what kinship should mean.

◆

## Germanic Art

The artistic production of nomadic peoples consists largely of easily transported objects such as carpets, jewelry, and weapons. Germanic folk often buried the most lavish of these items with their chieftains in boats that were cast out to sea (as described in *Beowulf*). In 1939,

archeologists at Sutton Hoo in Eastern England excavated a seventh-century Anglo-Saxon grave that contained weapons, coins, utensils, jewelry, and a small lyre. These treasures were packed, along with the corpse of their chieftain, into an 89-foot-long ship that served as a tomb. Among the remarkable metalwork items found at Sutton Hoo were gold buckles and shoulder clasps (Figure 11.1) adorned with semiprecious stones and *cloisonné*—enamelwork produced by pouring molten colored glass between thin gold partitions (Figure 11.2). A 5-pound gold belt buckle is ornamented with a dense pattern of interlaced snakes incised with a black sulfurous substance called **niello** (Figure 11.3). The high quality of so-called "barbarian" art, as evidenced at Sutton Hoo and elsewhere, shows that technical sophistication and artistic originality were by no means the monopoly of "civilized" societies. It also demonstrates the continuous diffusion and exchange of styles across Asia and into Europe. The **zoomorphic** (animal-shaped) motifs found on the artifacts at Sutton Hoo, along with many of the metalwork techniques used in their fabrication, are evidence of contact between the Germanic tribes and the populations of Central Asia, who actively maintained the decorative traditions of ancient Persian, Scythian, and Chinese craftspeople.

As the Germanic tribes poured into Europe, their art and their culture commingled with that of the people with whom they came into contact. A classic example is the fusion of Celtic and Anglo-Saxon styles. The Celts were a non-Germanic, Iron Age folk that had migrated throughout Europe between the fifth and third centuries B.C.E., settling in the British Isles before the time of Christ. A great flowering of Celtic art and literature occurred in Ireland and England following the conversion of the Celts to Christianity in the fifth century C.E.

**Figure 11.2** *Cloisonné* enameling process. From Richard Phipps and Richard Wink, *Introduction to the Gallery*. Copyright © 1987 Wm. C. Brown Publishers, Dubuque, Iowa. All rights reserved. Reprinted by permission.

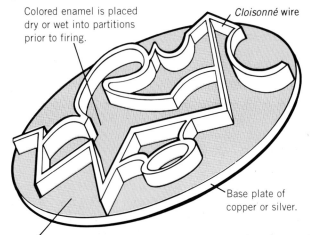

Colored enamel is placed dry or wet into partitions prior to firing.

*Cloisonné* wire

Base plate of copper or silver.

Base plate is enameled and permanently holds the partitions in place. They may also be soldered to the base metal before the first firing.

**Figure 11.3** Buckle, from Sutton Hoo, first half of seventh century C.E. Gold and niello, length 5¼ in., weight 5 lb. Reproduced by courtesy of the Trustees of the British Museum, London.

**Figure 11.4** Bishop Eadfrith (?), "Carpet Page," from the Lindisfarne Gospels, ca. 698–721 C.E. Vellum, 13½ × 9¾ in. Reproduced by courtesy of the Trustees of the British Museum, London.

The instrument of this conversion was the fabled Saint Patrick (ca. 385–461), the British monk who is said to have baptized more than 120,000 people and founded three hundred churches in Ireland. In the centuries thereafter, Anglo-Irish monasteries produced a number of extraordinary illuminated manuscripts, the decorative style of which is closely related to the dynamic linear ornamentation of the Sutton Hoo artifacts.

The visual masterpiece of an otherwise bleak period in the West, the seventh-century Lindisfarne Gospels, comes from a monastery located on an island off the east coast of England. In the pages of this remarkable Gospel book, naturalistic representation of the kind associated with classical culture has disappeared entirely. The precisely drawn Lindisfarne "carpet page"—so called for its resemblance to a woven fabric—is dominated by a magnificent **cruciform** (cross-shaped) design (Figure 11.4), but the entire spatial field writhes with knotted, ribbonlike shapes resembling those on the

Sutton Hoo belt buckle (see Figure 11.3). Looking every bit like a metalwork surface or a woven rug, the carpet page combines the illusion of compositional order with a sense of labyrinthine movement. Analysis of the design shows, however, that one's initial impression of perfect symmetry is mistaken, for the composition involves a complex system of mirror images and subtly varied shapes, lines, and colors. The influence of Germanic design in Christian manuscript illumination is a dramatic example of cultural syncretism (the combination of different practises and principles), but it also raises another matter—the similarity between Germanic and Islamic art styles. As did Islamic artists, the Germanic tribes distilled the decorative traditions of Persia, Egypt, and the Mediterranean into a style marked by complex, rhythmically meandering surface designs. Whether the sophisticated abstract vocabularies of these two bodies of art—Germanic and Islamic—are symbolic of the wandering lifestyles of these originally nomadic peoples

**Figure 11.5** Ardagh Chalice, from Ireland, early eighth century C.E. Silver, gilt bronze, gold wire, glass, and enamel. National Museum of Ireland, Dublin.

sacred rites, they received inordinate care in execution. The Ardagh Chalice, made of silver, **gilt** (gold-surfaced) bronze, gold wire, glass, and enamel, displays the technical virtuosity of early eighth-century metalworkers in Ireland (Figure 11.5). On the surface of the vessel, a band of interlace designs is offset by raised roundels worked in enamel and gold thread. Clearly, in the liturgical objects and illuminated manuscripts of the Early Middle Ages, the abstract, ornamental Germanic style provided Christian art with an aesthetic alternative to classical modes of representation.

## Charlemagne and the Carolingian Renaissance

From the time he came to the throne in 768 until his death in 814, the Frankish chieftain Charles the Great (in French, "Charlemagne") pursued the dream of restoring the Roman Empire under Christian leadership. A great warrior and an able administrator, the fair-haired heir to the Frankish kingdom conquered vast areas of land (Map 11.2). His holy wars—the Christian equivalent of the Muslim *jihad*—resulted in the forcible conversion of the Saxons east of the Rhine River, the Lombards of Northern Italy, and the Slavic peoples

(as some scholars have suggested), or whether closeness to nature generated a set of unique but similar design principles, may be left to speculation.

The Germanic style influenced not only the illumination of Christian manuscripts, but also the decoration of Christian liturgical objects, such as the **paten** (Eucharistic plate) and the **chalice** (Eucharistic cup). Employed in the celebration of the Mass, these objects usually commanded the finest and most costly materials; and, like the manuscripts that accompanied the

**Map 11.2** The Empire of Charlemagne, 814 C.E.

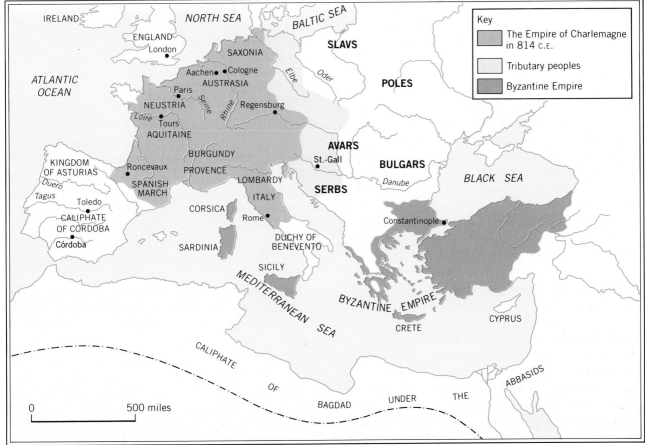

**Figure 11.6** Odo of Metz, Palatine Chapel of Charlemagne, Aachen, Germany, 792–805 C.E. © Deutscher Kunstverlag, Munich.

**Figure 11.7** Equestrian statuette of Charlemagne, ninth century C.E. Bronze with traces of gilt, height 9½ in. Louvre, Paris. Photo: © R.M.N., Paris.

along the Danube. Charlemagne's campaigns also pushed the Muslims back beyond the Pyrenees into Spain.

In the year 800, Pope Leo III crowned Charlemagne "Emperor of the Romans," thus establishing a firm relationship between Church and state. But, equally significantly, Charlemagne's role in creating a Roman Christian or "Holy" Roman Empire cast him as the prototype of Christian kingship. For the more than thirty years during which he waged wars in the name of Christ, Charlemagne sought to control conquered lands by placing them in the hands of local administrators— on whom he bestowed the titles "count" and "duke"— and by periodically sending out royal envoys to carry his edicts abroad. He revived trade with the East, stabilized the currency of the realm, and even pursued diplomatic ties with Baghdad, whose caliph, Harun al-Rashid, graced Charlemagne's court with the gift of an elephant.

Charlemagne's imperial mission was animated by a passionate interest in education and the arts. Having visited San Vitale in Ravenna (see Figures 9.15, 9.16), he had its architectural plan and decorative program imitated in the Palatine Chapel at Aachen (Figure 11.6). The topmost tier, crowned by a mosaic dome, represented Heaven and the bottom tier the earth; sitting in the gallery between, which was connected by a passageway to the royal palace, Charlemagne assumed his symbolic role as mediator between God and ordinary Christians. Alert to the legacy of his forebears, he revived the bronze-casting techniques of Roman sculptors,

though on a small scale (Figure 11.7). Despite the fact that he himself could barely read and write—his sword hand was, according to his biographers, so callused that he had great difficulty forming letters—he sponsored a revival of learning and literacy. To oversee this educational program, Charlemagne invited to his court missionaries and scholars from all over Europe. He established schools at Aachen (Aix-la-Chapelle), in town centers throughout the Empire, and in Benedictine monasteries such as that at Saint-Gall in Switzerland, where monks and nuns copied religious manuscripts, along with texts on medicine, drama, and other secular subjects. The scale of this **renaissance** or "rebirth" of learning is evident in that eighty percent of the oldest surviving classical Latin manuscripts exist in Carolingian copies.

Carolingian copyists rejected Roman script, which lacked punctuation and spaces between words, in favor of a neat, uniform writing style known as the minuscule (Figure 11.8), the ancestor of modern typography. The

Merovingian Script

*Cum autem audisset ihs quod iohan
nes traditus esset secessit in galileam.
Et relicta ciuitate nazareth uenit et habitauit in caphar
naum maritimam in finib: zabulon et nepthalim. ut
adimpleretur quod dictum e per esaiam prophetam:*

Caroline Minuscule

**Figure 11.8** Comparison of Merovingian (pre-Carolingian) Book script and Caroline (Carolingian) Minuscule.

decorative programs of many Carolingian manuscripts reflect the union of late Roman realism and Germanic abstraction. The former is revealed in the pictorial narrative that fills the capital letter in Figure **11.9**, while the latter is seen in the ribbonlike pattern of the initial itself. But the Carolingian Renaissance was not limited to the copying of manuscripts. Among the most magnificent artifacts of the period were liturgical and devotional objects, often made of ivory or precious metals. Dating from the decades shortly after Charlemagne's death, the book cover for the Lindau Gospels testifies to the superior technical abilities of Carolingian metalsmiths (Figure **11.10**). The surface of the back cover, worked in silver gilt, inlaid with *cloisonné* enamel, and encrusted with precious gems, consists of an ornate Greek cross that dominates a field of writhing, interlaced creatures similar to those found in Anglo-Saxon metalwork (see Figure 11.3) and Anglo-Irish manuscripts (see Figure 11.4). At the corners of the inner rectangle of the book cover are four tiny scenes showing the evangelists at their writing desks. These realistically conceived representations contrast sharply with the more stylized figural images that appear in the arms of the cross. The synthesis of Germanic, Roman, and Byzantine artistic traditions manifested in the cover of the Lindau Gospels typifies the Carolingian Renaissance, the glories of which would not be matched for at least three centuries.

## Feudal Society

When Charlemagne died in the year 814, the short-lived unity he had brought to Western Europe died with him. Although he had turned the Frankish kingdom into an empire, he failed to establish any legal and administrative machinery comparable with that of imperial Rome. There was no standing army, no system of taxation, and no single code of law to unify the

**Figure 11.9** *The Ascension*, from the Sacramentary of Archbishop Drogo of Metz, ca. 842 C.E. Bibliothèque Nationale, Paris, MS Lat. 9428, f.71v.

**Figure 11.10** Back cover of the Lindau Gospels, ca. 800 C.E. Silver gilt with enamel and precious stones, 13⅜ × 10⅜ in. © The J. Pierpont Morgan Library, New York.

widely diverse population. Inevitably, following his death, the fragile stability of the Carolingian Empire was shattered by Scandinavian seafarers known as north-men or Vikings. Charlemagne's sons and grandsons failed to repel the raids of these fierce invaders, who ravaged the Northern coasts of the Empire; at the same time, neither were his heirs able to arrest the repeated forays of the Muslims along the Mediterranean coast. Lacking effective leadership, the Carolingian Empire disintegrated. In the mid-ninth century, Charlemagne's three grandsons divided the Empire among themselves, separating French- from German-speaking territories. Increasingly, however, administration and protection fell to members of the local ruling aristocracy—heirs of the counts and dukes whom Charlemagne had appointed to administer portions of the realm, or simply those who had taken land by force. The fragmentation of the Empire and the insecurity generated by the Viking invasions caused people at all social levels to attach themselves to members of a military nobility who were capable of providing protection. These circum-stances enhanced the growth of a unique system of political and military organization known as **feudalism**.

Derived from Roman and Germanic traditions of rewarding warriors with the spoils of war, feudalism involved the exchange of land for military service. In return for the grant of land, known as a **fief** or *feudum* (the Germanic word for "property"), a **vassal** owed his **lord** a certain number of fighting days (usually forty) per year. The contract between lord and vassal also involved a number of other obligations, including the lord's provision of a court of justice, the vassal's contri-bution of ransom if his lord were captured, and the reciprocation of hospitality between the two. In an age of instability, feudalism provided a rudimentary form of local government, while answering the need for secu-rity against armed attack.

Those engaged in the feudal contract constituted roughly the upper ten percent of European society. The feudal nobility, which bore the twin responsibilities of military defense and political leadership, was a closed class of men and women whose superior status was inherited at birth. A male member of the nobility was first and foremost a mounted man-at-arms—a *chevalier* (from the French *cheval*, for "horse") or knight (from the Germanic *Knecht*, a youthful servant or soldier). The medieval knight was a cavalry warrior equipped with stirrups, protected by **chain mail** (a flexible armor made of interlinked metal rings), and armed with such weapons as broadsword and shield.

The knight's conduct and manners in all aspects of life were guided by a strict code of behavior called **chivalry**. Chivalry demanded that the knight be coura-geous in battle, loyal to his lord and fellow warriors, and reverent toward women. Feudal life was marked by

**Figure 11.11** Matthew Paris, *Vassal Paying Homage to his Lord*, from the Westminster Psalter, ca. 1250. Reproduced by permission of the British Library, London.

ceremonies and symbols almost as extensive as those of the Christian Church. For instance, a vassal received his fief by an elaborate procedure known as **investiture**, in which oaths of fealty were formally exchanged (Figure **11.11**). In warfare, adversaries usually fixed the time and place of combat in advance. Medieval warfare was both a profession and a pastime, as knights entertained themselves with **jousts** (personal combat between men on horseback) or war games that imitated the trials of combat (Figure 11.12).

Women helped to shape the chivalric society of the Middle Ages. In many parts of Europe they inherited land, which they usually defended by means of hired soldiers. A woman controlled her fief until she married, and regained it upon becoming a widow. Men and women took great pride in their aristocratic lineage and advertised the family name by means of heraldic devices emblazoned on tunics, pennants, and shields (see Figure 11.11).

**Figure 11.12** French plaque from a casket, fourteenth century. Ivory, $3\frac{7}{8} \times \frac{5}{8}$ in. The Metropolitan Museum of Art, New York. Gift of J. Pierpont Morgan, 1917.

## The Literature of the Feudal Nobility

The ideals of the fighting nobility in a feudal age are best exemplified in the oldest and greatest French epic poem, the *Song of Roland*. Based on an event that took place in 778—the ambush of Charlemagne's rear guard, led by his nephew Roland as Charlemagne returned from an expedition against the Muslims in Spain—this *chanson de geste* ("song of heroic deeds") captures the spirit of the Early Middle Ages. Transmitted orally for three centuries, the four-thousand-line poem was not written down until the early 1100s. Generation after generation of *jongleurs* (professional entertainers) wandered from court to court, chanting the story (and possibly embellishing it with episodes of folklore) to the accompaniment of a lyre. Though the music for the poem has not survived, it is likely that it consisted of a single and highly improvised line of melody. The melody was probably syllabic (one note to each syllable) and—like folk song—dependent on simple repetition. As with other works in the oral tradition (the *Epic of Gilgamesh* and the *Iliad*, for instance), the *Song of Roland* is grandiose in its dimensions and profound in its lyric power. Its rugged Old French verse describes a culture that prized the performance of heroic deeds that brought honor to the warrior, his lord, and his religion. The strong bond of loyalty between vassal and chieftain that characterized the Germanic way of life resonates in Roland's declaration of unswerving devotion to his temporal overlord, Charlemagne.

The *Song of Roland* brings to life such aspects of early medieval culture as the practice of naming one's battle gear and weapons (often considered sacred), the dependence on cavalry, the glorification of blood-and-thunder heroism, and the strong sense of comradeship among men-at-arms. Women play almost no part in the epic. The feudal contract did not exclude members of the clergy; hence a churchman like Archbishop Turpin fights, armed with a **mace** (a spike-headed club) by which he might defend himself without violating the Church law that forbade a member of the clergy to shed another man's blood. Roland's willingness to die for his religious beliefs, fired by the Archbishop's promise of admission into Paradise for those who fall fighting the infidels (in this case, the Muslims), suggests that the militant fervor of Muslims was matched by that of early medieval Christians. Indeed, the *Song of Roland* captures the powerful antagonism between Christians and Muslims that dominated all of medieval history and culminated in the Christian Crusades described later in this chapter.

The descriptive language of the *Song of Roland* is stark, unembellished, and vivid: "He feels his brain gush out," reports the poet in verse 168. Such directness and simplicity lend immediacy to the action. Characters are stereotypical ("Roland's a hero, and Oliver is wise," verse 87), and groups of people are characterized with epic expansiveness: *All* Christians are good and *all* Muslims are bad. The figure of Roland epitomizes the ideals of physical courage, religious devotion, and personal loyalty. Yet, in his refusal to call for assistance from Charlemagne and his troops, who have already retreated across the Pyrenees, he exhibits a foolhardiness—perhaps a "tragic flaw"—that leads him and his warriors to their deaths.

### READING 2.14

## From the *Song of Roland*

### 81

Count Oliver has climbed up on a hill;                           1
From there he sees the Spanish lands below,
And Saracens[1] assembled in great force.
Their helmets gleam with gold and precious stones,
Their shields are shining, their hauberks[2] burnished gold,      5
Their long sharp spears with battle flags unfurled.
He tries to see how many men there are:
Even battalions are more than he can count.
And in his heart Oliver is dismayed;
Quick as he can, he comes down from the height,                 10
And tells the Franks what they will have to fight.

### 82

Oliver says, "Here come the Saracens—
A greater number no man has ever seen!
The first host carries a hundred thousand shields,
Their helms are laced, their hauberks shining white,            15
From straight wood handles rise ranks of burnished spears.
You'll have a battle like none on earth before!
Frenchmen, my lords, now God give you the strength
To stand your ground, and keep us from defeat."
They say, "God's curse on those who quit the field!             20
We're yours till death—not one of us will yield."     AOI[3]

### 83

Oliver says, "The pagan might is great—
It seems to me, our Franks are very few!
Roland, my friend, it's time to sound your horn;
King Charles[4] will hear, and bring his army back."           25
Roland replies, "You must think I've gone mad!
In all sweet France I'd forfeit my good name!
No! I will strike great blows with Durendal,[5]
Crimson the blade up to the hilt of gold.
To those foul pagans I promise bitter woe—                     30
They all are doomed to die at Roncevaux!"[6]         AOI

### 84

"Roland, my friend, let the Oliphant[7] sound!
King Charles will hear it, his host will all turn back,
His valiant barons will help us in this fight."
Roland replies, "Almighty God forbid                           35
That I bring shame upon my family,
And cause sweet France to fall into disgrace!
I'll strike that horde with my good Durendal;
My sword is ready, girded here at my side,
And soon you'll see its keen blade dripping blood.             40
The Saracens will curse the evil day
They challenged us, for we will make them pay."      AOI

---

[1]Another name for Muslims.
[2]Long coats of chain mail.
[3]The letters AOI have no known meaning but probably signify a musical appendage or refrain that occurred at the end of each stanza.
[4]Charlemagne.
[5]Roland's sword.
[6]"The gate of Spain," a narrow pass in the Pyrenees where the battle takes place.
[7]A horn made from an elephant's tusk.

### 85

"Roland, my friend I pray you, sound your horn!
King Charlemagne, crossing the mountain pass,
Won't fail, I swear it, to bring back all his Franks."         45
"May God forbid!" Count Roland answers then.
"No man on earth shall have the right to say
That I for pagans sounded the Oliphant!
I will not bring my family to shame.
I'll fight this battle; my Durendal shall strike               50
A thousand blows and seven hundred more;
You'll see bright blood flow from the blade's keen steel.
We have good men; their prowess will prevail,
And not one Spaniard shall live to tell the tale."

### 86

Oliver says, "Never would you be blamed;                       55
I've seen the pagans, the Saracens of Spain.
They fill the valleys, cover the mountain peaks;
On every hill, and every wide-spread plain,
Vast hosts assemble from that alien race;
Our company numbers but very few."                             60
Roland replies, "The better, then, we'll fight!
If it please God and His angelic host,
I won't betray the glory of sweet France!
Better to die than learn to live with shame—
Charles loves us more as our keen swords win fame."            65

### 87

Roland's a hero, and Oliver is wise;
Both are so brave men marvel at their deeds.
When they mount chargers, take up their swords and shields,
Not death itself could drive them from the field.
They are good men; their words are fierce and proud.           70
With wrathful speed the pagans ride to war.
Oliver says, "Roland, you see them now.
They're very close, the king too far away.
You were too proud to sound the Oliphant:
If Charles were with us, we would not come to grief.           75
Look up above us, close to the Gate of Spain:
There stands the guards—who would not pity them!
To fight this battle means not to fight again."
Roland replies, "Don't speak so foolishly!
Cursed be the heart that cowers in the breast!                 80
We'll hold our ground; if they will meet us here,
Our foes will find us ready with sword and spear."   AOI

### 88

When Roland sees the fight will soon begin,
Lions and leopards are not so fierce as he.
Calling the Franks, he says to Oliver:                         85
"Noble companion, my friend, don't talk that way!
The Emperor Charles, who left us in command
Of twenty thousand he chose to guard the pass,
Made very sure no coward's in their ranks.
In his lord's service a man must suffer pain,                  90
Bitterest cold and burning heat endure;
He must be willing to lose his flesh and blood.
Strike with your lance, and I'll wield Durendal—
The king himself presented it to me—
And if I die, whoever takes my sword                           95
Can say its master has nobly served his lord."

### 89

Archbishop Turpin comes forward then to speak.
He spurs his horse and gallops up a hill,
Summons the Franks, and preaches in these words:
"My noble lords, Charlemagne left us here,                    100
And may our deaths do honor to the king!
Now you must help defend our holy Faith!
Before your eyes you see the Saracens.
Confess your sins, ask God to pardon you;
I'll grant you absolution to save your souls.                 105
Your deaths would be a holy martyrdom,
And you'll have places in highest Paradise."
The French dismount; they kneel upon the ground.
Then the archbishop, blessing them in God's name,
Told them, for penance, to strike when battle came.           110

. . . . . . . . . . .

### 91

At Roncevaux Count Roland passes by,
Riding his charger, swift-running Veillantif.[8]
He's armed for battle, splendid in shining mail.
As he parades, he brandishes his lance.
Turning the point straight up against the sky,               115
And from the spearhead a banner flies, pure white,
With long gold fringes that beat against his hands.
Fair to behold, he laughs, serene and gay.
Now close behind him comes Oliver, his friend,
With all the Frenchmen cheering their mighty lord.           120
Fiercely his eyes confront the Saracens;
Humbly and gently he gazes at the Franks,
Speaking to them with gallant courtesy:
"Barons, my lords, softly now, keep the pace!
Here come the pagans looking for martyrdom.                  125
We'll have such plunder before the day is out,
As no French king has ever won before!"
And at this moment the armies join in war.        AOI

. . . . . . . . . . .

### 161

The pagans flee, furious and enraged,
Trying their best to get away in Spain.                      130
Count Roland lacks the means to chase them now,
For he has lost his war-horse Veillantif;
Against his will he has to go on foot.
He went to give Archbishop Turpin help,
Unlaced his helmet, removed it from his head,               135
And then took off the hauberk of light mail;
The under-tunic he cut into long strips
With which he stanched the largest of his wounds.
Then lifting Turpin, carried him in his arms
To soft green grass, and gently laid him down.              140
In a low voice Roland made this request:
"My noble lord, I pray you, give me leave,
For our companions, the men we held so dear,
Must not be left abandoned now in death.
I want to go and seek out every one,                        145
Carry them here, and place them at your feet."
Said the archbishop, "I grant it willingly.
The field belongs, thank God, to you and me."

[8]Roland's horse.

### 162

Alone, Count Roland walks through the battlefield,
Searching the valleys, searching the mountain heights.       150
He found the bodies of Ivon and Ivoire,
And then he found the Gascon Engelier.
Gerin he found, and Gerier his friend,
He found Aton and then Count Bérengier,
Proud Anseïs he found, and then Samson,                      155
Gérard the Old, the Count of Roussillon.
He took these barons, and carried every one
Back to the place where the archbishop was,
And then he put them in ranks at Turpin's knees.
Seeing them, Turpin cannot restrain his tears;              160
Raising his hand, he blesses all the dead.
And then he says, "You've come to grief, my lords!
Now in His glory, may God receive your souls,
Among bright flowers set you in Paradise!
It's my turn now; death keeps me in such pain,              165
Never again will I see Charlemagne."

### 163

Roland goes back to search the field once more,
And his companion he finds there, Oliver.
Lifting him in his arms he holds him close,
Brings him to Turpin as quickly as he can,                  170
Beside the others places him on a shield;
Turpin absolves him, signing him with the cross,
And then they yield to pity and to grief.
Count Roland says, "Brother in arms, fair friend,
You were the son of Renier, the duke                        175
Who held the land where Runers valley lies.
For breaking lances, for shattering thick shields,
Bringing the proud to terror and defeat,
For giving counsel, defending what is right,
In all the world there is no better knight."                180

### 164

When Roland sees that all his peers are dead,
And Oliver whom he so dearly loved,
He feels such sorrow that he begins to weep;
Drained of all color, his face turns ashen pale,
His grief is more than any man could bear,                  185
He falls down, fainting whether he will or no.
Says the archbishop, "Baron, you've come to woe."

. . . . . . . . . . .

### 168

Now Roland knows that death is very near.
His ears give way, he feels his brain gush out.
He prays that God will summon all his peers;                190
Then, for himself, he prays to Gabriel.
Taking the horn, to keep it from all shame,
With Durendal clasped in his other hand,
He goes on, farther than a good cross-bow shot,
West into Spain, crossing a fallow field.                   195
Up on a hilltop, under two lofty trees.
Four marble blocks are standing on the grass.
But when he comes there, Count Roland faints once more,
He falls down backward; now he is at death's door.

. . . . . . . . . . .

**174**

Count Roland feels the very grip of death                    200
Which from his head is reaching for his heart.
He hurries then to go beneath a pine;
In the green grass he lies down on his face,
Placing beneath him the sword and Oliphant;
He turns his head to look toward pagan Spain.               205
He does these things in order to be sure
King Charles will say, and with him all the Franks,
The noble count conquered until he died.
He makes confession, for all his sins laments.
Offers his glove to God in penitence.            AOI        210

───────────◆───────────

## The Norman Conquest and the Arts

During the tenth century, the Viking seafarers who had terrorized Charlemagne's lands settled in Northwest France. Within one hundred years, these aggressive Northmen, or Normans, as they came to be called, made Normandy one of the strongest fiefs in France. In 1066 under the leadership of William of Normandy, some five thousand men crossed the English Channel; at the Battle of Hastings, William defeated the Anglo-Saxon Duke Harold and seized the throne of England. The Norman Conquest had enormous consequences for the histories of England and France, for it marked the transfer of power in England from Anglo-Saxon rulers to Norman noblemen who were already vassals of the king of France. The Normans brought feudalism to England. To raise money, William ordered a detailed census of all property in the realm—the *Domesday Book*—which laid the basis for the collection of taxes. The king controlled all aspects of government with the aid of the *Curia Regis*, a royal court and council consisting of his feudal barons. Under the Norman kings, England would become one of Europe's leading medieval states.

The Normans led the way in the construction of stone churches and castles. Atop hills and at such vulnerable sites as Dover on the southeast coast of England, Norman kings erected austere castle-fortresses (Figure **11.14**). The castle featured a **keep** (square tower) containing a dungeon, a main hall, and a chapel, and incorporated a central open space with workshops and storehouses (Figure **11.15**). The enclosing stone walls were usually surmounted by turrets with **crenellations** that provided archers with protection in defensive combat. A **moat** (a trench filled with water) often surrounded the castle walls to deter enemy invasion. The brilliance of the Normans' achievement in architecture, apparent in their fortresses and in some of the earliest Romanesque churches (see chapter 13), lies in the use of stone to replace earlier timber fortifications and in the clarity with which the form of the building reflects its function.

One of the most famous Norman artifacts is the Bayeux Tapestry, a visual record of the conquest of England by William of Normandy. This eleventh-century embroidered wallhanging, named for the city in Northwestern France where it was sewn and where it is still displayed today, documents the history and folklore of the Normans with the same energetic spirit that animates the *Song of Roland*. Sewn into the linen cloth, which is some 20 inches deep and 231 feet long, are lively pictorial representations of the incidents leading up to and including the Battle of Hastings (Figure **11.13**; see also Frontispiece, p. ii). Above and alongside the images are Latin captions that serve to identify characters, places, and events. The text in the scene in Figure 11.13 reads, "Here the English and French have fallen together in battle." In the margin below the spectacle appear fallen soldiers, weapons, and a bodiless head. The seventy-nine scenes progress in the manner of a

**Figure 11.13** *The Battle Rages*, detail from the Bayeux Tapestry, eleventh century. Wool embroidery on linen, depth approx. 20 in., entire length 231 ft. Ville de Bayeux, France. Photo: By special permission of the City of Bayeux.

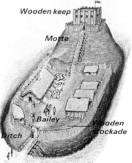

Wooden keep

Motte

Bailey

Ditch

Wooden stockade

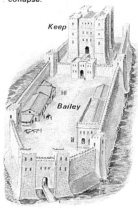

Keep

Bailey

**Figure 11.14** (above) Dover Castle, Kent, U.K., twelfth century. Photo: Ministry of Public Building and Works, London. NMR 1224/119 © Royal Commission on the Historical Monuments of England.

**Figure 11.15** (right) Development of the Norman Castle, from Patrick Rook, *The Normans.* Macdonald Education Ltd., 1977.

parchment scroll or a cartoon comic strip (although they also call to mind the style of ancient Assyrian narrative reliefs, pictured in chapter 3). Rendered in only eight colors of wool yarn, the ambitious narrative includes 626 figures, 190 horses, and over 500 other animals. Since embroidery was almost exclusively a female occupation, it is likely that the Bayeux Tapestry was the work of women—although women are depicted only four times throughout the entire piece.

The *Song of Roland* and the Bayeux Tapestry have much in common: Both are epic in theme and robust in style. Both consist of sweeping narratives whose episodes are irregular rather than uniform in length. Like the stereotypical (and almost exclusively male)

characters in the *chanson*, the figures of the Tapestry are delineated by means of expressive gestures and simplified physical features; the Normans, for instance, are distinguished by the shaved backs of their heads. Weapons and armor in both epic and embroidery are described with loving detail. Indeed, in the Bayeux Tapestry, scenes of combat provide a veritable encyclopedia of medieval battle gear: kite-shaped shields, conical iron helmets, hauberks, short bows, double-edged swords, battle axes, and lances. Both the *Song of Roland* and the Bayeux Tapestry offer a vivid record of feudal life in all its heroic splendor.

## The Lives of Medieval Serfs

Although the feudal class monopolized land and power within medieval society, this elite group represented only a tiny percentage of the total population. The vast majority of people—more than ninety percent—were unfree peasants or **serfs** who, along with freemen, farmed the soil. Medieval serfs lived quite differently from their noble landlords. Bound to large farms or manors they, like the farmers of the old Roman *latifundia* (see chapter 7), provided food in exchange for military protection furnished by the nobility. They owned no property. They were forbidden to leave the land, though, on the positive side, they could not be evicted. Their bondage to the soil assured them the protection of feudal lords who, in an age lacking effective central authority, were the sole sources of political authority.

During the Middle Ages, the reciprocal obligations of serfs and lords and the serf's continuing tenure on the land became firmly fixed. At least until the eleventh century, the interdependence between the two classes was beneficial to both; serfs needed protection, and lords, whose position as gentlemen-warriors excluded them from menial toil, needed food. For upper and lower classes alike, the individual's place in medieval society was inherited and bound by tradition.

The medieval fief usually included one or more manors. The average manor community comprised fifteen to twenty families, while a large manor of 5,000 acres might contain some fifty families. The lord usually appointed the local priest, provided a court of justice, and governed the manor from a fortified residence or castle. Between the eighth and tenth centuries, such residences were simple wooden structures but, by the twelfth century, elaborate stone manor houses with crenellated walls and towers became commonplace. On long winter nights, the lord's castle might be the scene of reveling and entertainment by *jongleurs* singing epic tales like the *Song of Roland* (see Reading 2.14).

The typical medieval manor consisted of farmlands, woodland, and pasture, and included a common mill, wine press, and oven (Figure **11.16**). Serfs cultivated the major crops of oats and rye on strips of arable land. In addition to the food they produced from fields reserved for the lord, they owed the lord a percentage—usually a third—of their own agricultural yield. They also performed services in the form of labor. In the medieval world, manor was isolated from manor, and a subsistence economy similar to that of the Neolithic village prevailed. The annual round of peasant labor, beset

**Figure 11.16** The Medieval Manor.

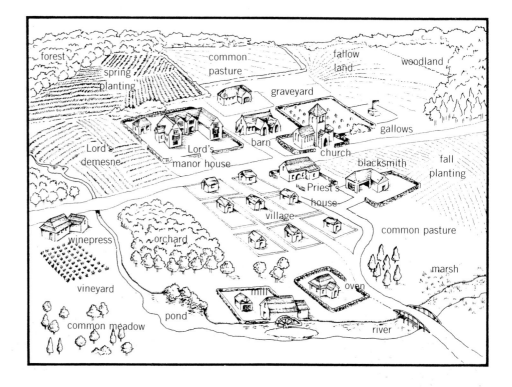

**Figure 11.17** Carpenters' Guild Signature window, detail, early thirteenth century. Stained glass. Chartres Cathedral, France. Photo: Sonia Halliday, Weston Turville, U.K.

**Figure 11.18** *Women and Men Reaping*, from the Luttrell Psalter, ca. 1340. Reproduced by permission of the British Library, London, Add. MS 42130, f.172.

by a continuing war with the elements, was harsh and demanding. Nevertheless, during the Early Middle Ages, serfs made considerable progress in farm technology and agricultural practices. They utilized the heavy-wheeled plow and the tandem harness, developed wind and water mills, recovered land by dredging swamps and clearing forests, and offset soil exhaustion by devising systems of crop rotation. The "three-field system," for example, left one-third of the land fallow to allow it to recover its fertility. Such innovations eventually contributed to the production of a food surplus, which in turn stimulated the revival of trade.

Medieval serfs were subject to perennial toil and constant privations, including those of famine and disease. Most could neither read nor write. Unfortunately, art and literature leave us little insight into the lives and values of the lower classes of medieval society. Occasionally, however, in the sculptures of laboring peasants found on medieval cathedrals, in stained glass windows (Figure 11.17), and in medieval manuscripts (Figure 11.18), we find visual representations of lower-class life. And although these examples may provide an idealized version of reality conceived by those who directed such programs of illustration, this type of evidence constitutes a valuable resource for our understanding of the Middle Ages.

| | |
|---|---|
| **900** | horse collars come into use in Europe |
| **1050** | crossbows are first used in France |
| **ca. 1150** | the first windmills appear in Europe |

## The Christian Crusades

During the eleventh century, numerous circumstances contributed to a change in the character of medieval life. The Normans effectively pushed the Muslims out of the Mediterranean Sea and, as the Normans and other marauders began to settle down, Europeans enjoyed a greater degree of security. At the same time, rising agricultural productivity and surplus encouraged trade and travel. The Christian Crusades of the eleventh to thirteenth centuries were directly related to these changes. They were both a cause of economic revitalization and a symptom of the increased freedom and new mobility of Western Europeans during the High Middle Ages (ca. 1000–1300).

The Crusades began in an effort to rescue Jerusalem from Muslim Turks who were threatening the Byzantine Empire and denying Christian pilgrims access to the Holy Land. At the request of the Byzantine emperor, the Roman Catholic Church launched a series of military expeditions designed to regain territories dominated by the Turks. The First Crusade, called by Pope Urban II in 1095, began in the spirit of a Holy War

but, unlike the Muslim *jihad*, the intention was to recover land, not to convert pagans. Thousands of people—both laymen and clergy—"took up the Cross" and marched overland through Europe to the Byzantine East (Map **11.3**). It soon became apparent, however, that the material benefits of the Crusades outweighed the spiritual ones, especially since the campaigns provided economic and military opportunities for the younger sons of the nobility. While the eldest son of an upper-class family inherited his father's fief under the principle of **primogeniture**, his younger brothers were left to seek their own fortunes. The Crusades stirred the ambitions of these disenfranchised young men. Equally ambitious were the Italian city-states. Eager to expand their commercial activities, they encouraged the Crusaders to become middlemen in trade between Italy and the East. In the course of the Fourth Crusade, Venetian profit seekers persuaded the Crusaders to sack Constantinople and capture trade ports in the Aegean in the interest of Venetian trade. Moral inhibitions failed to restrain the vampires of greed and, in 1204, the Fourth Crusade deteriorated into a contest for personal profit.

**Map 11.3** The Major Crusades, 1096–1204.

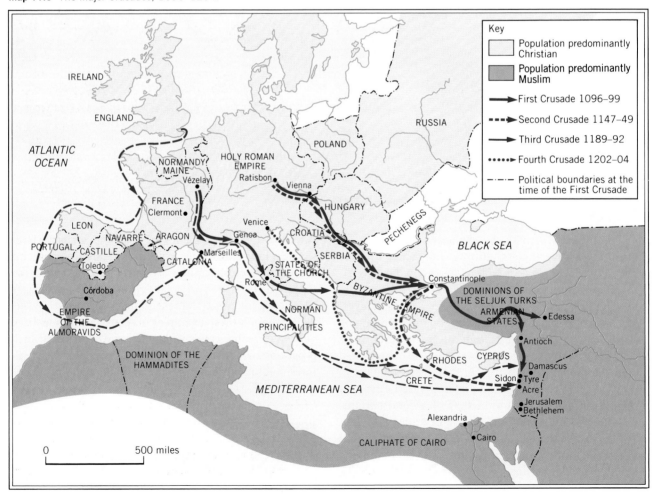

| | |
|---|---|
| ca. 1150 | magnetic compasses appear in Europe |
| 1233 | the first coal mines are opened in Newcastle, England |
| 1240 | European shipbuilders adopt the use of the rudder from the Arabs |
| 1249 | Muslims use gunpowder against Christian Crusaders |

Aside from such economic advantages as those enjoyed by individual Crusaders and the Italian city-states, the gains made by the Crusades were slight. In the first of the four major expeditions, the Crusaders did retake some important cities, including Jerusalem. But by 1291, all recaptured lands were lost again to the Muslims. Indeed, in over two hundred years of fighting, the Christian Crusaders did not secure any territory permanently, nor did they stop the westward advance of the Turks. Constantinople finally fell in 1453 to a later wave of Muslim Turks.

Despite their failure as religious ventures, the Crusades had enormous consequences for the West: The revival of trade between East and West enhanced European commercial life, encouraging the rise of towns and bringing great wealth to the cities of Venice, Genoa, and Pisa in Italy. Then, too, in the absence or death of crusading noblemen, feudal lords (including emperors and kings) seized every opportunity to establish greater authority over the lands within their domains, thus consolidating and centralizing political power in the embryonic nation-states of England and France. Finally, renewed contact with Byzantium promoted an atmosphere of commercial and cultural receptivity that had not existed since Roman times. Luxury goods, such as saffron, citrus, silks, and damasks, entered Western Europe, as did sacred relics associated with the lives of Jesus, Mary, and the Christian saints. And, to the delight of the literate, Arabic translations of Greek manuscripts poured into France, along with all genres of Islamic literature (see chapter 10).

## The Medieval Romance and the Code of Courtly Love

The Crusades inspired the writing of chronicles that were an admixture of historical fact, Christian lore, and stirring fiction. As such histories had broad appeal in an age of increasing upper-class literacy, they came to be written in the everyday language of the layperson—the vernacular—rather than in Latin. The Crusades also contributed to the birth of the **medieval romance**, a fictitious tale of love and adventure that became the most popular form of literary entertainment in the West between the years 1200 and 1500. Medieval romances first appeared in twelfth-century France in the form of rhymed verse, but later ones were written in prose.

While romances were probably recited before a small, courtly audience rather than read individually, the development of the form coincided with the rise of a European "textual culture," that is, a culture dependent on written language rather than on oral tradition. In this textual culture, vernacular languages gained importance for intimate kinds of literature, while Latin remained the official language of Church and state.

The "spice" of the typical medieval romance was an illicit relationship or forbidden liaison between a man and woman of the upper class. During the Middle Ages, marriage among members of the nobility was usually an alliance formed in the interest of securing land. Indeed, noble families might arrange marriages for offspring who were still in the cradle. In such circumstances, romantic love was more likely to flourish outside marriage. An adulterous affair between Lancelot, a knight of King Arthur's court, and Guinevere, the king's wife, is central to the popular twelfth-century verse romance *Lancelot*. Written in vernacular French by Chrétien de Troyes (d. ca. 1183), Lancelot belongs to a cycle of stories associated with a semilegendary sixth-century Welsh chieftain named Arthur. Chrétien's poem (a portion of which appears in prose translation in the following pages) stands at the beginning of a long tradition of Arthurian romance literature. Filled with bloody combat, supernatural events, and romantic alliances, medieval romances introduced a new and complex picture of human conduct and courtship associated with the so-called code of courtly love.

The code of courtly love, popularized in twelfth-century manuals of conduct for European aristocrats, held that love (whether requited or not) had a purifying and ennobling influence on the lover. To love was to suffer; witness, in the excerpt below, Queen Guinevere's distress upon hearing the false report of Lancelot's death. Courtly love was also associated with a variety of distressing physical symptoms, such as an inability to eat or sleep. The tenets of courtly love required that a knight prove his love for his lady by performing daring and often impossible deeds; he must even be willing to die for her. In these features, the medieval romance is far removed from the rugged, bellicose spirit of earlier literary works like the *Song of Roland*. Indeed, *Lancelot* dramatizes the feminization of the chivalric ideal. The *Song of Roland* pictures early medieval culture in terms of heroic idealism and personal loyalty between men. The Arthurian romance, however, redefined these qualities in the direction of sentiment and sensuality. Lancelot fights not for his country, nor even for his lord, but to win the love of his mistress. His prowess is not exercised, as with Roland, on a field of battle, but as individual combat undertaken in the courtyard of his host. While Roland is motivated by the ideal of glory in battle, Lancelot is driven by his love for Guinevere.

The courtly love tradition contributed to shaping modern Western concepts of gender and courtship. It also worked to define the romantic perception of women as objects, particularly objects of reward for the performance of extraordinary deeds. For although courtly love elevated the woman (and her prototype, the Virgin Mary) as worthy of adoration, it defined her exclusively in terms of the interests of men. Nevertheless, the medieval romance, which flattered and exalted the aristocratic lady as an object of desire, was directed toward a primarily female audience. A product of the aristocratic (and male) imagination, the lady of the medieval romance had no counterpart in the lower classes of society, where women worked side by side with men in the fields (see Figure 11.18) and in a variety of trades, including textiles, beermaking, and innkeeping. Despite the artificiality, however, the theme of courtly love and the romance itself had a significant influence on Western literary tradition. In that tradition, even into modern times, writers have tended to treat love more as a mode of spiritual purification or as an emotional affliction than as a condition of true affection and sympathy between the sexes.

## READING 2.15
## From Chrétien de Troyes' *Lancelot*

*[Gawain and Lancelot, knights of King Arthur's court, set out in quest of Queen Guinevere. In the forest, they meet a damsel, who tells them of the Queen's whereabouts.]*

Then the damsel relates to them the following story: 1
"In truth, my lords, Meleagant, a tall and powerful knight, son of the King of Gorre, has taken her off into the kingdom whence no foreigner returns, but where he must perforce remain in servitude and banishment." Then they ask her: "Damsel, where is this country? Where can we find the way thither?" She replies: "That you shall quickly learn; but you may be sure that you will meet with many obstacles and difficult passages, for it is not easy to enter there except with the permission of the king, whose name 10 is Bademagu; however, it is possible to enter by two very perilous paths and by two very difficult passage-ways. One is called 'the water-bridge,' because the bridge is under water, and there is the same amount of water beneath it as above it, so that the bridge is exactly in the middle; and it is only a foot and a half in width and in thickness. This choice is certainly to be avoided, and yet it is the less dangerous of the two. . . . The other bridge is still more impracticable and much more perilous, never having been crossed by man. It is just like a sharp sword, 20 and therefore all the people call it 'the sword-bridge.' Now I have told you all the truth I know. . . ."

*[They reach the sword-bridge.]*

At the end of this very difficult bridge they dismount from their steeds and gaze at the wicked-looking stream, which is as swift and raging, as black and turgid, as fierce and terrible as if it were the devil's stream; and it is so dangerous and bottomless that anything falling into it would be as completely lost as if it fell into the salt sea. And the bridge, which spans it, is different from any other bridge; for there never was such a one as this. If 30 any one asks of me the truth, there never was such a bad bridge, nor one whose flooring was so bad. The bridge across the cold stream consisted of a polished, gleaming sword; but the sword was stout and stiff, and was as long as two lances. At each end there was a tree-trunk in which the sword was firmly fixed. No one need fear to fall because of its breaking or bending, for its excellence was such that it could support a great weight . . . . [Lancelot] prepares, as best he may, to cross the stream, and he does a very marvelous thing in removing the armor from 40 his feet and hands. He will be in a sorry state when he reaches the other side [Figure **11.19**]. He is going to support himself with his bare hands and feet upon the sword, which was sharper than a scythe, for he had not kept on his feet either sole or upper[1] or hose. But he felt no fear of wounds upon his hands or feet; he preferred to maim himself rather than to fall from the bridge and be plunged in the water from which he could never escape. In accordance with this determination, he passes over with great pain and agony, being wounded in the hands, 50 knees, and feet. But even this suffering is sweet to him: for Love, who conducts and leads him on, assuages and relieves the pain. Creeping on his hands, feet, and knees, he proceeds until he reaches the other side. . . .

*[Lancelot confronts the Queen's captors: King Bademagu's son, Meleagant, refuses to make peace with Lancelot and promptly challenges him to battle.]*

. . . Very early, before prime[2] had yet been sounded, both of the knights fully armed were led to the place, mounted upon two horses equally protected. Meleagant was very graceful, alert, and shapely; the hauberk with its fine meshes, the helmet, and the shield hanging from his neck—all these became him well. . . . Then the 60 combatants without delay make all the people stand aside; then they clash the shields with their elbows, and thrust their arms into the straps, and spur at each other so violently that each sends his lance two arms' length through his opponent's shield, causing the lance to split and splinter like a flying spark. And the horses meet head on, clashing breast to breast, and the shields and helmets crash with such a noise that it seems like a mighty thunder-clap; not a breast-strap, girth, rein or surcingle[3] remains unbroken, and the saddle-bows, though strong, 70 are broken to pieces. The combatants felt no shame in falling to earth, in view of their mishaps, but they quickly spring to their feet, and without waste of threatening words rush at each other more fiercely than two wild boars, and deal great blows with their swords of steel like men whose hate is violent. Repeatedly they trim the helmets and shining hauberks so fiercely that after the sword the blood spurts out. They furnished an excellent battle, indeed, as they stunned and wounded each other

---

[1]Parts of the shoe or boot.
[2]The second of the Canonical Hours, around 6 A.M. The devout recited special devotional prayers at each of the Canonical Hours: lauds, prime, terce, sext, none, vespers, and compline.
[3]A band passing around a horse's body to bind the saddle.

**Figure 11.19** *Lancelot Crossing the Swordbridge and Guinevere in the Tower*, from the *Romance of Lancelot*, ca. 1300. 13½ × 10 in. © The J. Pierpont Morgan Library, New York, 1990, MS 806 f. 166.

with their heavy, wicked blows. Many fierce, hard, long 80
bouts they sustained with equal honor, so that the
onlookers could discern no advantage on either side. But
it was inevitable that he who had crossed the bridge
should be much weakened by his wounded hands. The
people who sided with him were much dismayed, for they
notice that his strokes are growing weaker, and they fear
he will get the worst of it; it seemed to them that he was
weakening, while Meleagant was triumphing, and they
began to murmur all around. But up at the window of the
tower there was a wise maiden who thought within herself 90
that the knight had not undertaken the battle either on
her account or for the sake of the common herd who had
gathered about the list, but that his only incentive had
been the Queen; and she thought that, if he knew that she
was at the window seeing and watching him, his strength
and courage would increase. . . . Then she came to the
Queen and said: "Lady, for God's sake and your own as
well as ours, I beseech you to tell me, if you know, the
name of yonder knight, to the end that it may be of some
help to him." "Damsel," the Queen replies, "you have 100
asked me a question in which I see no hate or evil, but
rather good intent; the name of the knight, I know, is
Lancelot of the Lake." "God, how happy and glad at heart
I am!" the damsel says. Then she leans forward and calls
to him by name so loudly that all the people hear:
"Lancelot, turn about and see who is here taking note of
thee!"

When Lancelot heard his name, he was not slow to
turn around: he turns and sees seated up there at the
window of the tower her whom he desired most in the 110
world to see. From the moment he caught sight of her,
he did not turn or take his eyes and face from her,
defending himself with backhand blows. . . . Lancelot's
strength and courage grow, partly because he has love's
aid, and partly because he never hated any one so much
as him with whom he is engaged. Love and mortal hate,
so fierce that never before was such hate seen, make
him so fiery and bold that Meleagant ceases to treat it as
a jest and begins to stand in awe of him, for he had
never met or known so doughty a knight, nor had any 120
knight ever wounded or injured him as this one does. . . .

*[Lancelot spares Meleagant but thereafter is taken prisoner. Rumor reaches the Queen that Lancelot is dead.]*

The news of this spread until it reached the Queen, who
was sitting at meat. She almost killed herself on hearing
the false report about Lancelot, but she supposes it to be
true, and therefore she is in such dismay that she almost
loses the power to speak; but, because of those present,
she forces herself to say: "In truth, I am sorry for his death,
and it is no wonder that I grieve, for he came into this
country for my sake, and therefore I should mourn for
him." Then she says to herself, so that the others should 130
not hear, that no one need ask her to drink or eat, if it is
true that he is dead, in whose life she found her own. Then
grieving she rises from the table, and makes her lament,
but so that no one hears or notices her. She is so beside
herself that she repeatedly grasps her throat with the
desire to kill herself; but first she confesses to herself, and
repents with self-reproach, blaming and censuring herself,
for the wrong she had done him, who, as she knew, had
always been hers, and would still be hers, if he were alive.
. . . "Alas how much better I should feel, and how much 140
comfort I should take, if only once before he died I had
held him in my arms! What? Yes, certainly, quite unclad,
in order the better to enjoy him. If he is dead, I am very
wicked not to destroy myself. Why? Can it harm my lover
for me to live on after he is dead, if I take no pleasure in
anything but in the woe I bear for him? In giving myself
up to grief after his death, the very woes I court would be
sweet to me, if he were only still alive. It is wrong for a
woman to wish to die rather than to suffer for her lover's
sake. It is certainly sweet for me to mourn him long. I 150
would rather be beaten alive than die and be at rest."

*[Once freed, Lancelot makes his way to the castle and Guinevere agrees to meet with him secretly.]*

Lancelot . . . was so impatient for the night to come that
his restlessness made the day seem longer than a hundred
ordinary days or than an entire year. If night had only come,
he would gladly have gone to the trysting place. Dark and
somber night at last won its struggle with the day, and
wrapped it up in its covering, and laid it away beneath
its cloak. When he saw the light of day obscured, he
pretended to be tired and worn, and said that, in view of
his protracted vigils, he needed rest. You, who have ever 160
done the same, may well understand and guess that he
pretends to be tired and goes to bed in order to deceive
the people of the house; but he cared nothing about his

bed, nor would he have sought rest there for anything, for he could not have done so and would not have dared, and furthermore he would not have cared to possess the courage or the power to do so. Soon he softly rose, and was pleased to find that no moon or star was shining, and that in the house there was no candle, lamp or lantern burning. Thus he went out and looked about, but there    170 was no one on the watch for him, for all thought that he would sleep in his bed all night. Without escort or company he quickly went out into the garden, meeting no one on the way, and he was so fortunate as to find that a part of the garden-wall had recently fallen down. Through this break he passes quickly and proceeds to the window, where he stands, taking good care not to cough or sneeze, until the Queen arrives clad in a very white chemise. She wore no cloak or coat, but had thrown over her a short cape of scarlet cloth and shrew-mouse fur. As soon as    180 Lancelot saw the Queen leaning on the window-sill behind the great iron bars, he honored her with a gentle salute. She promptly returned his greeting, for he was desirous of her, and she of him. Their talk and conversation are not of vulgar, tiresome affairs. They draw close to one another, until each holds the other's hand. But they are so distressed at not being able to come together more completely, that they curse the iron bars. Then Lancelot asserts that, with the Queen's consent, he will come inside to be with her, and that the bars cannot    190 keep him out. And the Queen replies: "Do you not see how the bars are stiff to bend and hard to break? You could never so twist, pull or drag at them as to dislodge one of them." "Lady," says he, "have no fear of that. It would take more than these bars to keep me out. . . ."

Then the Queen retires, and he prepares to loosen the window. Seizing the bars, he pulls and wrenches them until he makes them bend and drags them from their places. But the iron was so sharp that the end of his little finger was cut to the nerve, and the first joint of the next    200 finger was torn; but he who is intent upon something else paid no heed to any of his wounds or to the blood which trickled down. Though the window is not low, Lancelot gets through it quickly and easily . . . then he comes to the bed of the Queen, whom he adores and before whom he kneels, holding her more dear than the relic of any saint. And the Queen extends her arms to him and, embracing him, presses him tightly against her bosom, drawing him into the bed beside her and showing him every possible satisfaction: her love and her heart go out to him. It is    210 love that prompts her to treat him so; and if she feels great love for him, he feels a hundred thousand times as much for her. For there is no love at all in other hearts compared with what there is in his; in his heart love was so completely embodied that it was niggardly toward all other hearts. Now Lancelot possesses all he wants, when the Queen voluntarily seeks his company and love, and when he holds her in his arms, and she holds him in hers. Their sport is so agreeable and sweet, as they kiss and fondle each other, that in truth such a marvellous joy    220 comes over them as was never heard or known. But their joy will not be revealed by me, for in a story it has no place. Yet, the most choice and delightful satisfaction was precisely that of which our story must not speak. That night Lancelot's joy and pleasure was very great. But, to

his sorrow, day comes when he must leave his mistress' side. It cost him such pain to leave her that he suffered a real martyr's agony. His heart now stays where the Queen remains; he has not the power to lead it away, for it finds such pleasure in the Queen that it has no desire to leave    230 her: so his body goes, and his heart remains; . . .

———————◆———————

## The Cult of the Virgin Mary

From the earliest years of its formation as a religion, Christianity exalted the Virgin Mary as an object of veneration; but, beginning in the twelfth century, Mary's roles as Mother of God, Queen of Heaven, and principal intercessor between Jesus and the humble Christian received great attention in literature, music, and art (Figure **11.20**; see also Part Opener, p. 64, and Figures 13.25, 13.31). In the High Middle Ages, the impulse that led to the exaltation of Mary seems to have kindled a new affection for women in general—especially in literature and song (see "The Motet," p. 139). Lancelot's worship of Guinevere and his repeated references to her "saintliness" illustrate the confusion of sensual and spiritual passions that characterized the culture of the High Middle Ages. The fact that Lancelot uses the terminology of religious worship to flatter an unfaithful wife reflects the paradoxical nature of the so-called "religion

**Figure 11.20** *Yolande de Soissons Kneeling Before a Statue of the Virgin and Child*, from a French psalter and Book of Hours, ca. 1290. 7¼ × 5⅓ in. © The J. Pierpont Morgan Library, New York, MS 729, f.232v.

of love." However one explains this phenomenon, *Lancelot* remains representative of the climate of shifting values and the degeneration of feudal ideals, especially those of honor and loyalty among gentleman-warriors.

## The Poetry of the *Troubadours*

During the Early Middle Ages, few men and women could read or write. But by the eleventh century, literacy was spreading beyond the cathedral schools and monasteries. The popularity of such forms of vernacular literature as lyric poetry, the chronicle, and the romance gives evidence of the increasing lay literacy among upper-class men and women. To entertain the French nobility, *trouvères* (in the North) and *troubadours* (in the South) composed and performed poems devoted to courtly love, chivalry, religion, and politics. *Minnesingers* provided a similar kind of entertainment at German-speaking courts, while *Meistersingers*, masters of the guilds of poets and musicians, flourished somewhat later in

**Figure 11.21** "Herr Konrad von Altretten," *Medieval Lovers*, from the Manesse Codex, Zürich, ca. 1315–1330. Universitätsbibliothek, Heidelberg, Germany, MS Pal. germ. 848, f.84. Rheinisches Köln Bildarchiv, Cologne, Germany.

German towns. Unlike the minstrels of old, *troubadours* were usually men and women of noble birth. Their poems, like the *chansons* of the Early Middle Ages, were monophonic and syllabic, but they were more expressive in content and more delicate in style, betraying their indebtedness to Arab poetic forms. Often, *troubadours* (or the professional musicians who recited their poems) accompanied themselves on a lyre or a lute (see Figure 10.15). Many of the 2,600 extant *troubadour* poems exalt the passionate affection of a gentleman for a lady, or, as in those written by the dozen or so identifiable female *troubadours*, the reverse (Figure 11.21).

Influenced by Islamic verse such as that found in chapter 10, *troubadour* poems generally manifest a positive, even joyous, response to physical nature and the world of the senses. An eleventh-century poem by William IX, Duke of Aquitaine and one of the first *troubadours*, compares the anticipation of sexual fulfillment with the coming of spring. It opens with these high-spirited words:

> In the sweetness of the new season
> when woods burst forth and birds
> sing, each in its own voice
> to the lyrics of a new song,
> *then* should one seize
> the pleasures one most desires.

In a more melancholic vein, the mid-twelfth-century poet Bernart de Ventadour explored the popular theme of unrequited love in the poem "When I behold the lark."[*] Occasionally, *troubadour* verse gives evidence of hostility between upper and lower social classes. Such is the case with the second of the poems printed here, in which the *troubadour* Peire Cardenal levels a fierce attack on social inequity and upper-class greed.

[*]See Music Listening Selection at end of chapter.

# READING 2.16
## *Troubadour* Poems

### Bernart de Ventadour's "When I behold the lark"

When I behold the lark arise    1
with wings of gold for heaven's height,
to drop at last from flooded skies,
lost in its fullness of delight,
such sweetness spreads upon the day    5
I envy those who share the glee.
My heart's so filled with love's dismay
I wait its breaking suddenly.

I thought in love's ways I was wise,
yet little do I know aright.    10
I praised a woman as love's prize
and she gives nothing to requite.
My heart, my life she took in theft,

she took the world away from me,
and now my plundered self is left    15
only desire and misery.

Her rule I'm forced to recognize
since all my broken joys took flight.
I looked within her lifted eyes,
that mirror sweet with treacherous might:    20
O mirror, here I weep and dream
of depths once glimpsed and now denied.
I'm lost in you as in the stream
comely Narcissus looked and died.

Now trust in indignation dies    25
and womanhood I henceforth slight.
I find that all her worths are lies.
I thought her something made of light.
And no one comes to plead for me
with her who darkens all my days.    30
Woman I doubt and now I see
that she like all the rest betrays.

Aye, pity women all despise.
Come face the truth and do not fight.
The smallest kindness she denies,    35
yet who but she should soothe my plight?
So gentle and so fair is she,
it's hard for others to believe.
She, who could save, in cruelty
watches her wasting lover grieve.    40

My love has failed and powerless lies;
devotion bears for me no right.
She laughs to hear my deepest sighs—
then silently I'll leave her sight.
I cast my love of her away.    45
She struck and I accept the blow.
She will not speak and I must stray
in exile. Where, I do not know.

Tristan, I've made an end, I say.
I'm going—where, I do not know.    50
My song is dying, and away
all love and joy I cast, and go.

### Peire Cardenal's "Lonely the rich need never be"

Lonely the rich need never be,
they have such constant company.
For Wickedness in front we see,
behind, all round, and far and wide.
The giant called Cupidity    5
is always hulking at their side.
Injustice waves the flag, and he
is led along by Pride . . .

If a poor man has snitched a bit of rag,
he goes with downcast head and frightened eye.    10
But when the rich thief fills his greedy bag,
he marches on with head still held as high.
The poor man's hanged, he stole a rotten bridle.
The man who hanged him stole the horse. O fie.
To hang poor thieves the rich thieves still aren't idle.    15
That kind of justice arrow-swift will fly . . .

The rich are charitable? Yes,
as Cain who slew his brother Abel.

They're thieves, no wolves as merciless.
They're liars, like a whoreshop-babel.                                    20
O stick their ribs, O stick their souls!
No truth comes bubbling from the holes,
but lies. Their greedy hearts, abhorrent,
are rabid as a mountain-torrent . . .

With loving-kindness how they quicken,                                    25
what hoards of charity they spread.
If all the stones were loaves of bread,
if all the streams with wine should thicken,
the hills turn bacon or boiled chicken,
they'd give no extra crumb. That's flat,                                  30
    Some people are like that.

---

## The Rise of Medieval Towns

Observing the plight of the poor at the hands of the rich, Peire Cardenal condemns a universal condition; but his poem discloses a new social consciousness associated with economic change. During the High Middle Ages, a class of people "midway" between serfs and landlords—the middle class—was emerging. Many factors, including increased agricultural production and the reopening of trade routes, encouraged the rise of the middle class. During the eleventh century, merchants (often younger sons of noble families) engaged in commercial enterprises that promoted the growth of local markets. Usually established near highways or rivers, trade markets became an essential part of manorial life. The permanent market (or *fauberg*) provided the basis for the medieval town—an urban center that attracted farmers and artisans who might buy freedom from their lord or simply run away from the manor. "City air makes a man free" was the cry of those who had discovered the urban alternative to manorial life.

In the newly established towns, the middle class pursued profit from commercial exchange. Merchants and craftspeople in like occupations formed **guilds** for the mutual protection of buyers and sellers. The guilds regulated prices, fixed wages, established standards of quality in the production of goods, and provided training for newcomers in each profession. During the eleventh and twelfth centuries, urban dwellers purchased charters of self-government from lords in whose fiefs their towns were situated. Such charters allowed townspeople (in French, *bourgeois*; in German, *Burghers*) to establish municipal governments and regulate their own economic activities. Such commercial centers as Milan, Florence, and Venice became completely self-governing city-states similar to those of ancient Greece and Rome. The Flemish cities of Bruges and Antwerp exported fine linen and wool to England and to towns along the Baltic Sea. The spirit of urban growth was manifested in the construction of defensive stone walls that protected the citizens, as at Carcassonne in Southwestern France (Figure **11.22**), and in the building of cathedrals and guildhalls that flanked the open marketplace. Although by the twelfth century town dwellers constituted less than fifteen percent of the total European population, the middle class continued to expand and ultimately came to dominate Western society.

Middle-class values differed considerably from those of the feudal nobility. Whereas warfare and chivalry preoccupied the nobility, financial prosperity and profit were the principal concerns of the middle class. In European cities, there evolved a lively vernacular literature

**Figure 11.22** The walled city of Carcassonne, France, twelfth–thirteenth centuries. Arch. Phot. Paris/S.P.A.D.E.M.

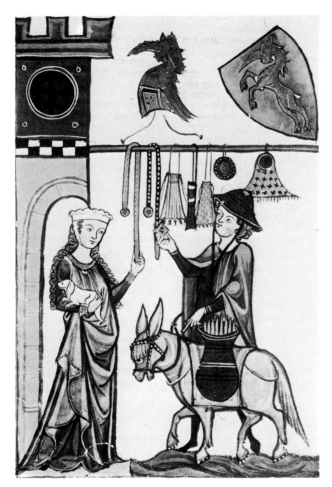

**Figure 11.23** *Young Lady Shopping for Belts and Purses*, from the Manesse Codex, Zürich, ca. 1315-1333. Universitätsbibliothek, Heidelberg, Germany, MS Pal. germ. 848, f.64. Rheinisches Köln Bildarchiv, Cologne, Germany.

He who takes a wife trades peace for strife,
Long weariness, despair, oppress his life,
A heavy load, a barrel full of chatter,
Uncorkable, her gossip makes a clatter,
Now, ever since I took a wife,
Calamity has marred my life.*

## SUMMARY

The progress of the medieval West reflects the commingling of three cultural ingredients: classical, Christian, and Germanic. The westward migrations of the Germanic tribes threatened the stability of the already waning Roman civilization. Nevertheless, these tribes introduced customs and values that came to shape the character of the European Middle Ages. In the first five hundred years of the first millennium, Germanic languages, laws, and forms of artistic expression fused with those of the late Roman and newly Christianized world to fix the patterns of early medieval life. The epic *Beowulf* and the art of Sutton Hoo are two examples of Germanic cultural achievement. By the eighth century, the Empire of the Frankish ruler Charlemagne had become the cultural oasis of the West. Under Charlemagne's influence, much of Europe converted to Christianity, while members of his court worked to encourage education and the arts. In the turbulent century following the fragmentation of the Carolingian Empire, feudalism—the exchange of land for military service—gave upper-class warriors the power to rule locally while providing protection from outside attack. The artistic monuments of the Early Middle Ages—the *Song of Roland*, the Norman castle, and the Bayeux Tapestry—all describe a heroic age that glorified feudal combat, male prowess, and the conquest of land. Manorialism, the economic basis for medieval society, offered the lower classes physical protection in exchange for food production, but it left in its wake little tangible evidence of the lives and values of the majority of the population.

The Christian Crusades—the definitive expression of Christian-Muslim hostility—altered early medieval patterns of economic and cultural life, even as they reflected the new mobility of Europe's High Middle Ages. In the literature of the medieval court, sentiment and sensuousness replaced heroic idealism and chivalric chastity. Romantic love, a medieval invention, dominated both the vernacular romance and *troubadour* poetry. The Crusades also encouraged the rise of towns and trade dominated by a new middle class, whose ambitions were distinctly materialistic and profit oriented. The values of merchants and craftspeople differed from

expressive of middle-class concerns. It included humorous narrative tales (*fabliaux*) and poems (*dits*) describing urban occupations, domestic conflict, and street and tavern life (Figure **11.23**). These popular genres, which feature such stereotypes as the miserly husband and the lecherous monk, slyly reflect many of the social tensions and sexual prejudices of the day. A favorite theme of medieval *fabliaux* and *dits* was the antifemale diatribe, a denunciation of women as bitter as Juvenal's (see chapter 7), and one that was rooted in a long tradition of misogyny (the hatred of women). While medieval romances generally cast the female in the role of Mary, Mother of God, *fabliaux* and *dits* often described all women as descended from the sinful and seductive Eve. The hostile attitude toward womankind, intensified perhaps by women's increasing participation in some of the commercial activities traditionally dominated by men, is readily apparent in the popular literature of the late thirteenth century. The following verse, based on a widely circulated proverb, voices a popular male complaint:

*"The Vices of Women," in *Three Medieval Views of Women*, translated by Gloria K. Fiero et al. New Haven: Yale University Press, 1989, 129, 131.

those of the feudal nobility, for whom land provided the basis of wealth and chivalry dictated manners and morals. Vernacular tales and poems often satirized inequality between classes and antagonism between sexes. Whereas medieval romances generally pictured their heroines as figures of the Virgin Mary, *fabliaux* and *dits* condemned women as the daughters of Eve. Changing patterns of secular life between the years 750 and 1300 reflect the shift from a feudal society to an urban one distinguished by increasingly complex social interactions between male and female, lord and vassal, farmer and merchant.

## SUGGESTIONS FOR READING

Brooke, Christopher. *The Structure of Medieval Society*. New York: McGraw-Hill, 1971.

Bruce-Mitford, Rupert. *The Sutton Hoo Ship-Burial: A Handbook*. London: British Museum, 1972.

Dodwell, C. R. *The Pictorial Arts of the West 800–1200*. New Haven: Yale University Press, 1992.

Drew, Katherine F., ed. The *Barbarian Invasions*. New York: Holt, 1970.

Duby, George. *Love and Marriage in the Middle Ages*, translated by Jane Dunnett. Chicago: University of Chicago Press, 1994.

Erickson, Carolly. *The Medieval Vision: Essays in History and Perception*. New York: Oxford University Press, 1976.

———. *Life in a Medieval City*. New York: Harper, 1981.

Gies, Frances, and J. Gies. *Life in a Medieval Village*. New York: Harper, 1991.

Gies, Joseph, and F. Gies. *Women in the Middle Ages*. New York: Barnes and Noble, 1980.

Herlihy, David. *Opera Muliera: Women and Work in Medieval Europe*. New York: McGraw-Hill, 1990.

Lewis, Archibald R. *Knights and Samurai: Feudalism in Northern France and Japan*. London: Temple Smith, 1974.

Maalouf, Amin. *The Crusades Through Arab Eyes*. New York: Schocken, 1984.

Macauley, David. *Castle*. Boston: Houghton Mifflin, 1982.

Riche, Pierre. *Daily Life in the World of Charlemagne*, translated by J. MacNamara. Philadelphia: University of Pennsylvania Press, 1978.

Stephenson, Carl. *Medieval Feudalism*. Ithaca, N.Y.: Cornell University Press, 1973.

Strayer, J. R. *Western Europe in the Middle Ages*. Glenview, Ill.: Scott-Foresman, 1982.

Trevor-Roper, Hugh. *The Rise of Christian Europe*. New York: Norton, 1989.

## MUSIC LISTENING SELECTION

**Cassette I Selection 5**   Bernart de Ventadour, "Can vei la lauzeta mover" ("When I behold the lark"), ca. 1150, excerpt.

## GLOSSARY

**chain mail**   a flexible medieval armor made of interlinked metal rings

**chalice**   a goblet; in Christian liturgy, the Eucharistic cup

**chanson de geste**   (French, "song of heroic deeds") an epic poem of the Early Middle Ages

**chivalry**   a code of behavior practiced by upper-class men and women of medieval society

**cloisonné**   (French, *cloison*, meaning "fence") an enameling technique produced by pouring molten colored glass between thin metal strips secured to a metal surface; any object ornamented in this manner (see Figure 11.2)

**common law**   the body of unwritten law developed primarily from judicial decisions based on custom and precedent; the basis of the English legal system and that of all states in the United States with the exception of Louisiana

**crenellations**   tooth-shaped battlements surmounting a wall and used for defensive combat

**cruciform**   cross-shaped

**fealty**   loyalty; the fidelity of the warrior to his chieftain

**feudalism**   the system of political organization prevailing in Europe between the ninth and fifteenth centuries and having as its basis the exchange of land for military defense

**fief**   in feudal society, land or property given to a warrior in return for military service

**gilt**   gold-surfaced; covered with gold paint or gold foil

**guild**   an association of merchants or craftspeople organized according to occupation

**investiture**   the procedure by which a feudal lord granted a vassal control over a fief

**jongleur**   a professional entertainer who wandered from court to court in medieval Europe

**joust**   a form of personal combat, usually with lances on horseback, between men-at-arms

**keep**   a square tower, the strongest and most secure part of the medieval castle (see Figure 11.14)

**kenning**   a two-term metaphor used in Old English verse

**lord**   any member of the feudal nobility who invested a vassal with a fief

**mace**   a heavy, spike-headed club used as a weapon in medieval combat

**medieval romance**   a tale of adventure that supplanted the older *chanson de geste* and that deals with knights, kings, and ladies acting under the impulse of love, religious faith, or the desire for adventure

**moat**   a wide trench, usually filled with water, surrounding a fortified place such as a castle (see Figure 11.14)

**niello**   a black sulfurous substance used as a decorative inlay for incised metal surfaces; the art or process of decorating metal in this manner

**paten**   a shallow dish; in Christian liturgy, the Eucharistic plate

**primogeniture**   the principle by which a fief was passed from father to eldest son

**renaissance**   (French, "rebirth") a revival of the learning of former and especially classical culture

**serf**   an unfree peasant

**vassal**   any member of the feudal nobility who vowed to serve a lord in exchange for control of a fief

**zoomorphic**   animal-shaped; having the form of an animal

# 12
# Christianity and
# the Medieval Mind

For a thousand years after the fall of Rome (ca. 500–1500), the Catholic Church was the primary source of spiritual authority and religious leadership in the European West. Longstanding disagreements over doctrinal and liturgical matters resulted, in 1054, in a permanent breach between the Roman Catholic Church in the West and the Greek Orthodox Church in the East. Both churches, however, shared the view that the terrestrial world mirrored a divine order that was sustained through the ministry of God's representatives on earth. Church doctrine and liturgy gave coherence and meaning to everyday life. More important, the Church offered the sole means by which the medieval Christian might achieve life everlasting.

## The Church and
## the Promise of Salvation

The promise of personal immortality was central to the medieval worldview. That promise must be understood in the context of the profound and universal fact of death, or nonbeing, and of the human inability to imagine the condition of nonbeing. In both the physical and the intellectual sense, death represents humankind's ultimate vulnerability. Almost all religious belief systems in history offer the promise of personal immortality—the ultimate act of controlling (even defying) nature.

With the exception of the purest forms of Hinduism and Buddhism, which anticipate the extinction of the Self, most world religions have met the human fear of death with an ideology (a body of doctrine supported by myth and symbols) that promises the survival of some aspect of the Self in a life hereafter. The nature of that hereafter usually depends on the moral status of the believer—that is, his or her conduct on earth.

Christianity addressed the question of personal extinction more effectively than any other world religion. The Christian immortality ideology* provided a system by which medieval Christians achieved final

victory over death. Through the **sacraments**, a set of sacred acts that impart **grace** (the free and unearned favor of God), medieval Christians were assured of the soul's redemption from sin and, ultimately, of immortality in a world to come. The seven sacraments—the number fixed by the Fourth Lateran Council of 1215—touched every significant phase of human life.[1] At birth, baptism purified the recipient of Original Sin;[2] confirmation admitted the baptized to full church privileges;[3] ordination invested those entering the clergy with priestly authority;[4] matrimony blessed the union of man and woman;[5] penance acknowledged repentance of sins and offered absolution;[6] Eucharist—the central and most important of the sacraments—joined human beings to God by means of the body and blood of Jesus;[7] and finally, just prior to death, extreme unction provided final absolution from sins.

By way of sacraments, the Church participated in virtually every major aspect of the individual's life, enforcing a set of values that determined the collective spirituality of Christendom. Since only Church officials could administer the sacraments, the clergy held a "monopoly" on personal salvation. Medieval Christians thus looked to representatives of the Mother Church as shepherds guiding the members of their flock on their long and hazardous journey through life. Their conduct on earth determined whether their souls went to Heaven, Hell, or Purgatory (the place of purification from sins). But only by way of the clergy might they receive the gifts of grace that made salvation possible.

By the twelfth century, the Christian concepts of sin and divine justice had become ever more complex: Church councils defined Purgatory as an intermediate state after death (and before the Last Judgment) where punishment was imposed for the unexpiated sins committed in mortal life. While ordinary Christians might suffer punishment in Purgatory, they might also benefit from prayers and good works offered on their behalf. The role of the priesthood in providing such forms of remission from sin would give the medieval Church unassailable power and authority.

---

*The phrase is from Ernest Becker, *The Denial of Death*. New York: The Free Press, 1973.

## Medieval Literature and the Promise of Salvation

The Christian immortality ideology shaped all forms of medieval expression. However, three works stand out as definitive of that ideology: a papal sermon, an allegorical drama, and an epic poem. The first of these, the classic medieval sermon entitled *On the Misery of the Human Condition*, was written by one of Christendom's most influential popes, Innocent III (d. 1216). Innocent's sermon is a compelling description of the natural sinfulness of humankind and a scathing condemnation of the "vile and filthy [human] condition." Innocent's imagery proceeds from the medieval view of the human body: Weighed down by the burden of the flesh, the body was subject to corruption, disease, and carnal desire. As the temple of the soul, the body would be resurrected on Judgment Day, but not before it suffered the trials of mortality. Warning of the "nearness of death," Innocent's sermon functions as a *memento mori*, a device by which listeners in a predominantly oral culture might "remember death" and thus prepare themselves for its inevitable arrival. Innocent's portrayal of the decay of the human body reflects the medieval disdain for the world of matter, a major theme in most medieval didactic literature. During the Late Middle Ages, especially after the onslaught of the bubonic plague (see chapter 15), the motif of the body as "food for worms"—one of Innocent's most vivid images—became particularly popular in gruesomely forthright tomb sculptures (Figure 12.1).

**Figure 12.1** Detail of *transi* (effigy of the dead) of François de la Sarra, ca. 1390. La Sarraz, Switzerland. Photo: De Jongh, Lausanne. © Musée de l'Elysée, Lausanne, Switzerland.

Innocent's vivid account of the Christian Hell transforms the concept of corruption into an image of eternal punishment for unabsolved sinners—a favorite subject matter for medieval artists (Figure 12.2). The contrast that Innocent draws between physical death and spiritual life has its visual counterpart in the representations of the Last Judgment depicted in medieval manuscripts and on Romanesque and Gothic church portals (see Figure 13.9).

## READING 2.17

### From Pope Innocent III's *On the Misery of the Human Condition*

**Of the Miserable Entrance upon the Human Condition**

. . . Man was formed of dust, slime, and ashes: what is even more vile, of the filthiest seed. He was conceived from the itch of the flesh, in the heat of passion and the stench of lust, and worse yet, with the stain of sin. He was born to toil, dread, and trouble; and more wretched still, was born only to die. He commits depraved acts by which he offends God, his neighbor, and himself; shameful acts by which he defiles his name, his person, and his conscience; and vain acts by which he ignores all things important, useful, and necessary. He will become fuel for those fires which are forever hot and burn forever bright; food for the worm which forever nibbles and digests; a mass of rottenness which will forever stink and reek. . . .

**On the Nearness of Death**

A man's last day is always the first in importance, but his first day is never considered his last. Yet it is fitting to live always on this principle, that one should act as if in the moment of death. For it is written: "Remember that death is not slow."[1] Time passes, death draws near. In the eyes of the dying man a thousand years are as yesterday, which is past. The future is forever being born, the present forever dying and what is past is utterly dead. We are forever dying while we are alive; we only cease to die when we cease to live. Therefore it is better to die to life than to live waiting for death, for mortal life is but a living death. . . .

**On the Putrefaction of the Dead Body**

. . . Man is conceived of blood made rotten by the heat of lust; and in the end worms, like mourners, stand about his corpse. In life he produced lice and tapeworms; in death he will produce worms and flies. In life he produced dung and vomit; in death he produces rottenness and stench. In life he fattened one man; in death he fattens a multitude of worms. What then is more foul than a human corpse? What is more horrible than a dead man? He whose embrace was pure delight in life will be a gruesome sight in death.

Of what advantage, then, are riches, food, and honors? For riches will not free us from death, neither food protect us from the worm nor honors from the stench.

[1]Ecclesiastes 14:12.

**Figure 12.2** *The Mouth of Hell*, from the Psalter of Henry of Blois, Bishop of Winchester, twelfth century. Reproduced by permission of the British Library, London, MS Cotton Nero, C.IV, f.39.

That man who but now sat in glory upon a throne is now looked down on in the grave; the dandy who once glittered in his palace lies now naked and vile in his tomb; and he who supped once on delicacies in his hall is now in his sepulcher food for worms. . . .    40

**That Nothing Can Help the Damned**

. . . O strict judgment!—not only of actions, but "of every idle word that men shall speak, they shall render an account";[2] payment with the usurer's interest will be exacted to the last penny. "Who hath showed you to flee from the wrath to come?"[3]

"The Son of Man shall send his angels and they shall gather out of his kingdom all scandals, and them that work iniquity, and they will bind them as bundles to be    50 burnt, and shall cast them into the furnace of fire. There shall be weeping and gnashing of teeth,"[4] there shall be groaning and wailing, shrieking and flailing of arms and screaming, screeching, and shouting; there shall be fear and trembling, toil and trouble, holocaust and dreadful stench, and everywhere darkness and anguish; there shall be asperity, cruelty, calamity, poverty, distress, and utter wretchedness; they will feel an oblivion of loneliness and namelessness; there shall be twistings and piercings, bitterness, terror, hunger and thirst, cold    60 and hot, brimstone and fire burning, forever and ever world without end. . . .

———————————◆———————————

²Matthew 12:36.        ³Luke 3:7.        ⁴Matthew 13:41–42.

## The Medieval Morality Play

While medieval churches rang with sermons like those preached by Innocent III, town squares (often immediately adjacent to a cathedral) became open-air theaters for the dramatization of Christian history and legend. To these urban spaces, people flocked to see dramatic performances that might last from sunrise to sunset. The **mystery play** dramatized biblical history from the fall of Lucifer to the Last Judgment, while the **miracle play** enacted stories from the Life of Christ, the Virgin, or the saints. The **morality play**, the last to evolve among the three types of medieval play, dealt with such themes as the conflict between good and evil and the fall of humankind. Usually performed by members of the craft guilds and produced on **pageants** (roofed wagon-stages) that were rolled into the town square, medieval plays were a popular form of local entertainment, as well as a source of religious and moral instruction.

Just as ancient Greek drama originated in religious ritual, so medieval drama had its roots in the performance of Church liturgy. The Catholic Mass, the principal rite of Christian worship, admitted all of the trappings of theater: colorful costumes, symbolic props, solemn processions, dramatic gestures, and ceremonial music. It is likely that the gradual dramatization of Church liturgy (see chapter 13) influenced the genesis of mystery and miracle plays. The morality play, however, had clear precedents in allegorical poetry and sermon literature. In keeping with most medieval writing, the morality play featured allegory—a literary device encountered in Plato's *Republic* (see chapter 5) and in Augustine's *City of God* (see chapter 9)—that depends on symbolic representation to capture the essence of a person, thing, or idea. The characters of the morality play are personifications of abstract qualities and universal conditions. In the play *Everyman*, for instance, the main character represents all Christian souls, Fellowship stands for friends, Goods for worldly possessions, and so forth.

Although *Everyman* has survived only in fifteenth-century Dutch and English editions, plays similar to it originated considerably earlier. The most popular of all medieval morality plays, *Everyman* symbolically recreates the pilgrimage of the Christian soul to its ultimate destiny. The play opens with the Messenger, who expounds on the transitory nature of human life. The subsequent conversation between Death and God, somewhat reminiscent of that between Satan and God in the Book of Job (see chapter 2), shows God to be an angry, petulant figure who regards human beings as "drowned in sin." If left to their own devices, he opines, "they will become much worse than beasts."

As the action unfolds, Everyman realizes that Death has come for him. He soon discovers that his best friends, his kin, his worldly possessions—indeed, all that he so treasured in life—will not accompany him to the grave. Knowledge, Wits, Beauty, and Discretion may point the way to redemption, but they cannot save him. Ultimately, only Good-Deeds will accompany him to confront judgment by "eternal God." *Everyman* is essentially a moral allegory that illustrates the Christian immortality ideology; but, typical of its time, it is also an exposition on the importance of the Catholic priesthood in helping the medieval Christian achieve salvation. Like Pope Innocent's sermon, *Everyman* teaches that all things contributing to worldly pleasure are ultimately valueless, that life is transient, and that sin can be mitigated solely by salvation earned through grace as dispensed by the Church.

## READING 2.18

### From *Everyman*

**Characters**

| | | |
|---|---|---|
| Messenger | Cousin | Strength |
| God (Adonai) | Goods | Discretion |
| Death | Good-Deeds | Five-Wits |
| Everyman | Knowledge | Angel |
| Fellowship | Confession | Doctor |
| Kindred | Beauty | |

HERE BEGINNETH A TREATISE HOW THE HIGH FATHER OF HEAVEN SENDETH DEATH TO SUMMON EVERY CREATURE TO COME AND GIVE ACCOUNT OF THEIR LIVES IN THIS WORLD AND IS IN MANNER OF A MORAL PLAY.

**MESSENGER:** I pray you all give your audience, 1
And hear this matter with reverence,
By figure a moral play—
The *Summoning of Everyman* called it is,
That of our lives and ending shows
How transitory we be all day.[1]
This matter is wondrous precious,
But the intent of it is more gracious,
And sweet to bear away.
The story saith—Man, in the beginning, 10
Look well, and take good heed to the ending,
Be you never so gay!
Ye think sin in the beginning full sweet,
Which in the end causeth thy soul to weep,
When the body lieth in clay.
Here shall you see how *Fellowship* and *Jollity*,
Both *Strength*, *Pleasure*, and *Beauty*,
Will fade from thee as flower in May.
For ye shall hear, how our heaven king
Calleth *Everyman* to a general reckoning: 20
Give audience, and hear what he doth say.
**GOD:** I perceive here in my majesty,
How that all creatures be to me unkind,[2]

Living without dread in worldly prosperity:
Of ghostly[3] sight the people be so blind,
Drowned in sin, they know me not for their God:
In worldly riches is all their mind,
They fear not my right wiseness, the sharp rod:
My law that I shewed, when I for them died,
They forget clean, and shedding of my blood red: 30
I hanged between two, it cannot be denied:
To get them life I suffered to be dead:
I healed their feet, with thorns hurt was my head:
I could do no more than I did truly,
And now I see the people do clean forsake me,
They use the seven deadly sins damnable;
As pride, covetise, wrath, and lechery,
Now in the world be made commendable;
And thus they leave of angels the heavenly company;
Everyman liveth so after his own pleasure, 40
And yet of their life they be nothing sure:
I see the more that I them forbear
The worse they be from year to year;
All that liveth appaireth[4] fast,
Therefore I will in all the haste
Having a reckoning of Everyman's person
For and[5] I leave the people thus alone
In their life and wicked tempests,
Verily they will become much worse than beasts;
For now one would by envy another up eat; 50
Charity they all do clean forget.
I hoped well that Everyman
In my glory should make his mansion,
And thereto I had them all elect;
But now I see, like traitors deject,
They thank me not for the pleasure that I to them meant
Nor yet for their being that I them have lent;
I proffered the people great multitude of mercy,
And few there be that asketh it heartily;
They be so combered with worldly riches, 60
That needs of them I must do justice,
On Everyman living without fear.
Where art thou, Death, thou mighty messenger?
**DEATH:** Almighty God, I am here at your will,
Your commandment to fulfil.
**GOD:** Go thou to Everyman,
And show him in my name
A pilgrimage he must on him take,
Which he in no wise may escape:
And that he bring with him a sure reckoning 70
Without delay or any tarrying.
**DEATH:** Lord, I will in the world go run over all,
And cruelly outsearch both great and small;
Every man will I beset that liveth beastly
Out of God's laws, and dreadeth not folly:
He that loveth riches I will strike with my dart,
His sight to blind, and from heaven to depart,
Except that alms be his good friend,
In hell for to dwell, world without end.
Lo, yonder I see Everyman walking; 80
Full little he thinketh on my coming;
His mind is on fleshly lusts and his treasure,

---

[1]Always.
[2]Ungrateful.

[3]Spiritual.
[4]Decays.
[5]If.

And great pain it shall cause him to endure
Before the Lord Heaven King.
Everyman, stand still; whither art thou going
Thus gaily? Hast my Maker forgot?
 **EVERYMAN:** Why askst thou?
Wouldest thou wete?[6]
 **DEATH:** Yea, sir, I will show you;
In great haste I am sent to thee     90
From God out of his majesty.
 **EVERYMAN:** What, sent to me?
 **DEATH:** Yea, certainly.
Though thou have forget him here,
He thinketh on thee in the heavenly sphere,
As, or we depart, thou shalt know.
 **EVERYMAN:** What desireth God of me?
 **DEATH:** That shall I show thee;
A reckoning he will needs have
Without any longer respite.     100
 **EVERYMAN:** To give a reckoning longer leisure I crave;
This blind matter troubleth my wit.
 **DEATH:** On thee thou must take a long journey:
Therefore thy book of count with thee thou bring:
For turn again thou can not by no way.
And look thou be sure of thy reckoning:
For before God thou shalt answer, and show
Thy many bad deeds and good but a few;
How thou hast spent thy life, and in what wise,
Before the chief lord of paradise.    110
Have ado that we were in that way,
For, wete thou well, thou shalt make none attournay.[7]
 **EVERYMAN:** Full unready I am such reckoning to give.
I know thee not: what messenger art thou?
 **DEATH:** I am Death, that no man dreadeth.
For every man I rest[8] and no man spareth;
For it is God's commandment
That all to me should be obedient.
 **EVERYMAN:** O Death, thou comest when I had thee least
  in mind,
In thy power it lieth me to save,    120
Yet of my good[s] will I give thee, if ye will be kind,
Yea, a thousand pound shalt thou have,
And defer this matter till another day.
 **DEATH:** Everyman, it may not be by no way;
I set not by gold, silver, nor riches,
Ne by pope, emperor, king, duke, ne princes,
For and I would receive gifts great,
All the world I might get;
But my custom is clean contrary.
I give thee no respite: come hence, and not tarry. 130
 **EVERYMAN:** Alas, shall I have no longer respite?
I may say Death giveth no warning:
To think on thee, it maketh my heart sick,
For all unready is my book of reckoning.
But twelve year and I might have abiding,
My counting book I would make so clear,
That my reckoning I should not need to fear.
Wherefore, Death, I pray thee, for God's mercy.
Spare me till I be provided of remedy.
 **DEATH:** Thee availeth not to cry, weep, and pray: 140

But haste thee lightly that you were gone the journey.
And prove thy friends if thou can.
For, wete thou well, the tide abideth no man,
And in the world each living creature
For Adam's sin must die of nature.
 **EVERYMAN:** Death, if I should this pilgrimage take,
And my reckoning surely make,
Show me, for saint charity,
Should I not come again shortly?
 **DEATH:** No, Everyman; and thou be once there, 150
Thou mayst never more come here,
Trust me verily.
 **EVERYMAN:** O gracious God, in the high seat celestial,
Have mercy on me in this most need;
Shall I have no company from this vale terrestrial
Of mine acquaintance that way me to lead?
 **DEATH:** Yea, if any be so hardy,
That would go with thee and bear thee company.
Hie thee that you were gone[9] to God's magnificence,
Thy reckoning to give before his presence. 160
What, weenest[10] thou thy life is given thee,
And thy worldly goods also?
 **EVERYMAN:** I had wend[11] so, verily.
 **DEATH:** Nay, nay; it was but lent thee;
For as soon as thou art go,
another awhile shall have it, and then go therefrom
Even as thou has done.
Everyman, thou art mad; thou hast thy wits five,
And here on earth will not amend thy life,
For suddenly I do come.    170
 **EVERYMAN:** O wretched caitiff, whither shall I flee,
That I might scape this endless sorrow!
Now, gentle Death, spare me till to-morrow,
That I may amend me
With good advisement.
 **DEATH:** Nay, thereto I will not consent,
Nor no man will I respite,
But to the heart suddenly I shall smite
Without any advisement.
And now out of thy sight I will me nie; 180
See thou make thee ready shortly,
For thou mayst say this is the day
That no man living may scape away.
 **EVERYMAN:** Alas, I may well weep with sighs deep,
Now have I no manner of company
To help me in my journey, and me to keep;
And also my writing is full unready.
How shall I do now for to excuse me?
I would to God I had never be gete![12]
To my soul a full great profit it had be; 190
For now I fear pains huge and great.
The time passeth; Lord, help that all wrought;
For though I mourn it availeth nought.
The day passeth, and is almost a-go;
I wot not well what for to do.
To whom were I best my complaint to make?
What, and I to Fellowship thereof spake,
And showed him of this sudden chance?
For in him is all mine affiance;[13]

---

[6]Know.
[7]Mediator.
[8]Arrest.

[9]Hurry and go.  [10]Do you suppose.
[11]Supposed.  [12]Been born.
[13]Trust.

We have in the world so many a day 200
Be on good friends in sport and play.
I see him yonder, certainly;
I trust that he will bear me company;
Therefore to him will I speak to ease my sorrow.
Well met, good Fellowship, and good morrow!
    **FELLOWSHIP:** Everyman, good morrow by this day.
Sir, why lookest thou so piteously?
If any thing be amiss, I pray thee, me say,
That I may help to remedy.
    **EVERYMAN:** Yea, good Fellowship, yea. 210
I am in great jeopardy.
    **FELLOWSHIP:** My true friend, show to me your mind;
I will not forsake thee, unto my life's end,
In the way of good company.
    **EVERYMAN:** That was well spoken, and lovingly.
    **FELLOWSHIP:** Sir, I must needs know your heaviness;
I have pity to see you in any distress;
If any have ye wronged he shall revenged be,
Though I on the ground be slain for thee—
Thou that I know before that I should die. 220
    **EVERYMAN:** Verily, Fellowship, gramercy.[14]
    **FELLOWSHIP:** Tush! by thy thanks I set not a straw;
Show me your grief, and say no more.
    **EVERYMAN:** If my heart should to you break,
And then you to turn your mind from me,
And would not me comfort, when you hear me speak,
Then should I ten times sorrier be.
    **FELLOWSHIP:** Sir, I say as I will do in deed.
    **EVERYMAN:** Then be you a good friend at need:
I have found you true here before. 230
    **FELLOWSHIP:** And so ye shall evermore;
For, in faith, and thou go to Hell,
I will not forsake thee by the way!
    **EVERYMAN:** Ye speak like a good friend: I believe you well;
I shall deserve[15] it, and I may.
    **FELLOWSHIP:** I speak of no deserving, by this day.
For he that will say and nothing do
Is not worthy with good company to go;
Therefore show me the grief of your mind,
As to your friend most loving and kind. 240
    **EVERYMAN:** I shall show you how it is;
Commanded I am to go a journey,
A long way, hard and dangerous,
And give a strait count without delay
Before the high judge Adonai.[16]
Wherefore I pray you, bear me company,
As ye have promised, in this journey.
    **FELLOWSHIP:** That is matter indeed! Promise is duty,
But, and I should take such a voyage on me,
I know it well, it should be to my pain: 250
Also it make me afeard, certain.
But let us take counsel here as well as we can,
For your words would fear[17] a strong man.
    **EVERYMAN:** Why, ye said, if I had need,
Ye would me never forsake, quick nor dead,
Though it were to Hell truly.
    **FELLOWSHIP:** So I said, certainly,
But such pleasures be set aside, thee sooth to say:

And also, if we took such a journey,
When should we come again? 260
    **EVERYMAN:** Nay, never again till the day of doom.
    **FELLOWSHIP:** In faith, then will not I come there!
Who hath you these tidings brought?
    **EVERYMAN:** Indeed, Death was with me here.
    **FELLOWSHIP:** Now, by God that all hath bought,
If Death were the messenger,
For no man that is living today
I will not go that loath journey—
Not for the father that begat me!
    **EVERYMAN:** Ye promised other wise, pardie.[18] 270
    **FELLOWSHIP:** I wot well I say so truly
And yet if thou wilt eat, and drink, and make good cheer,
Or haunt to women, the lusty company,
I would not forsake you, while the day is clear,
Trust me verily!
    **EVERYMAN:** Yea, thereto ye would be ready;
To go to mirth, solace, and play
Your mind will sooner apply
Than to bear me company in my long journey.
    **FELLOWSHIP:** Now, in good faith, I will not that way. 280
But and thou wilt murder, or any man kill,
In that I will help thee with a good will!
    **EVERYMAN:** O that is a simple advice indeed!
Gentle fellow: help me in my necessity;
We have loved long, and now I need,
And now, gentle Fellowship, remember me.
    **FELLOWSHIP:** Whether ye have loved me or no,
By Saint John, I will not with thee go.
    **EVERYMAN:** Yet I pray thee, take the labour, and do so
       much for me
To bring me forward, for saint charity, 290
And comfort me till I come without the town.
    **FELLOWSHIP:** Nay, and thou would give me a new gown,
I will not a foot with thee go;
But and you had tarried I would not have left thee so.
And as now, God speed thee in thy journey,
For from thee I will depart as fast as I may.
    **EVERYMAN:** Whither away, Fellowship? Will you forsake me?
    **FELLOWSHIP:** Yea, by my fay,[19] to God I betake thee.
    **EVERYMAN:** Farewell, good Fellowship; for this my heart
       is sore;
Adieu for ever, I shall see thee no more. 300
    **FELLOWSHIP:** In faith, Everyman, farewell not at the end;
For you I will remember that parting is mourning.
    **EVERYMAN:** Alack! shall we thus depart indeed?
Our Lady, help, without any more comfort,
Lo, Fellowship forsaketh me in my most need:
For help in this world whither shall I resort?
Fellowship herebefore with me would merry make;
And now little sorrow for me doth he take.
It is said, in prosperity men friends may find,
Which in adversity be full unkind. 310
Now whither for succour shall I flee,
[since] Fellowship hath forsaken me?
To my kinsmen I will truly,
Praying them to help me in my necessity:
I believe that they will do so,

---

[14]Many thanks.     [15]Repay.
[16]God.     [17]Terrify.

[18]By God.
[19]Faith.

For kind will creep where it may not go,
Where be ye now, my friends and kinsmen?
   **KINDRED:** Here be we now at your commandment.
Cousin, I pray you show us your intent
In any wise, and not spare.              320
   **COUSIN:** Yea, Everyman, and to us declare
If ye be disposed to go any whither,
For wete you well, we will live and die together.
   **KINDRED:** In wealth and woe we will with you hold,
For over his kin a man may be bold.
   **EVERYMAN:** Gramercy, my friends and kinsmen kind.
Now shall I show you the grief of my mind:
I was commanded by a messenger,
That is an high king's chief officer;
He bade me go a pilgrimage to my pain,      330
And I know well I shall never come again;
Also I must give a reckoning straight,
For I have a great enemy, that hath me in wait,
Which intendeth me for to hinder.
   **KINDRED:** What account is that which ye must render?
That would I know.
   **EVERYMAN:** Of all my works I must show
How I have lived and my days spent;
Also of ill deeds, that I have used
In my time, sith[20] life was me lent;       340
And of all virtues that I have refused.
Therefore I pray you go thither with me,
To help to make mine account, for saint charity.
   **COUSIN:** What, to go thither? Is that the matter?
Nay, Everyman, I had liefer[21] fast bread and water
All this five year and more.
   **EVERYMAN:** Alas, that ever I was bore![22]
For now shall I never be merry
If that you forsake me.
   **KINDRED:** Ah, sir, what, ye be a merry man!    350
Take good heart to you, and make no moan.
But one thing I warn you, by Saint Anne,
As for me, ye shall go alone.
   **EVERYMAN:** My Cousin, will you not with me go?
   **COUSIN:** No, by our Lady; I have the cramp in my toe.
Trust not to me, for, so God me speed,
I will deceive you in your most need.
   **KINDRED:** It availeth not us to tice.[23]
Ye shall have my maid with all my heart;
She loveth to go to feasts, there to be nice,   360
And to dance, and abroad to start:
I will give her leave to help you in that journey,
If that you and she may agree.
   **EVERYMAN:** Now show me the very effect of your mind.
Will you go with me, or abide behind?
   **KINDRED:** Abide behind? Yea, that I will and I may!
Therefore farewell until another day.
   **EVERYMAN:** How should I be merry or glad?
For fair promises to me make,
But when I have most need, they me forsake.   370
I am deceived; that maketh me sad.
   **COUSIN:** Cousin Everyman, farewell now,
For verily I will not go with you;
Also of mine own an unready reckoning
I have to account: therefore I make tarrying.

Now, God keep thee, for now I go.
   **EVERYMAN:** Ah, Jesus, is all come hereto?
Lo, fair words maketh fools feign;
They promise and nothing will do certain.
My kinsmen promised me faithfully     380
For to abide with me steadfastly,
And now fast away do they flee:
Even so Fellowship promised me.
What friend were best me of to provide?
I lose my time here longer to abide.
Yet in my mind a thing there is:—
All my life I have loved riches;
If that my goods now help me might,
He would make my heart full light.
I will speak to him in this distress.—    390
Where art thou, my Goods and riches?
   **GOODS:** Who calleth me? Everyman? What haste thou
      hast!
I lie here in corners, trussed and piled so high,
And in chests I am locked so fast,
Also sacked in bags, thou mayst see with thine eye,
I cannot stir; in packs low I lie,
What would ye have, lightly me say.[24]
   **EVERYMAN:** Come hither, Good, in all the haste thou
      may,
For of counsel I must desire thee.
   **GOODS:** Sir, and ye in the world have trouble or adversity.  400
That can I help you to remedy shortly.
   **EVERYMAN:** It is another disease that grieveth me;
In this world it is not, I tell thee so.
I am sent for another way to go,
To give a straight account general
Before the highest Jupiter of all;
And all my life I have had joy and pleasure in thee.
Therefore I pray thee go with me,
For, peradventure, thou mayst before God Almighty
My reckoning help to clean and purify;    410
For it is said ever among,
That money maketh all right that is wrong.
   **GOODS:** Nay, Everyman, I sing another song.
I follow no man in such voyages;
For and I went with thee
Thou shouldst fare much the worse for me;
For because on me thou did set thy mind,
Thy reckoning I have made blotted and blind
That thine account thou cannot make truly;
And that has thou for the love of me.    420
   **EVERYMAN:** That would grieve me full sore,
When I should come to that fearful answer.
Up, let us go thither together.
   **GOODS:** Nay, no so, I am too brittle, I may not endure:
I will follow no man one foot, be ye sure.
   **EVERYMAN:** Alas, I have thee loved, and had great
pleasure
All my life-days on good and treasure.
   **GOODS:** That is to thy damnation without lesing,[25]
For my love is contrary to the love everlasting
But if thou had me loved moderately during,   430
As, to the poor give part of me,
Then shouldst thou not in this dolour[26] be,

---

[20]Since.      [21]Rather.      [22]Born.
[23]It is useless to try to entice us.

[24]Quickly tell me.      [25]Loosing, releasing.
[26]Distress.

Nor in this great sorrow and care.
EVERYMAN: Lo, now was I deceived or I was ware,
And all I may wyte[27] my spending of time.
GOODS: What, weenest thou that I am thine?
EVERYMAN: I had wend so.
GOODS: Nay, Everyman, I say no;
As for a while I was lent thee,
A season thou hast had me in prosperity          440
My condition is man's soul to kill;
If I save one, a thousand I do spill;[28]
Weenest thou that I will follow thee?
Nay, from this world, not verily.
EVERYMAN: I had wend otherwise.
GOODS: Therefore to thy soul Good is a thief;
For when thou art dead, this is my guise
Another to deceive in the same wise
As I have done thee, and all to his soul's reprief.[29]
EVERYMAN: O false Good, cursed thou be!          450
Thou traitor to God, that has deceived me,
And caught me in thy snare.
GOODS: Marry,[30] thou brought thyself in care,
Whereof I am glad,
I must needs laugh, I cannot be sad.
EVERYMAN: Ah, Goods, thou has had long my heartly love;
I gave thee that which should be the Lord's above.
But wilt thou not go with me in deed?
I pray thee truth to say.
GOODS: No, so God me speed,          460
Therefore farewell, and have good day.
EVERYMAN: O, to whom shall I make moan
For to go with me in that heavy journey?
First Fellowship said he would with me gone;
His words were very pleasant and gay,
But afterward he left me alone.
Then spake I to my kinsmen all in despair,
And also they gave me words fair,
They lacked no fair speaking,
But all forsake me in the ending.          470
Then went I to my Goods that I loved best,
In hope to have comfort, but there had I least:
For my Goods sharply did me tell
That he bringeth many into hell.
Then of myself I was ashamed;
And so I am worthy to be blamed;
Thus may I well myself hate,
Of whom shall I now counsel take?
I think that I shall never speed
Till that I go to my Good-Deed,          480
But alas, she is so weak,
That she can neither go nor speak,
Yet will I venture on her now.—
My Good-Deeds, where be you?
GOOD-DEEDS: Here I lie cold on the ground,
Thy sins hath me sore bound,
That I cannot stir.
EVERYMAN: O, Good-Deeds, I stand in fear;
I must you pray of counsel,
For help now should come right well.          490
GOOD-DEEDS: Everyman, I have understanding
That ye be summoned account to make

Before Messias, of Jerusalem King;
And you by me[31] that journey what[32] you will I take.
EVERYMAN: Therefore I come to you, my moan to make;
I pray you, that ye will go with me.
GOOD-DEEDS: I would full fain,[33] but I cannot stand verily.
EVERYMAN: Why, is there anything on you fall?
GOOD-DEEDS: Yea, sir, I may think you of all;
If ye had perfectly cheered me,          500
Your book of account now full ready had be.
Look, the books of your works and deeds eke;[34]
Oh, see how they lie under the feet,
To your soul's heaviness.
EVERYMAN: Our Lord Jesus, help me!
For one letter here I can not see.
GOOD-DEEDS: There is a blind reckoning in time of
distress!
EVERYMAN: Good-Deeds, I pray you, help me in this need,
Or else I am for ever damned indeed;
Therefore help me to make reckoning          510
Before the redeemer of all thing,
That king is, and was, and ever shall.
GOOD-DEEDS: Everyman, I am sorry of your fall,
And fain would I help you, and I were able.
EVERYMAN: Good-Deeds, your counsel I pray you give me.
GOOD-DEEDS: That shall I do verily;
Though that on my feet I may not go,
I have a sister, that shall with you also,
Called Knowledge, which shall with you abide,
To help you to make that dreadful reckoning.          520

*[Knowledge guides Everyman to Confession, Discretion,
Strength, Beauty, and Five-Wits, who direct him to
receive the sacrament of extreme unction.]*

KNOWLEDGE: Everyman, hearken what I say;
Go to priesthood, I you advise,
And receive of him in any wise
The holy sacrament and ointment together;
Then shortly see ye turn again hither;
We will all abide you here.
FIVE-WITS: Yea, Everyman, hie[35] you that ye ready were,
There is no emperor, king, duke, ne baron,
That of God hath commission,
As hath the least priest in the world being;          530
For of the blessed sacraments pure and benign,
He beareth the keys and thereof hath the cure
For man's redemption, it is ever sure;
Which God for our soul's medicine
Gave us out of his heart with great pine;[36]
Here in this transitory life, for thee and me
The blessed sacraments seven there be.
Baptism, confirmation, with priesthood good,
And the sacrament of God's precious flesh and blood,
Marriage, the holy extreme unction, and penance;          540
These seven be good to have in remembrance,
Gracious sacraments of high divinity.
EVERYMAN: Fain would I receive that holy body
And meekly to my ghostly father I will go.
FIVE-WITS: Everyman, that is the best that ye can do:
God will you to salvation bring,
For priesthood exceedeth all other thing;

---

[27]Blame.     [28]Ruin.     [29]Shame.
[30]The Virgin Mary! (An interjection of surprise or agreement.)

[31]If you do as I advise.     [32]With.     [33]Very willingly.
[34]Also.     [35]Hasten.     [36]Suffering.

To us Holy Scripture they do teach,
And converteth man from sin heaven to reach;
God hath to them more power given, 550
Than to any angel that is in heaven;
With five words he may consecrate
God's body in flesh and blood to make,
And handleth his maker between his hands;
The priest bindeth and unbindeth all bands,
Both in earth and in heaven;
Thou ministers all the sacraments seven;
Though we kissed thy feet thou were worthy;
Thou art surgeon that cureth sin deadly:
No remedy we find under God 560
But all only priesthood.
Everyman, God gave priest that dignity,
And setteth them in his stead among us to be;
Thus be they above angels in degree.

    **KNOWLEDGE:** If priests be good it is so surely;
But when Jesus hanged on the cross with great smart
There he gave, out of his blessed heart,
The same sacrament in great torment:
He sold them not to us, that Lord Omnipotent.
Therefore Saint Peter the apostle doth say 570
That Jesu's curse hath all they
Which God their Savior do buy or sell,
Or they for any money do take or tell.
Sinful priests giveth the sinners example bad;
Their children sitteth by other men's fires, I have heard;
And some haunteth women's company,
With unclean life, as lusts of lechery:
These be with sin made blind.

    **FIVE-WITS:** I trust to God no such may we find;
Therefore let us priesthood honour, 580
And follow their doctrine for our souls' succour;
We be their sheep, and they shepherds be
By whom we all be kept in surety.
Peace, for yonder I see Everyman come,
Which hath made true satisfaction.

    **GOOD-DEEDS:** Methinketh it is he indeed.

    **EVERYMAN:** Now Jesu be our alder speed.[37]
I have received the sacrament for my redemption,
And then mine extreme unction:
Blessed be all they that counselled me to take it! 590
And now, friends, let us go without longer respite;
I thank God that ye have tarried so long.
Now set each of you on this rood[38] your hand,
And shortly follow me:
I go before, there I would be; God be our guide.

*[All but Good-Deeds then abandon Everyman.]*

    **EVERYMAN:** Methinketh, alas, that I must be gone
To make my reckoning and my debts pay,
For I see my time is nigh spent away.
Take example, all ye that this do hear or see,
How they that I loved best do forsake me, 600
Except my Good-Deeds that bideth truly.

    **GOOD-DEEDS:** All earthly things is but vanity:
Beauty, Strength, and Discretion, do man forsake,
Foolish friends and kinsmen, that fair spake,
All fleeth save Good-Deeds, and that am I.

    **EVERYMAN:** Have mercy on me, God most mighty;
And stand by me, thou Mother and Maid, holy Mary.

    **GOOD-DEEDS:** Fear not, I will speak for thee.

    **EVERYMAN:** Here I cry God mercy.

    **GOOD-DEEDS:** Short our end, and minish[39] our pain; 610
Let us go and never come again.

    **EVERYMAN:** Into thy hands, Lord, my soul I commend;
Receive it, Lord, that it be not lost;
As thou me boughtest, so me defend,
And save me from the fiend's boast,
That I may appear with that blessed host
That shall be saved at the day of doom.
*In mannus tuas*—of might's most
For ever—*commendo spiritum meum.*[40]

    **KNOWLEDGE:** Now hath he suffered that we all shall 620
        endure:
The Good-Deeds shall make all sure.
Now hath he made ending;
Methinketh that I hear angels sing
And make great joy and melody,
Where Everyman's soul received shall be.

    **ANGEL:** Come, excellent elect spouse to Jesu:[41]
Hereabove thou shalt go
Because of thy singular virtue:
Now the soul is taken the body fro;
Thy reckoning is crystal-clear. 630
Now shalt thou into the heavenly sphere,
Unto the which all ye shall come
That liveth well before the day of doom.

    **DOCTOR:** This moral men may have in mind;
Ye hearers, take it of worth, old and young,
And forsake pride, for he deceiveth you in the end,
And remember Beauty, Five-Wits, Strength, and
    Discretion,
They all at the last do Everyman forsake,
Save his Good-Deeds, there doth he take.
But beware, and they be small 640
Before God, he hath not help at all.
None excuse may be there for Everyman:
Alas, how shall he do then?
For after death amends may no man make,
For then mercy and pity do him forsake.
If his reckoning be not clear when he do come,
God will say—*ite maledicti in ignem aeternum.*[42]
And he that hath his account whole and sound,
High in heaven he shall be crowned;
Unto which place God brings us all thither 650
That we may live body and soul together.
Thereto help the Trinity,
Amen, say ye, for saint Charity
THUS ENDETH THIS MORALL PLAY OF EVERYMAN.

———————◆———————

---

[37]Speed in help of all.
[38]Cross.

[39]Diminish.
[40]Into your hands I commend my spirit.
[41]Bride of Christ, a term symbolizing the soul's union with God.
[42]Be damned to the eternal fire.

## Dante's *Divine Comedy*

The medieval view of life on earth as a vale of tears was balanced by the triumphant belief in the divine promise of deliverance and eternal bliss. By far the most profound and imaginative statement of these ideas is the epic poem known as the *Commedia Divina* or *Divine Comedy*. Begun in the year 1312 by the Florentine poet Dante Alighieri (1265–1321), the *Commedia* records, on the literal level, the poet's adventure-packed journey through the realm of the dead (Figure 12.3). On a symbolic level, the poem describes the spiritual pilgrimage of the Christian soul from sin (Hell), through purification (Purgatory), to salvation (Paradise) (Figure 12.4). The *Divine Comedy* exposes the intellectual architecture of the medieval mind: It brings to life with epic grandeur both the Christian immortality ideology and the medieval perception of nature as the mirror of God's plan. In addition, it provides an invaluable picture of the ethical, political, and theological concerns of Dante's own time.

Every aspect of Dante's *Commedia* carries symbolic meaning. For instance, Dante is accompanied through Hell by the Roman poet Virgil, who stands for human reason. Dante deeply admired Virgil's great epic, the *Aeneid*, and was familiar with the hero's journey to the underworld included in the sixth book of the poem. As Dante's guide, Virgil may travel only as far as the top of Mount Purgatory, for while human reason serves as the pilgrim's initial guide to salvation, it cannot penetrate the divine mysteries of the Christian faith. In Paradise, Dante is escorted by Beatrice, the symbol of Divine Wisdom, modeled on a Florentine woman who had, throughout the poet's life, been the object of his physical desire and spiritual devotion. Dante structured the *Commedia* according to a strict moral hierarchy. The three parts of the poem correspond to the Aristotelian divisions of the human psyche: reason, will, and love. They also represent the potential moral conditions of the Christian soul: perversity, repentance, and grace.

Sacred numerology—especially the number 3, symbolic of the Trinity—permeates the design of the *Commedia*. The poem is divided into three canticles (books); and each canticle has thirty-three **cantos**, to which Dante added one introductory canto to total a sublime one hundred (the number symbolizing plenitude and perfection). Each canto consists of stanzas composed in *terza rima*—interlocking lines that rhyme a/b/a, b/c/b, c/d/c. There are three guides to escort Dante, three divisions of Hell and Purgatory, three main rivers in Hell. Three squared (9) are the regions of sinners in Hell, the circles of penitents in Purgatory, and the spheres of Heaven.

**Figure 12.3** Domenico di Michelino, *Dante and His Poem*, 1465. Fresco, 10 ft. 6 in. × 9 ft. 7 in. Florence Cathedral, Italy. Dante, with an open copy of the *Commedia*, points to Hell with his right hand. The mount of Purgatory with its seven terraces is behind him. Florence's cathedral (with its newly finished dome) represents Paradise on the poet's left. Alinari/Art Resource, New York.

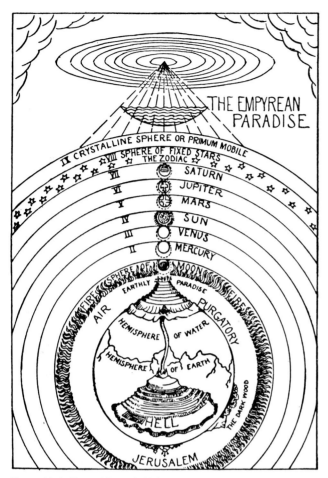

**Figure 12.4** Plan of Dante's Universe.

the Latin of churchmen and scholars and wrote in his native Italian, the language of everyday speech. Dante called his poem a comedy because the piece begins with affliction (Hell) and ends with joy (Heaven). Later admirers added the adjective "divine" to the title, not simply to describe its religious character, but also to praise its sublime lyrics and its artful composition.

The most lively of the canticles, and the one that best manifests Dante's talent for creating realistic images with words, is the "Inferno," the first book of the *Commedia*. With grim moral logic, the sinners are each assigned to one of the nine rings in Hell (Figure **12.5**), where they are punished according to the nature of their sins: The violent are immersed for eternity in boiling blood and the gluttons wallow like pigs in their own excrement. By the law of symbolic retribution, the sinners are punished not *for* but *by* their sins. Those condemned for sins of passion—the least grave of sins—inhabit the conical rings at the top of Hell, while those who have committed sins of the will lie farther down.

**Figure 12.5** Plan of Dante's "Inferno."

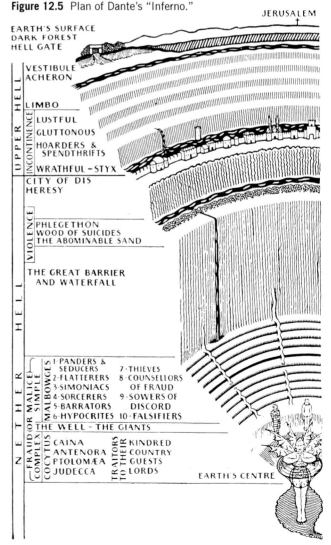

The elaborate numerology of the *Commedia* is matched by multileveled symbolism that draws into relationship theological, scientific, and historical information based in ancient and medieval sources. Given this wealth of symbolism, it is remarkable that the language of the poem is so sharply realistic. For, while the characters in the *Commedia*, like those in *Everyman*, serve an allegorical function, they are, at the same time, convincing flesh-and-blood creatures. The inhabitants of Dante's universe are real people, some drawn from history and legend, others from his own era—citizens of the bustling urban centers of Italy through which Dante had wandered for nineteen years after his exile from his native Florence for political offenses. By framing the poem on both a literal level and an allegorical level, Dante reinforces the medieval (and essentially Augustinian) view of the bond between the City of Man and the City of God. At the same time, he animates a favorite theme of medieval sermons: the warning that actions in this life bring inevitable consequences in the next.

Well versed in both classical and Christian literature, Dante had written Latin treatises on political theory and on the origins and development of language. But for the poem that constituted his epic masterpiece, he rejected

**Figure 12.6** *Satan Eating and Excreting the Souls of the Damned in Hell.* Louvre, Paris. Photo: Roger Viollet, Paris.

Those guilty of sins of the intellect are imprisoned still lower, deep within the pit ruled by Satan (Figure **12.6**). Thus, Dante's Hell proclaims a moral hierarchy and a divinely graded system in which the damned assume their proper destiny.

In the last canto of the "Inferno," Dante describes the ninth circle of Hell, the very bottom of the infernal pit. Lodged in ice up to his chest, a three-faced Satan beats his six batlike wings to create a chilling wind—the setting provides sharp contrast with the flaming regions of Upper Hell. Surrounding Satan, whom Dante calls "the Emperor of the Universe of Pain," those guilty of treachery—the most foul of all sins, according to Dante—are imprisoned in the ice, "like straws in glass." Satan, weeping tears "mixed with bloody froth and pus," chews with "rake-like teeth" on the bodies of the three most infamous traitors of Christian and classical history respectively: Judas, Brutus, and Cassius. The mood of darkness and brooding despair that pervades the "Inferno" reflects the medieval view of Hell as the condition of the soul farthest from the light of God. Nevertheless, the last canto of the "Inferno" ends with

Dante and Virgil climbing from the frozen pit "into the shining world," a motif of ascent that pervades the second and third canticles.

Satan's domain stands in grim contrast to the blissful and brilliant experience of God enjoyed by those in Paradise. Light, the least material of natural elements, is a prime image in Dante's evocation of Heaven, and light imagery—as central to the *Commedia* as it is to Saint Ambrose's hymn (see chapter 9)—pervades Dante's vision of God's mystery and majesty. The last eight stanzas of Canto 33 of "Paradiso" (reproduced below) are the culminating phase of that vision. In the perfect shape of the circle, as in a cathedral rose window, Dante sees the image of humankind absorbed into the substance of God. And as that wheel of love turns, the poet discovers the redemptive radiance of God.

It is impossible to recreate the grandeur of the *Commedia* by means of a single canto, especially since, translated into English, a great deal of the richness of the original Tuscan dialect is lost. Nevertheless, some of the majesty of Dante's poem may be conveyed by the excerpts reproduced here.

## READING 2.19

# From Dante's *Divine Comedy*

### The Dark Wood of Error ("Inferno," Canto 1)

Midway in our life's journey, I went astray
  from the straight road and woke to find myself
  alone in a dark wood. How shall I say      3

what wood that was! I never saw so drear,
  so rank, so arduous a wilderness!
  Its very memory gives a shape to fear.      6

Death could scarce be more bitter than that place!
  But since it came to good, I will recount
  all that I found revealed there by God's grace.      9

How I came to it I cannot rightly say,
  so drugged and loose with sleep had I become
  when I first wandered there from the True Way.      12

But at the far end of the valley of evil
  whose maze had sapped my very heart with fear!
  I found myself before a little hill      15

and lifted up my eyes. Its shoulders glowed
  already with the sweet rays of that planet
  whose virtue leads men straight on every road,      18

and the shining strengthened me against the fright
  whose agony had wracked the lake of my heart
  through all the terrors of that piteous night.      21

Just as a swimmer, who with his last breath
  flounders ashore from perilous seas, might turn
  to memorize the wide water of his death—      24

so did I turn, my soul still fugitive
  from death's surviving image, to stare down
  that pass that none had ever left alive.      27

And there I lay to rest from my heart's race
  till calm and breath returned to me. Then rose
  and pushed up that dead slope at such a pace      30

each footfall rose above the last. And lo!
  almost at the beginning of the rise
  I faced a spotted Leopard, all tremor and flow      33

and gaudy pelt. And it would not pass, but stood
  so blocking my every turn that time and again
  I was on the verge of turning back to the wood.      36

This fell at the first widening of the dawn
  as the sun was climbing Aries with those stars
  that rode with him to light the new creation.      39

Thus the holy hour and the sweet season
  of commemoration did much to arm my fear
  of that bright murderous beast with their good omen.      42

Yet not so much but what I shook with dread
  at sight of a great Lion that broke upon me
  raging with hunger, its enormous head      45

held high as if to strike a mortal terror
  into the very air. And down his track,
  a She-Wolf drove upon me, a starved horror      48

ravening and wasted beyond all belief.
  She seemed a rack for avarice, gaunt and craving.
  Oh many the souls she has brought to endless grief!      51

She brought such heaviness upon my spirit
  at sight of her savagery and desperation,
  I died from every hope of that high summit.      54

And like a miser—eager in acquisition
  but desperate in self-reproach when Fortune's wheel
  turns to the hour of his loss—all tears and attrition      57

I wavered back; and still the beast pursued,
  forcing herself against me bit by bit
  till I slid back into the sunless wood.      60

And as I fell to my soul's ruin, a presence
  gathered before me on the discolored air,
  the figure of one who seemed hoarse from long silence.      63

At sight of him in that friendless waste I cried:
  "Have pity on me, whatever thing you are,
  whether shade or living man." And it replied:      66

"Not man, though man I once was, and my blood
  was Lombard, both my parents Mantuan.
  I was born, though late, *sub Julio*, and bred      69

in Rome under Augustus in the noon
  of the false and lying gods. I was a poet
  and sang of old Anchises' noble son      72

who came to Rome after the burning of Troy.
  But you—why do *you* return to these distresses
  instead of climbing that shining Mount of Joy      75

which is the seat and first cause of man's bliss?"
  "And are you then that Virgil and that fountain
  of purest speech?" My voice grew tremulous:      78

"Glory and light of poets! now may that zeal
  and love's apprenticeship that I poured out
  on your heroic verses serve me well!      81

For you are my true master and first author,
  the sole maker from whom I drew the breath
  of that sweet style whose measures have brought me      84
              honor.

See there, immortal sage, the beast I flee.
  For my soul's salvation, I beg you, guard me from her,
  for she has struck a mortal tremor through me."      87

And he replied, seeing my soul in tears:
  "He must go by another way who would escape
  this wilderness, for that mad beast that fleers*      90

before you there, suffers no man to pass.
  She tracks down all, kills all, and knows no glut,
  but, feeding, she grows hungrier than she was.      93

She mates with any beast, and will mate with more
  before the Greyhound comes to hunt her down.
  He will not feed on lands nor loot, but honor      96

and love and wisdom will make straight his way.
  He will rise between Feltro and Feltro, and in him
  shall be the resurrection and new day      99

---

*sneers

of that sad Italy for which Nisus died,
   and Turnus, and Euryalus, and the maid Camilla.
   He shall hunt her through every nation of sick pride   102

till she is driven back forever to Hell
   whence Envy first released her on the world.
   Therefore, for your own good, I think it well   105

you follow me and I will be your guide
   and lead you forth through an eternal place.
   There you shall see the ancient spirits tried   108

in endless pain, and hear their lamentation
   as each bemoans the second death of souls.
   Next you shall see upon a burning mountain   111

souls in fire and yet content in fire,
   knowing that whensoever it may be
   they yet will mount into the blessed choir.   114

To which, if it is still your wish to climb,
   a worthier spirit shall be sent to guide you.
   With her shall I leave you, for the King of Time,   117

who reigns on high, forbids me to come there
   since, living, I rebelled against his law.
   He rules the waters and the land and air   120

and there holds court, his city and his throne.
   Oh blessed are they he chooses!" And I to him:
   "Poet, by that God to you unknown,   123

lead me this way. Beyond this present ill
   and worse to dread, lead me to Peter's gate
   and be my guide through the sad halls of Hell."   126

And he then: "Follow." And he moved ahead
in silence, and I followed where he led.

## Notes to "Inferno" (Canto 1)

line 1 *midway in our life's journey*: The biblical life span is three-score years and ten. The action opens in Dante's thirty-fifth year, i.e., 1300 C.E.

line 17 *that planet*: The sun. Ptolemaic astronomers considered it a planet. It is also symbolic of God as He who lights man's way.

line 31 *each footfall rose above the last*: The literal rendering would be: "So that the fixed foot was ever the lower." "Fixed" has often been translated "right" and an ingenious reasoning can support that reading, but a simpler explanation offers itself and seems more competent: Dante is saying that he climbed with such zeal and haste that every footfall carried him above the last despite the steepness of the climb. At a slow pace, on the other hand, the rear foot might be brought up only as far as the forward foot. This device of selecting a minute but exactly-centered detail to convey the whole of a larger action is one of the central characteristics of Dante's style.

lines 33, 44, 48 *Leopard, Lion, She-Wolf*: These three beasts are undoubtedly taken from Jeremiah 5.6. Many additional and incidental interpretations have been advanced for them, but the central interpretation must remain as noted. They foreshadow the three divisions of Hell (incontinence, violence, and fraud) which Virgil explains at length in Canto 11, 16–111. I am not at all sure but what the She-Wolf is better interpreted as Fraud and the Leopard as Incontinence. Good arguments can be offered either way.

lines 38–39 *Aries . . . that rode with him to light the new creation*: The medieval tradition had it that the sun was in Aries at the time of the Creation. The significance of the astronomical and religious conjunction is an important part of Dante's intended allegory. It is just before dawn of Good Friday 1300 when he awakens in the Dark Wood. Thus his new life begins under Aries, the sign of creation, at dawn (rebirth) and in the Easter season (resurrection). Moreover the moon is full and the sun is in the equinox, conditions that did not fall together on any Friday of 1300.

Dante is obviously constructing poetically the perfect Easter as a symbol of his new awakening.

line 69 *sub Julio*: In the reign of Julius Caesar.

lines 95–98 *the Greyhound . . . Feltro and Feltro*: Almost certainly refers to Can Grande della Scala (1290–1329), a great Italian leader born in Verona, which lies between the towns of Feltre and Montefeltro.

lines 100–101 *Nisus, Turnus, Euryalus, Camilla*: All were killed in the war between the Trojans and the Latians when, according to legend, Aeneas led the survivors of Troy into Italy. Nisus and Euryalus (*Aeneid* IX) were Trojan comrades-in-arms who died together. Camilla (*Aeneid* XI) was the daughter of the Latian king and one of the warrior women. She was killed in a horse charge against the Trojans after displaying great gallantry. Turnus (*Aeneid* XII) was killed by Aeneas in a duel.

line 110 *the second death*: Damnation. "This is the second death, even the lake of fire." (Revelation 20.14)

lines 118–119 *forbids me to come there since, living, etc.*: Salvation is only through Christ in Dante's theology. Virgil lived and died before the establishment of Christ's teachings in Rome, and therefore cannot enter Heaven.

line 125 *Peter's gate*: The gate of Purgatory. (See "Purgatorio" 9, 76 ff.) The gate is guarded by an angel with a gleaming sword. The angel is Peter's vicar (Peter, the first pope, symbolized all popes; i.e., Christ's vicar on earth) and is entrusted with the two great keys.

Some commentators argue that this is the gate of Paradise, but Dante mentions no gate beyond this one in his ascent to Heaven. It should be remembered, too, that those who pass the gate of Purgatory have effectively entered Heaven.

The three great gates that figure in the entire journey are: the gate of Hell (Canto 3, 1–11), the gate of Dis (Canto 8, 79–113, and Canto 9, 86–87), and the gate of Purgatory, as above.

## The Ninth Circle of Hell ("Inferno," Canto 34)

"On march the banners of the King of Hell,"
   my Master said. "Toward us. Look straight ahead:
   can you make him out at the core of the frozen shell?"   3

Like a whirling windmill seen afar at twilight,
   or when a mist has risen from the ground—
   just such an engine rose upon my sight   6

stirring up such a wild and bitter wind
   I cowered for shelter at my Master's back
   there being no other windbreak I could find.   9

I stood now where the souls of the last class
   (with fear my verses tell it) were covered wholly:
   they shone below the ice like straws in glass.   12

Some lie stretched out; others are fixed in place
   upright, some on their heads, some on their
   soles; another, like a bow, bends foot to face.   15

When we had gone so far across the ice
   that it pleased my Guide to show me the foul creature
   which once had worn the grace of Paradise,   18

he made me stop, and, stepping aside, he said:
   "Now see the face of Dis! This is the place
   where you must arm your soul against all dread."   21

Do not ask, Reader, how my blood ran cold
   and my voice choked up with fear. I cannot write it:
   this is a terror that cannot be told.   24

I did not die, and yet I lost life's breath:
   imagine for yourself what I became,
   deprived at once of both my life and death.   27

The Emperor of the Universe of Pain
   jutted his upper chest above the ice;
   and I am closer in size to the great mountain     30

the Titans make around the central pit,
   than they to his arms. Now starting from this part,
   imagine the whole that corresponds to it.     33

If he was once as beautiful as now
   he is hideous, and still turned on his Maker,
   well may he be the source of every woe!     36

With what a sense of awe I saw his head
   towering above me! for it had three faces:
   one was in front, and it was fiery red,     39

the other two, as weirdly wonderful,
   merged with it from the middle of each shoulder
   to the point where all converged at the top of the skull;  42

the right was something between white and bile;
   the left was about the color that one finds
   on those who live along the banks of the Nile.     45

Under each head two wings rose terribly,
   their span proportioned to so gross a bird:
   I never saw such sails upon the sea.     48

They were not feathers—their texture and their form
   were like a bat's wings—and he beat them so
   that three winds blew from him in one great storm:     51

it is these winds that freeze all Cocytus. [The final pit
     of Hell.]
   He wept from his six eyes, and down three chins
   the tears ran mixed with bloody froth and pus.     54

In every mouth he worked a broken sinner
   between his rake-like teeth. Thus he kept three
   in eternal pain at his eternal dinner.     57

For the one in front the biting seemed to play
   no part at all compared to the ripping: at times
   the whole skin of his back was flayed away.     60

"That soul that suffers most," explained the Guide,
   "is Judas Iscariot, he who kicks his legs
   on the fiery chin and has his head inside.     63

Of the other two, who have their heads thrust forward
   the one who dangles down from the black face
   is Brutus: note how he writhes without a word.     66

And there, with the huge and sinewy arms, is the soul
   of Cassius. But the night is coming on
   and we must go, for we have seen the whole."     69

Then, as he bade, I clasped his neck, and he,
   watching for a moment when the wings
   were opened wide, reached over dexterously     72

and seized the shaggy coat of the king demon;
   then grappling matted hair and frozen crusts
   from one tuft to another, clambered down.     75

When we had reached the joint where the great thigh
   merges into the swelling of the haunch,
   my Guide and Master, straining terribly,     78

turned his head to where his feet had been
   and began to grip the hair as if he were climbing;
   so that I thought we moved toward Hell again.     81

"Hold fast!" my Guide said, and his breath came shrill
   with labor and exhaustion. "There is no way
   but by such stairs to rise above such evil."     84

At last he climbed out through an opening
   in the central rock, and he seated me on the rim;
   then joined me with a nimble backward spring.     87

I looked up, thinking to see Lucifer
   as I had left him, and I saw instead
   his legs projecting high into the air.     90

Now let all those whose dull minds are still vexed
   by failure to understand what point it was
   I had passed through, judge if I was perplexed.     93

"Get up. Up on your feet," my Master said.
   "The sun already mounts to middle tierce,
   and a long road and hard climbing lie ahead."     96

It was no hall of state we had found there,
   but a natural animal pit hollowed from rock
   with a broken floor and a close and sunless air.     99

"Before I tear myself from the Abyss,"
   I said when I had risen, "O my Master,
   explain to me my error in all this:     102

where is the ice? and Lucifer—how has he
   been turned from top to bottom: and how can the sun
   have gone from night to day so suddenly?"     105

And he to me: "You imagine you are still
   on the other side of the center where I grasped
   the shaggy flank of the Great Worm of Evil     108

which bores through the world—you *were* while I climbed down,
   but when I turned myself about, you passed
   the point to which all gravities are drawn.     111

You are under the other hemisphere where you stand;
   the sky above us is the half opposed
   to that which canopies the great dry land.     114

Under the mid-point of that other sky
   the Man who was born sinless and who lived
   beyond all blemish, came to suffer and die.     117

You have your feet upon a little sphere
   which forms the other face of the Judecca. [Named
     for Judas Iscariot.]
   There it is evening when it is morning here.     120

And this gross Fiend and Image of all Evil
   who made a stairway for us with his hide
   is pinched and prisoned in the ice-pack still.     123

On this side he plunged down from heaven's height,
   and the land that spread here once hid in the sea
   and fled North to our hemisphere for fright;     126

and it may be that moved by that same fear,
   the one peak that still rises on this side
   fled upward leaving this great cavern here."     129

Down there, beginning at the further bound
   of Beelzebub's dim tomb, there is a space
   not known by sight, but only by the sound     132

of a little stream descending through the hollow
   it has eroded from the massive stone
   in its endlessly entwining lazy flow.     135

My Guide and I crossed over and began
   to mount that little known and lightless road
   to ascend into the shining world again.        138

He first, I second, without thought of rest
   we climbed the dark until we reached the point
   where a round opening brought in sight the blest    141

and beauteous shining of the Heavenly cars.
And we walked out once more beneath the Stars.

### Notes to "Inferno" (Canto 34)

line 1 *On march the banners of the King*: The hymn ("Vexilla regis prodeunt") was written in the sixth century by Venantius Fortunatus, Bishop of Poitiers. The original celebrates the Holy Cross, and is part of the service for Good Friday to be sung at the moment of uncovering the cross.

line 17 *the foul creature*: Satan.

line 38 *three faces*: Numerous interpretations of these three faces exist. What is essential to all explanations is that they be seen as perversions of the qualities of the Trinity.

line 54 *bloody froth and pus*: The gore of the sinners he chews which is mixed with his slaver.

line 62 *Judas*: Note how closely his punishment is patterned on that of the Simoniacs (Canto 19).

line 67 *huge and sinewy arms*: The Cassius who betrayed Caesar was more generally described in terms of Shakespeare's "lean and hungry look." Another Cassius is described by Cicero (*Catiline* III) as huge and sinewy. Dante probably confused the two.

line 68 *the night is coming on*: It is now Saturday evening.

line 82 *his breath came shrill*: Cf. Canto 23, 85, where the fact that Dante breathes indicates to the Hypocrites that he is alive. Virgil's breathing is certainly a contradiction.

line 95 *middle tierce*: In the canonical day tierce is the period from about six to nine a.m. Middle tierce, therefore, is seven-thirty. In going through the center point, they have gone from night to day. They have moved ahead twelve hours.

line 128 *the one peak*: The Mount of Purgatory.

line 129 *this great cavern*: The natural animal pit of line 98. It is also "Beelzebub's dim tomb," line 131.

line 133 *a little stream*: Lethe. In classical mythology, the river of forgetfulness, from which souls drank before being born. In Dante's symbolism it flows down from Purgatory, where it has washed away the memory of sin from the souls who are undergoing purification. That memory it delivers to Hell, which draws all sin to itself.

line 143 *Stars*: As part of his total symbolism Dante ends each of the three divisions of the *Commedia* with this word. Every conclusion of the upward soul is toward the stars, God's shining symbols of hope and virtue. It is just before dawn of Easter Sunday that the Poets emerge—a further symbolism.

### From The Vision of God ("Paradiso," Canto 33)

O Light Eternal fixed in Itself alone,
   by Itself alone understood, which from Itself
   loves and glows, self-knowing and self-known;    126

that second aureole which shone forth in Thee,
   conceived as a reflection of the first—
   or which appeared so to my scrutiny—    129

seemed in Itself of Its own coloration
   to be painted with man's image. I fixed my eyes
   on that alone in rapturous contemplation.    132

Like a geometer wholly dedicated
   to squaring the circle, but who cannot find,
   think as he may, the principle indicated—    135

so did I study the supernal face.
   I yearned to know just how our image merges
   into that circle, and how it there finds place;    138

but mine were not the wings for such a flight.
   Yet, as I wished, the truth I wished for came
   cleaving my mind in a great flash of light.    141

Here my powers rest from their high fantasy,
   but already I could feel my being turned—
   instinct and intellect balanced equally    144

as in a wheel whose motion nothing jars—
by the Love that moves the Sun and the other stars.

### Notes to "Paradiso" (Canto 33)

lines 130-144 *seemed in Itself of Its own coloration . . . instinct and intellect balanced equally*: The central metaphor of the entire *Comedy* is the image of God and the final triumphant in Godding of the elected soul returning to its Maker. On the mystery of that image, the metaphoric symphony of the *Comedy* comes to rest.

In the second aspect of Triple-unity, in the circle reflected from the first, Dante thinks he sees the image of mankind woven into the very substance and coloration of God. He turns the entire attention of his soul to that mystery, as a geometer might seek to shut out every other thought and dedicate himself to squaring the circle. In *Il Convivio II*, 14, Dante asserted that the circle could not be squared, but that impossibility had not yet been firmly demonstrated in Dante's time and mathematicians still worked at the problem. Note, however, that Dante assumes the impossibility of squaring the circle as a weak mortal example of mortal impossibility. How much more impossible, he implies, to resolve the mystery of God, study as man will.

The mystery remains beyond Dante's mortal power. Yet, there in Heaven, in a moment of grace, God revealed the truth to him in a flash of light—revealed it, that is, to the God-enlarged power of Dante's emparadised soul. On Dante's return to the mortal life, the details of that revelation vanished from his mind but the force of the revelation survives in its power on Dante's feelings.

So ends the vision of the *Comedy* and yet the vision endures, for ever since that revelation, Dante tells us, he feels his soul turning ever as one with the perfect motion of God's love.

———————————————◆———————————————

# The Power and Prestige of the Medieval Church

During the High Middle Ages, the Catholic Church exercised great power and authority not only as a religious force, but also as a political institution. The papacy took strong measures to ensure the independence of the Church from secular interference, especially that of the emerging European states. In 1022, for instance, the Church formed the College of Cardinals as the sole agency responsible for the election of popes. Medieval pontiffs functioned much like secular monarchs, governing a huge and complex bureaucracy that incorporated financial, judicial, and disciplinary branches. The Curia, the papal council and highest Church court, headed a vast network of ecclesiastical courts, while the Camera (the papal treasury) handled financial matters. The Church was enormously wealthy in the medieval period. Over the centuries, Christians had donated and bequeathed to Christendom so many thousands of acres of land that, by the end of the twelfth century, the

Catholic Church was the largest single landholder in Western Europe.

Among lay Christians of every rank the Church commanded religious obedience. It enforced religious conformity by means of such spiritual penalties as **excommunication** (exclusion from the sacraments) and **interdict**, the excommunication of an entire city or state—used to dissuade secular rulers from opposing papal policy. In spite of these spiritual weapons, **heresy** (the denial of the revealed truths of the Christian faith) spread rapidly within the increasingly cosmopolitan centers of twelfth-century Europe. Such anticlerical groups as the Waldensians, followers of the French thirteenth-century reformer Peter Waldo, denounced the growing worldliness of the Church. Waldo proposed that lay Christians administer the sacraments and that the Bible—sole source of religious authority—should be translated into the vernacular.

Condemning such views as threats to civil and religious order, the Church launched antiheretical crusades that were almost as violent as those advanced against the Muslims. Further, in 1233, the pope established the Inquisition, a special court designed to stamp out heresy. The Inquisition brought to trial individuals whom local townspeople denounced as heretics. The accused were deprived of legal counsel and were usually tried in secret. Inquisitors might use physical torture to obtain confession, for the Church considered injury to the body preferable to the eternal damnation of the soul. If the Inquisition failed to restore accused heretics to the faith, it might impose such penalties as exile or excommunication, or it might turn over the defendants to the state to be hanged or burned at the stake—the preferred punishment for female heretics. With the same energy that the Church persecuted heretics, it acted as a civilizing agent. It preserved order by enforcing periods in which warfare was prohibited. It assumed moral and financial responsibility for the poor, the sick, and the homeless; and it provided for the organization of hospitals, refuges, orphanages, and other charitable institutions.

The power and prestige of the Church were enhanced by the outstanding talents of some popes as diplomats, canon lawyers, and administrators. Under the leadership of the lawyer/pope Innocent III, the papacy emerged as the most powerful political institution in Western Europe. Pope Innocent enlarged the body of canon law and refined the bureaucratic machinery of the Church. He used his authority to influence secular rulers and frequently intervened in the political, financial, and personal affairs of heads of state. At the Fourth Lateran Council (1215), he endorsed the establishment of the Franciscans, a monastic order that would revive the humane candor and devotional simplicity of the Sermon on the Mount.

The Franciscans followed the example of one of the most remarkable personalities of the Middle Ages, Francis of Assisi (ca. 1181–1226). The son of a wealthy Italian cloth merchant, Francis renounced physical comforts and dedicated himself to a life of preaching and service to the poor. In imitation of the apostles, he practiced absolute poverty and begged for his food and lodging as he traveled from town to town. Unlike Saint Benedict (see chapter 9) and other cloistered followers of Christ, however, Francis rejected the world-denying life of withdrawal. His affection for the poor, the sickly, and for all forms of life inspired a wave of humanitarianism that swept through late thirteenth-century culture and was especially evident in the visual arts (Figure **12.7**). During the same century, the followers of the well-educated Spanish priest Saint Dominic (ca. 1170–1221) founded a second mendicant ("begging") order. Deeply committed to the study of theology, the Dominicans educated many renowned preachers and scholars, including Thomas Aquinas, discussed later in this chapter. The Franciscan and Dominican friars ("brothers") and their female counterparts, the Poor Clares and the Dominican nuns, earned longlasting respect and acclaim for educating the young, fighting heresy, and ministering to the sick and needy (Figure **12.8**).

**Figure 12.7** Giotto, *Sermon to the Birds*, ca. 1290. Fresco. Upper Church, Assisi, Italy. Photo: Dagli Orti, Paris.

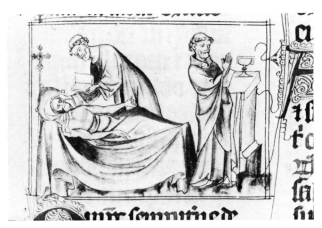

**Figure 12.8** *Mass for One who is Close to Death*, from a French Franciscan missal, early fourteenth century. Bodleian Library, Oxford, MS Douce 313, f.39S.

## The Conflict Between Church and State

As secular rulers grew in power among the burgeoning nation-states of medieval Europe, the early medieval alliance between Church and state deteriorated. The attempts of kings and emperors to win the allegiance of their subjects—especially those in the newly formed towns—and to enlarge their financial resources often interfered with papal ambitions and Church decree. When, for example, King Philip IV ("the Fair") of France (1268–1314) attempted to tax the clergy as citizens of the French realm, Pope Boniface VIII (ca. 1234–1302) protested, threatening to excommunicate and depose the king. In the dispute that followed, Pope Boniface issued the edict *Unam sanctam* ("One [and] Holy [Church]"), the boldest assertion of spiritual authority ever published. The edict rested upon the centuries-old papal claim that the Church held primacy over the state, since, while the Church governed the souls of all Christians, the state governed only their bodies. Although in the ensuing struggle between popes and kings, the latter emerged victorious, *Unam sanctam* remained the classic justification for Church supremacy in both temporal and spiritual realms.

## The Medieval University

Of the many lasting contributions of the Middle Ages to modern Western society—including trial by jury and the Catholic Church itself—one of the most significant was the university. Education in medieval Europe was almost exclusively a religious enterprise, and monastic schools had monopolized learning for many centuries. By the twelfth century, however, spurred by the resurgence of economic activity and the rise of towns, education shifted from monastic and parish schools to cathedral schools located in the new urban centers of

Western Europe. Growing out of these schools, groups of students and teachers formed guilds for higher learning; the Latin word *universitas* describes a guild of learners and teachers.

In medieval Europe, as in our own day, universities were arenas for intellectual inquiry and debate. At Bologna, Paris, Oxford, and Cambridge, to name but four among some eighty universities founded during the Middle Ages, the best minds of Europe grappled with the compelling ideas of their day, often testing those ideas against the teachings of the Church. The universities offered a basic Liberal Arts curriculum divided into two parts: the *trivium*, consisting of grammar, logic, and rhetoric; and the *quadrivium*, which included arithmetic, geometry, astronomy, and music. Programs in professional disciplines, such as medicine, theology, and law, were also available. Textbooks—that is, handwritten manuscripts—were expensive and difficult to obtain, therefore teaching took the form of oral instruction, and students took copious notes based on class lectures (Figure 12.9). Exams for the bachelor of arts (B.A.) degree, usually taken upon completion of a three- to five-year course of study, were oral. Beyond the B.A. degree, one might pursue additional study leading to mastery of a specialized field. The master of arts (M.A.) degree qualified the student to teach theology or practice law or medicine. Still another four years of study were usually required for the doctoral candidate, whose efforts culminated in his defense of a thesis before a board of learned masters. (Tradition required the successful candidate to honor his examiners with a banquet.)

Among the first universities was that founded at Bologna in Northern Italy in 1159. Bologna was a center for the study of law. Its curriculum was run by students who hired professors to teach courses in law and other fields. University students brought pressure on townsfolk to maintain reasonable prices for food and lodging. They controlled the salaries and teaching schedules of their professors, requiring a teacher to obtain permission from his students for even a single day's absence and docking his pay if he was tardy. In contrast to the student-run university at Bologna, the university in

| | | |
|---|---|---|
| 1120 | the English introduce the use of latitude and longitude measured in degrees and minutes |
| 1120s | Arabic works on mathematics, optics, and astronomy are introduced into Europe |
| 1249 | Roger Bacon (English) uses glass lenses to correct faulty eyesight |
| 1250s | Albertus Magnus (German) produces a biological classification of plants based on Aristotle |
| 1250s | returning Crusaders introduce Arabic numbering and the decimal system to Europe |

**Figure 12.9** *University Lecture by Henry of Germany*, from a medieval German edition of Aristotle's *Ethics*, second half of fourteenth century. Manuscript illumination, parchment, 7 × 8¾ in. Staatliche Museen, Berlin. Preussischer Kulturbesitz, Kupferstichkabinett. Photo: Bildarchiv Preussischer Kulturbesitz, Berlin.

Paris was a guild of teachers organized primarily for instruction in theology. This university, which grew out of the cathedral school of Notre Dame, became independent of Church control by a royal charter issued in the year 1200. Its respected degree in theology drew an international student body that made Paris the intellectual melting pot of the medieval West.

Until the thirteenth century, upper-class men and women received basically the same kinds of formal education. But with the rise of the university women were excluded from receiving a higher education, much as they were forbidden from entering the priesthood. Ranging between the ages of seventeen and forty, students often held minor orders in the Church, and the intellectual enterprise of the most famous of the theologically trained schoolmen or scholastics, as they came to be called, inspired an important movement in medieval intellectual life known as Scholasticism.

## Medieval Scholasticism

Before the twelfth century, intellectuals (as well as ordinary men and women) considered Scripture and the writings of the church fathers the major repositories of knowledge. Faith in these established sources superseded rational inquiry and preempted the empirical examination of the physical world. Indeed, most intellectuals upheld the Augustinian credo that faith preceded reason. They maintained that since both faith and reason derived from God, the two could never stand in contradiction. When, in the late twelfth century, Arabic copies of the writings of Aristotle and commentaries filtered into the West from Muslim Spain and Southwest Asia, a new intellectual challenge confronted churchmen and scholars. How were they to reconcile Aristotle's rational and dispassionate views of physical reality with the supernatural truths of the Christian faith? The Church's initial reaction was to ban Aristotle's works (with the exception of the *Logic*, which had long been available in the West), but by the early thirteenth century, all of the writings of the venerated Greek philosopher were in the hands of medieval scholars. For the next hundred years, the scholastics engaged in an effort to reconcile the two primary modes of knowledge: faith and reason, the first as defended by theology, the second as exalted in Greek philosophy.

Even before the full body of Aristotle's works was available, a brilliant logician and popular teacher at the University of Paris, Peter Abelard (1079–1142), had inaugurated a rationalist approach to Church dogma. In his treatise *Sic et Non* (*Yes and No*), written several years before the high tide of Aristotelian influence, Abelard puts into practice one of the principal devices of the scholastic method—that of balancing opposing points of view. *Sic et Non* presents 150 conflicting opinions on important religious matters from such sources as the Old Testament, the Greek philosophers, the Latin Fathers, and the decrees of the Church. Abelard's methodical compilation of Hebrew, classical, and Christian thought is an expression of the scholastic inclination to collect and reconcile vast amounts of information. This impulse toward synthesis—the combination of independent parts to form a coherent whole—also inspired the many *compendia* (collections), *specula* ("mirrors" of knowledge), and *summa* (comprehensive treatises) that were written during the twelfth and thirteenth centuries.

The greatest of the scholastics and the most influential teacher of his time was the Dominican theologian Thomas Aquinas (ca. 1225–1274). Aquinas lectured and wrote on a wide variety of theological and biblical subjects, but his major contribution was the *Summa Theologica*, a vast compendium of virtually all of the major theological issues of the High Middle Ages. In this unfinished work, which exceeds Abelard's *Sic et Non* in both size and conception, Aquinas poses 631 questions on topics ranging from the nature of God to the ethics of money lending. The comprehensiveness of Aquinas' program is suggested by the following list of queries drawn arbitrarily from the *Summa*:

Whether God exists
Whether God is the highest good
Whether God is infinite
Whether God wills evil
Whether there is a trinity in God
Whether it belongs to God alone to create
Whether good can be the cause of evil
Whether angels assume bodies
Whether woman should have been made in the first production of things
Whether woman should have been made from man

Whether the soul is composed of matter and form
Whether man has free choice
Whether paradise is a corporeal place
Whether there is eternal law
Whether man can merit eternal life without grace
Whether it is lawful to sell a thing for more than it is worth

In dealing with each question, Aquinas follows Abelard's method of marshaling opinions that seem to oppose or contradict each other. But where Abelard merely mediates, Aquinas offers carefully reasoned answers; he brings to bear all the intellectual ammunition of his time in an effort to prove that the truths of reason (those proceeding from the senses and from the exercise of logic) are compatible with the truths of revelation (those that have been divinely revealed). Aquinas begins by posing an initial question—for instance, "Whether woman should have been made in the first production of things"; then he offers objections or negations of the proposition, followed by positive responses drawn from a variety of authoritative sources—mainly Scripture and the works of the early church fathers (see chapter 9). The exposition of these "seeming opposites" is followed by Aquinas' own opinion, a synthesis that invariably resolves the contradictions. Finally, Aquinas answers the original objections to the question, with a definitive concluding statement.

In the following excerpt, Aquinas deals with the question of whether and to what purpose God created women, whom most medieval churchmen regarded as the "daughters of Eve" (see chapter 11) and hence the source of humankind's depravity. Following Aristotle, Aquinas concludes that, though inferior to man in "the discernment of reason," woman was created as man's helpmate in reproducing the species. Significantly, however, Aquinas denies Aristotle's claim that woman is a defective male and, elsewhere in the *Summa*, he holds that women should retain property rights and their own earnings. Even this brief examination of the *Summa Theologica* reveals its majestic intellectual sweep, its hierarchic rigor, and its power of synthesis—three of the principal characteristics of medieval cultural expression.

## READING 2.20

## From Aquinas' *Summa Theologica*

Whether Woman Should Have Been Made in the First    1
Production of Things?
We proceed thus to the First Article:
   *Objection 1.* It would seem that woman should not have been made in the first production of things. For the Philosopher[1] says that the *female is a misbegotten male.*

---

[1]Aristotle.

But nothing misbegotten or defective should have been in the first production of things. Therefore woman should not have been made at that first production.

*Objection 2.* Further, subjection and limitation were a result of sin, for to the woman was it said after sin (*Gen.* iii. 16): *Thou shalt be under the man's power;* and Gregory[2] says that, *Where there is no sin, there is no inequality.* But woman is naturally of less strength and dignity than man, *for the agent is always more honorable than the patient*, as Augustine says. Therefore woman should not have been made in the first production of things before sin.

*Objection 3.* Further, occasions of sin should be cut off. But God foresaw that woman would be an occasion of sin to man. Therefore He should not have made woman.

*On the contrary*, It is written (*Gen.* ii. 18): *It is not good for man to be alone; let us make him a helper like to himself.*

*I answer that*, It was necessary for woman to be made, as the Scripture says, as a *helper* to man; not, indeed, as a helpmate in other works, as some say, since man can be more efficiently helped by another man in other works: but as a helper in the work of generation. . . . Among perfect animals, the active power of generation belongs to the male sex, and the passive power to the female. And as among animals there is a vital operation nobler than generation, to which their life is principally directed, so it happens that the male sex is not found in continual union with the female in perfect animals, but only at the time of coition; so that we may consider that by coition the male and female are one, as in plants they are always united, even though in some cases one of them preponderates, and in some the other. But man is further ordered to a still nobler work of life, and that is intellectual operation. Therefore there was greater reason for the distinction of these two powers in man; so that the female should be produced separately from the male, and yet that they should be carnally united for generation. Therefore directly after the formation of woman, it was said: *And they shall be two in one flesh* (*Gen.* ii. 24).

*Reply Objection 1.* As regards the individual nature, woman is defective and misbegotten, for the active power in the male seed tends to the production of a perfect likeness according to the masculine sex; while the production of woman comes from defect in the active power, or from some material indisposition, or even from some external influence, such as that of a south wind, which is moist, as the Philosopher observes. On the other hand, as regards universal human nature, woman is not misbegotten, but is included in nature's intention as directed to the work of generation. Now the universal intention of nature depends on God, Who is the universal Author of nature. Therefore, in producing nature, God formed not only the male but also the female.

*Reply Objection 2.* Subjection is twofold. One is servile, by virtue of which a superior makes use of a subject for his own benefit; and this kind of subjection began after sin. There is another kind of subjection, which is called economic or civil, whereby the superior makes use of his subjects for their own benefit and good; and this kind of subjection existed even before sin. For the good of order would have been wanting in the human family if some were not governed by others wiser than themselves. So by such a kind of subjection woman is naturally subject to man, because in man the discernment of reason predominates. Nor is inequality among men excluded by the state of innocence, as we shall prove.

*Reply Objection 3.* If God had deprived the world of all those things which proved an occasion of sin, the universe would have been imperfect. Nor was it fitting for the common good to be destroyed in order that individual evil might be avoided; especially as God is so powerful that He can direct any evil to a good end.

———————◆———————

The scholastics aimed at producing a synthesis of Christian and classical learning, but the motivation for and the substance of their efforts were still largely religious. Despite their attention to Aristotle's writings and their respect for his methods of inquiry, medieval scholastics created no system of knowledge that completely dispensed with supernatural assumptions of faith. Nevertheless, the scholastics were the humanists of the medieval world; they held that the human being, the noblest of God's creatures, was the link between the created universe and divine intelligence. They believed that human reason was the handmaiden of faith, and that reason—though incapable of transcending revelation—was humankind's finest means of understanding God's divine plan.

## SUMMARY

The Catholic Church was the dominant political, spiritual, and cultural force of the European Middle Ages. As spiritual caretaker of the Christian soul, the Church guided medieval men and women through the rites of passage in anticipation of personal immortality. The Christian immortality ideology taught that life on earth was woeful and transient and that, depending on their conduct on earth, Christian souls would reap reward or punishment in an eternal hereafter. These concepts dominated medieval literary and artistic expression.

Medieval sermons and morality plays warned Christians of the perpetual struggle between good and evil and reminded them of the need to prepare for death. As the allegorical play *Everyman* illustrates, the medieval mind interpreted reality in symbolic and hierarchic terms: Everything in God's universe held a predesigned place that was fixed and unchanging. The literary work that best reflects the spirit of the Late Middle Ages is Dante's *Commedia,* an epic poem that offers a sublime moral and intellectual vision of the Christian universe.

[2]Gregory the Great (see chapter 9).

Wealthy and powerful, the medieval Church governed vast lands, a complex bureaucracy, and a large body of secular and regular clergymen. By means of excommunication, interdict, and the Inquisition, the Church challenged a rising tide of heresy and enforced a climate of conformity and stability. And despite the challenge of increasingly powerful secular rulers among the European states, the Church maintained a position of political dominance in the West until the sixteenth century.

With the rise of universities in twelfth-century Bologna, Paris, and elsewhere, intellectual life flourished. Inspired by the writings of Aristotle, scholastics tried to synthesize the fundamental precepts of Christianity with the teachings of the Greek and Arab philosophers. Abelard and Aquinas, both of whom taught at the University of Paris, were proponents of Scholasticism, an intellectual movement aimed at reconciling faith and reason. The scholastics considered the truths of reason subordinate to the truths of revelation. Among medieval scholastics, as among less learned Christians, matters concerning the eternal destiny of the soul and the fulfillment of God's design took precedence over the pursuit of finite knowledge.

## GLOSSARY

**canto** one of the main divisions of a long poem

**excommunication** ecclesiastical censure that excludes the individual from receiving the sacraments

**grace** the free, unearned favor of God

**heresy** the denial of the revealed truths or orthodox doctrine by a baptized member of the Church; an opinion or doctrine contrary to Church dogma

**interdict** the excommunication of an entire city, district, or state

**memento mori** (Latin, "remember death") a warning of the closeness of death and the need to prepare for one's own death

**miracle play** a type of medieval play that dramatized the lives of, and especially the miracles performed by, Christ, the Virgin Mary, or the saints

**morality play** a type of medieval play that dramatized moral themes, such as the conflict between good and evil

**mystery play** a type of medieval play originating in Church liturgy and dramatizing biblical history from the fall of Satan to the Last Judgment

**pageant** a roofed wagon-stage on which medieval plays and spectacles were performed

**sacrament** a sacred act or pledge; in medieval Christianity, a visible sign (instituted by Jesus Christ) to signify God's grace

## SUGGESTIONS FOR READING

Adams, Henry. *Mont-Saint-Michel and Chartres.* Garden City, N.Y.: Doubleday, 1959.

Daly, Lowrie J. *The Medieval University: 1200–1400.* New York: Sheed and Ward, 1961.

Duby, George. *The Age of the Cathedrals: Art and Society: 980–1420*, translated by E. Levieux and B. Thompson. Chicago: University of Chicago Press, 1981.

Heer, Frederick. *The Medieval World.* New York: New American Library, 1963.

LeGoff, Jacques. *The Medieval Imagination*, translated by A. Goldhammer. Chicago: University of Chicago Press, 1992.

Mazzotta, Giuseppe. *Dante's Vision and the Circle of Knowledge.* Princeton, N.J.: Princeton University Press, 1994.

Oakley, Francis. *The Medieval Experience: Foundations of Western Cultural Singularity.* New York: Scribner, 1974.

Rowling, Marjorie. *Everyday Life in Medieval Times.* New York: Putnam's, 1968.

Sayers, Dorothy L. *Introductory Papers on Dante.* New York: Harper, 1954.

Vittorini, Domenico. *The Age of Dante.* New York: Citadel, 1964.

# 13
# The Medieval Synthesis in the Arts

If the Catholic Church was the major source of moral and spiritual instruction in the West, it was also the wellspring of artistic productivity and the patron of some of the most glorious works of art ever created. The great monastic complexes and majestic cathedrals, the spirited sculptures and radiant stained glass windows, the richly illuminated manuscripts, and the polyphonic Masses and motets—all reflect the irrepressible religious vitality of an age of faith. Although each of these genres is distinct from every other, they all functioned in close relationship to form a grand synthesis—a combination of separate elements that formed an all-embracing whole. In the arts, as in Aquinas' *Summa* or Dante's *Commedia*, the enterprise of synthesis harmonized many diverse components, which nevertheless retained their individual identities. Church architecture, sculpture, stained glass, and painted altarpieces, for instance, along with the liturgy and the music of the Mass, formed the synthesis or "whole" of Christian worship. The medieval synthesis was the product of an age that believed that God, the Master Architect, had ordered the universe so that no part of it could stand independent of the whole (Figure **13.2**). The arts of the Middle Ages, then, not only pointed the way to salvation; they worked to link temporal and transcendental realms.

## The Carolingian Abbey Church

During the Carolingian Renaissance of the ninth century (see chapter 11), Charlemagne authorized the construction of numerous Benedictine monasteries, or abbeys. Central to each abbey was a church that served as a place of worship and as a shrine that housed sacred relics. Though built on a smaller scale than that of early Christian churches, most abbey churches of the Carolingian Era were simple basilicas with square towers added at the west entrance and at the crossing of the nave and transept.

In the construction of the abbey church, as in the arrangement of the monastic complex as a whole,

Carolingian architects pursued a strict geometry governed by classical principles of symmetry and order. The plan for an ideal monastery (Figure **13.1**) found in a manuscript in the library of the monastery of Saint-Gall, Switzerland, reflects these concerns: Each part of the complex, from **refectory** (dining hall) to cemetery, is fixed on the gridlike plan according to its practical function. Monks gained access to the church, for example,

**Figure 13.1** Plan for an ideal monastery, ninth century. 13½ × 10¼ in. Monastery Library of Saint-Gall, Switzerland.

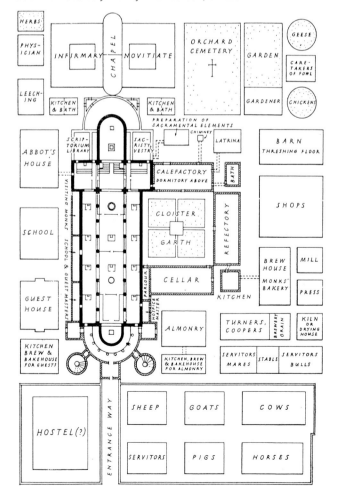

**Figure 13.2** *God as Architect of the Universe*, from the Bible Moralisée, thirteenth century. Österreichische Nationalbibliothek, Vienna, MS Cod. 2554, f.1.

by means of both the adjacent dormitory and the cloister. At the abbey church of Saint-Gall, where a second transept provided longitudinal symmetry, the monks added chapels along the aisles and transepts to house relics of saints and martyrs whose bones had been exhumed from the Roman catacombs.

## The Romanesque Pilgrimage Church

After the year 1000, devout Christians, who had expected the return of Jesus at the end of the millennium, reconciled themselves to the advent of a new age.

The Benedictine abbey of Cluny in Southeastern France launched a movement for monastic revitalization that resulted—within a period of 150 years—in the construction of more than one thousand monasteries and abbey churches throughout Western Europe. The new churches, most of which were modeled on Cluny itself, enshrined relics brought back from the Holy Land by the Crusaders. Such relics—the remains of saints and martyrs, a piece of the cross on which Jesus was crucified, and the like—were objects of holy veneration and were housed in elaborate containers, or **reliquaries**, some in the shape of the body part they held. A reliquary head like that pictured in Figure **13.3** held a skull

**Map 13.1** Romanesque and Gothic Sites in Western Europe.

or part of one belonging to a favorite local saint; on feast days, the reliquary, embellished with gilded copper and semiprecious stones, was carried through the streets in sacred procession. The churches that housed the holy relics of saints and martyrs attracted thousands of Christian pilgrims. Some traveled to the shrine to seek pardon from sins or pay homage to a particular saint. Suppliants afflicted with blindness, leprosy, and other illnesses often slept near the saint's tomb in hope of a healing vision or a miraculous cure.

There were four major pilgrimage routes that linked the cities of France with the favorite shrine of Christian pilgrims: the church of Santiago de Com-

postela in Northwestern Spain (Map 13.1). Santiago, that is, Saint James Major (brother of Saint John the Evangelist), was said to have brought Christianity to Spain and then have been martyred upon his return to Judea. His body was miraculously recovered in the early ninth century and buried at Compostela, where repeated miracles made his shrine a major pilgrimage center. Along the roads that carried pilgrims from Paris across to the Pyrenees, old churches were rebuilt and new churches erected, prompting one eleventh-century chronicler to observe, "The whole world seems to have shaken off her slumber, cast off her old rags, and clothed herself in a white mantle of new churches."

Like the Crusades themselves, pilgrimages were an expression of increased mobility and economic revitalization (see chapter 11). Since pilgrims, like modern tourists, constituted a major source of revenue for European towns and churches, parishes competed for them by enlarging church interiors and by increasing the number of reliquary chapels. The practical requirement for additional space in which to house these relics safely and make them accessible to Christian pilgrims determined the character of the pilgrimage church. In the early Christian church, as in the Carolingian abbey, the width of the nave was inhibited by the size and availability of roofing timber, and the wooden superstructure itself was highly susceptible to fire. The use of cut stone as the primary vaulting medium provided a solution to both of these problems. Indeed, the medieval architect's return to stone barrel and groin vaults of the kinds first used by the Romans (see chapter 7) inaugurated the *Romanesque style.*

**Figure 13.3** Rhenish reliquary in the shape of a head, early twelfth century. Reproduced by courtesy of the Trustees of the British Museum, London.

**Figure 13.4** West facade of the Abbey of Jumièges, on the lower Seine near Rouen, France, 1037–1067. Height of towers 141 ft.

Romanesque architects employed round arches and a uniform system of stone vaults in the upper zones of the nave and side aisles. While the floor plan of the typical Romanesque church followed the Latin cross pattern of early Christian and Carolingian churches, the new system of stone vaulting allowed medieval architects to build on a grander scale than ever before. To provide additional space for shrines, architects enlarged the eastern end of the church to include a number of radiating chapels. They also extended the side aisles around the transept and behind the apse to form an ambulatory (walkway) by which the chapels might be reached. In the construction of these new, all-stone structures, the Normans led the way. The technical superiority of Norman stonemasons, apparent in their castles (see Figure 11.13), is reflected in the abbey churches at Caen and Jumièges in Northwestern France. At the abbey of Jumièges, consecrated in 1067 in the presence of William the Conqueror, little remains other than the **westwork** (west facade), with its 141-foot-high twin towers (Figure 13.4). This austere entrance portal, with its **tripartite** (three-part) division and three round arches, captures the geometric simplicity and

**Figure 13.5** Saint-Sernin, Toulouse, France, ca. 1080–1120 (tower enlarged in the thirteenth century). Photo: Roger Viollet, Paris.

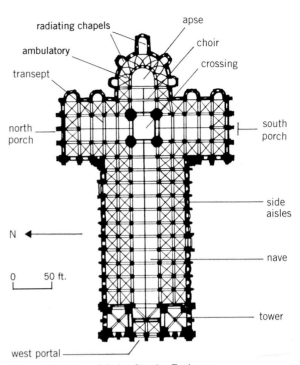

**Figure 13.6** Plan of Saint-Sernin, Toulouse.

rugged severity that was typical of the Romanesque style in France and England.

The church of Saint-Sernin at Toulouse, on the southernmost pilgrimage route to Compostela, is one of the largest of the French pilgrimage churches (Figure 13.5). Constructed of magnificent pink granite, Saint-Sernin's spacious nave is covered by a barrel vault divided by ornamental transverse arches (Figure 13.7). Thick stone walls and heavy piers carry the weight of the vault and provide lateral support (see Figure 13.18).

**Figure 13.7** Nave and choir of Saint-Sernin, Toulouse. Pink granite, length of nave 377 ft. 4 in. Photo: © Snider/The Image Works, Inc.

Since window openings might have weakened the walls that buttressed the barrel vault, the architects of Saint-Sernin eliminated the clerestory. Beneath the vaults over the double side-aisles, a gallery that served weary pilgrims as a place of overnight refuge provided additional lateral buttressing.

The formal design of Saint-Sernin follows rational and harmonious principles: The square represented by the crossing of the nave and transept is the module for the organization of the building and its parts (Figure **13.6**). Each nave **bay** (vaulted compartment) equals one-half the module, while each side-aisle bay equals one-fourth of the module. Clarity of design is also visible in the ways in which the exterior reflects the geometry of the interior: At the east end of the building, for instance, five reliquary chapels protrude uniformly from the ambulatory, while at the crossing of the nave and transept, a tower (enlarged in the thirteenth century) rises as both a belfry and a beacon to approaching pilgrims (see Figure 13.5). Massive and stately in its exterior, dignified and somber in its interior, Saint-Sernin conveys the effect of a monumental spiritual fortress.

Romanesque architects experimented with a wide assortment of regional variation in stone vaulting techniques. At the pilgrimage church of Sainte Madeleine (Mary Magdalene) at Vézelay in France—the site from which the Second Crusade was launched—the nave was covered with groin vaults separated by pronounced transverse arches. The concentration of weight along the arches, along with lighter masonry, allowed the architect to enlarge the width of the nave to 90 feet and to include a clerestory that admitted light into the dark interior (Figure **13.8**). The alternating light and dark stone **voussoirs** (wedges) in the arches of this dramatic interior indicate the influence of Muslim architecture (see Figure 10.10) on the development of the Romanesque church.

**Figure 13.8** Nave of Sainte Madeleine, Vézelay, France, ca. 1104–1132. Width 90 ft. © C.N.M.H.S./S.P.A.D.E.M.

**Figure 13.9** (above) Gislebertus, *Last Judgment*, ca. 1130–1135. West tympanum, Autun Cathedral, France. Giraudon, Paris.

**Figure 13.10** (right) Diagram of a portal.

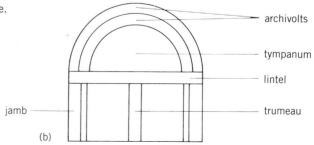

archivolts

tympanum

lintel

jamb

trumeau

(b)

## Romanesque Sculpture

Pilgrimage churches of the eleventh and twelfth centuries heralded the revival of monumental stone sculpture—a medium that, for the most part, had been abandoned since Roman antiquity. Scenes from the Old and New Testaments—carved in high relief and brightly painted—usually appeared on the entrance portals of the church, as well as in the capitals of columns throughout the basilica and its cloister. The entrance portal, normally located at the west end of the church, marked the dividing point between the earthly city and the City of God. Passage through the portal marked the beginning of the symbolic journey from sin (darkness/west) to salvation (light/east). As they passed beneath the elaborately carved west portal of the church of Saint Lazarus at Autun in France, medieval Christians were powerfully reminded of the inevitability of sin, death, and judgment. The forbidding image of Christ as Judge greeted them from the center of the **tympanum** (the semicircular space within the arch of the portal) just above their heads (Figures **13.9**, **13.10**). Framed by an almond-shaped halo, Jesus displays his wounds and points to the realms of the afterlife: Heaven (on his right) and Hell (on his left). Surrounding the awesome Christ, flamelike saints and angels and grimacing devils await the souls of the resurrected. Saint Michael weighs a soul in order to determine its eternal destiny, a motif that recalls late Egyptian art (see chapter 2), while a wraithlike devil tries to tip the scales in his own favor (Figure **13.11**). In the **lintel** (the horizontal band below the tympanum), the resurrected are pictured rising from their graves. Just beneath the mouth of Hell, a pair of disembodied claws clutch at the damned, who cower in anticipation of eternal punishment. Like a medieval morality play, the tympanum at Autun served as a *memento mori*, reminding Christians of the inevitability of divine judgment. Indeed, beneath his signature, the artist Gislebertus added the warning, "Let this terror frighten those bound by earthly sin."

The tympanum at Autun preserves the tradition of abstract stylization that evolved in early medieval manuscripts. With graphic subtlety, Gislebertus carved his figures to fit the shapes of the stone segments that comprise the portal. These lively, elongated figures bend and twist, as if animated by the restless energy that suffused the age. Similarly, at the abbey church of Saint Pierre at Moissac in France, the Hebrew prophet Jeremiah

**Figure 13.11** Gislebertus, detail of *Last Judgment*, ca. 1130–1135. Autun Cathedral. Photo: Bulloz, Paris.

**Figure 13.12** *Jeremiah the Prophet*, early twelfth century. Trumeau of south portal, Saint Pierre, Moissac, France. Giraudon, Paris.

**Figure 13.13** *The Flight to Egypt*, late eleventh century. Capital, Saint Benoît-sur-Loire, France. Photo: James Austin, Cambridge, U.K.

stretches and twists like taffy to conform to the shape of the **trumeau** (the post that supports the superstructure) of the west portal (Figure **13.12**). The Moissac sculptor unites form and content symbolically: The post supports the superstructure just as the Old Testament prophets were said to "support" the New Testament revelation of Last Judgment.

Among the most compelling examples of Romanesque sculpture are those that adorn the capitals of columns in churches and cloisters. These so-called **historiated capitals** feature narrative scenes depicting the life of Christ. One of the largest extant groups of historiated capitals comes from the west porch of the pilgrimage church of Saint Benoît-sur-Loire in France, which housed the relics of Saint Benedict. In the *Flight to Egypt*, an oval-faced Mary sits awkwardly upon a toy-like donkey led by a bearded Joseph (Figure **13.13**). The cookielike star above Mary's right shoulder and the naively shortened figures—altered to fit into the shape of the capital—give the scene a whimsical quality. Romanesque artisans plumbed their imaginations to generate the legions of fantastic beasts and hybrid demons that embellish church portals and capitals. The popularity of such imagery moved medieval churchmen to debate whether the visual arts inspired or distracted the faithful from contemplation and prayer. Nevertheless, the fusion of dogma and fantasy that characterizes so much Romanesque sculpture must have made a tremendous impact on the great percentage of people who could neither read nor write.

## The Gothic Cathedral

Romanesque architects drew on Greco-Roman principles and building techniques. Gothic architects, on the other hand, implemented a clear break with the classical past. Whereas classical temples seemed to hug the earth, Gothic cathedrals soared heavenward; whereas classical structures enforced a static relationship between building parts, Gothic structures engaged a dynamic system of thrusts and counterthrusts; and whereas classical architects rationalized form, Gothic architects infused form with symbolism. Seventeenth-century neoclassicists coined the term "Gothic" to condemn a style they judged to be a "rude and barbarous" alternative to the classical style. But modern critics have recognized the *Gothic style* as the sophisticated and majestic expression of an age of faith.

The Gothic style was born in Northern France and spread quickly throughout medieval Europe. In France alone, 80 Gothic cathedrals and nearly 500 cathedral-class churches were constructed between 1170 and 1270. Like all Christian churches, the Gothic cathedral was the religious center in which priests conducted Masses for all occasions. But, reflecting a shift of intellectual life from the monastery to the town, the Gothic cathedral was also the administrative seat or throne (*cathedra*) of a bishop, the site of ecclesiastical authority, and an educational center—a fount of theological doctrine and divine precept. The Gothic cathedral was a monumental shrine that honored one or more saints, including and especially the Virgin Mary—the principal intercessor between God and the Christian believer. Indeed, most of the prominent churches of the Middle Ages were dedicated to Notre Dame ("Our Lady"). On a symbolic level, the church was both the Heavenly Jerusalem, the City of God, and a model of the Virgin as Womb of Christ and Queen of Heaven. In the cathedral, the various types of religious expression converged: Sculpture appeared in its portals, capitals, and choir screens; stained glass diffused divine light through its windows; painted altarpieces embellished its chapels; religious drama was enacted both within its walls and outside its portals; liturgical music filled its choirs.

Finally, the Gothic cathedral, often large enough to hold the entire population of a town, was a municipal center. If the Romanesque church constituted a rural

**Figure 13.14** Chartres Cathedral, France, begun 1194.

**Figure 13.15** *Thirteenth-Century Masons*, French miniature from an Old Testament building scene, ca. 1240. 15⅓ × 11⅞ in. © The J. Pierpont Morgan Library, New York, 1991, MS 638 f.3. Stones, shaped by the two men (bottom right), are lifted by a hoisting engine powered by the treadwheel on the left. Another man is carrying mortar up the ladder on his back.

retreat for monastics and pilgrims, the Gothic cathedral served as the focal point for an urban community. Physically dominating the town, its spires soaring above the houses and shops below (Figure 13.14), the cathedral attracted civic events, public festivals, and even local business. The construction of a Gothic cathedral was a town effort, supported by the funds and labors of local citizens and guild members, including stonemasons (Figure 13.15), carpenters, metalworkers, and glaziers.

The definitive features of the Gothic style were first assembled in a monastic church just outside the gates of Paris: the abbey church of Saint-Denis—the church that held the relics of the patron saint of France and, for centuries, the burial place of French royalty. Between 1122 and 1144, Abbot Suger (1085–1151), a personal friend and adviser of the French kings Louis VI and VII, enlarged and remodeled the old Carolingian church of Saint-Denis. Suger's designs for the east end of the church called for a combination of three architectural innovations that had been employed only occasionally or experimentally: the pointed arch, the rib vault, and stained glass windows. The result was a spacious choir and ambulatory, free of heavy stone supports and flooded with light (Figure 13.16).

While Gothic cathedrals followed Saint-Denis in adopting a new look, their floor plan—the Latin cross—remained basically the same as that of the Romanesque church; only the transept might be moved further west to create a larger choir area (Figure 13.17). The ingenious combination of rib vault and pointed arch, however, had a major impact on the size and elevation of Gothic structures. Stone ribs replaced the heavy stone masonry of Romanesque vaults, and pointed arches raised these vaults to new heights. Whereas the rounded vaults of the Romanesque church demanded extensive lateral buttressing, the steeply pointed arches of the Gothic period, which directed weight downward, required only the combination of slender vertical piers and thin lateral ("flying") buttresses (Figures 13.18, 13.19). In place of masonry, broad areas of glass filled the interstices of this "cage" of stone. The nave wall consisted of an arcade of pier bundles that swept from floor to ceiling, an ornamental **triforium** gallery (the arcaded passage between the nave arcade and

**Figure 13.16** Choir and ambulatory of the Abbey Church of Saint-Denis, France, 1140-1144. © Hirmer Fotoarchiv, Munich.

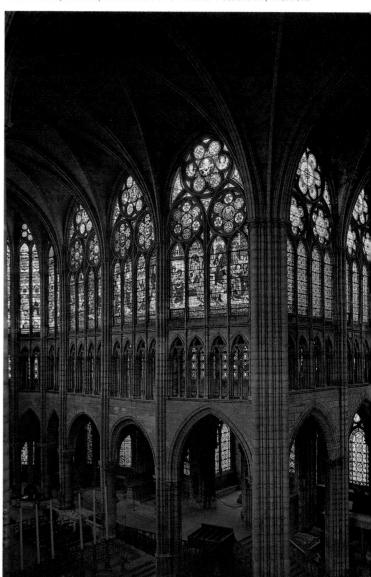

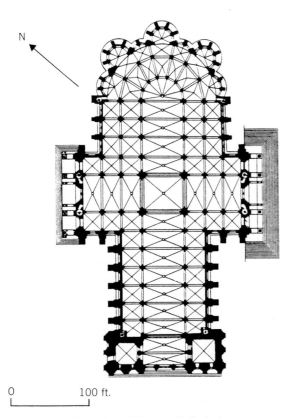

0      100 ft.

**Figure 13.17** Floor plan of Chartres Cathedral.

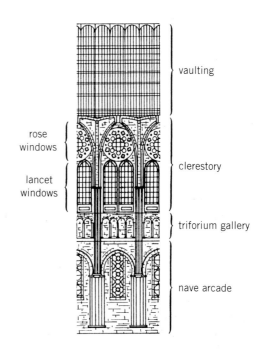

**Figure 13.18** Round and pointed arches and vaults. The round arch (a) spreads the load laterally, while the pointed arch (b) thrusts its load more directly toward the ground. The pointed arch can rise to any height while the height of the semicircular arch is governed by the space it spans. Round arches create a dome-shaped vault (c). The Gothic rib-vault (d) permits a lighter and more flexible building system with larger wall-openings that may accommodate windows.

the clerestory), and a large clerestory consisting of **rose** (from the French *roue*, "wheel") and **lancet** (vertically pointed) windows (see Figure 13.19). Above the clerestory hung elegant canopies of **quadripartite** (four-part; Figure 13.20) or **sexpartite** (six-part) rib vaults. Lighter and more airy than Romanesque churches, Gothic interiors seem to expand and unfold in vertical space. The pointed arch, the rib vault, and stained glass

windows, along with the flying buttress (first used at the cathedral of Notre Dame in Paris around 1170), became the fundamental ingredients of the Gothic style.

Medieval towns competed with one another in the grandeur of their cathedrals: At Chartres, a town located 50 miles southwest of Paris (see Map 13.1), the nave of the cathedral rose to a height of 122 feet (Figure **13.21**; see also Figures 13.14, 13.20); architects at

**Figure 13.19** Diagram of vaulting and section of nave wall, Chartres Cathedral.

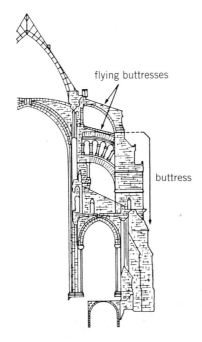

flying buttresses

buttress

vaulting

rose windows

clerestory

lancet windows

triforium gallery

nave arcade

**Figure 13.20** Nave facing east, Chartres Cathedral. Height of nave 122 ft.

Amiens (see Figure 13.24) took the space from the floor to the apex of the vault to a breathtaking 144 feet. At Beauvais, the 157-foot vault of the choir (the equivalent of a fourteen-story high-rise) collapsed twelve years after its completion and had to be reconstructed over a period of forty years. These major enterprises in engineering design and craftsmanship often took decades to build, and many were never finished. In contrast to the Romanesque church, with its well-defined cubic volumes and its simple geometric harmonies, the Gothic cathedral was an intricate web of stone, a dynamic network of open and closed spaces that evoked a sense of unbounded extension. Despite its visual complexity, however, the Gothic interior revealed its principal divisions in the articulation of the facade. At the cathedral of Notre Dame in Paris, for instance, the height of the nave arcade corresponds to that of the west portals; the triforium arcade is echoed in the rows of saints standing above those portals; and the clerestory is marked by a majestic rose window (Figure 13.22).

Gothic architects embellished the structural extremities of the cathedral with stone **crockets** (stylized

| 1122 | Abbot Suger combines pointed arches and rib vaults in remodeling the abbey church of Saint-Denis |
|---|---|
| ca. 1175 | flying buttresses are first used in the cathedral of Notre Dame in Paris |
| ca. 1225 | Villard de Honnecourt (French) begins a sketchbook of architectural plans, elevations, and engineering devices |
| 1291 | Venetian glassmakers produce the first clear (as opposed to colored) glass |

leaves) and **finials** (crowning ornamental details). At the upper portions of the building, **gargoyles**—waterspouts in the form of grotesque human beings or hybrid beasts—were believed to ward off evil (Figure **13.23**). During the thirteenth century and thereafter, cathedrals increased in structural and ornamental complexity (Figure **13.24**). Flying buttresses became ornate stone wings terminating in minichapels that housed individual statues of saints and martyrs. Crockets and finials sprouted in greater numbers from gables and spires (compare the facades of Chartres and Amiens; see

**Figure 13.21** West facade of Chartres Cathedral, lower parts 1134–1150, mainly after 1194.

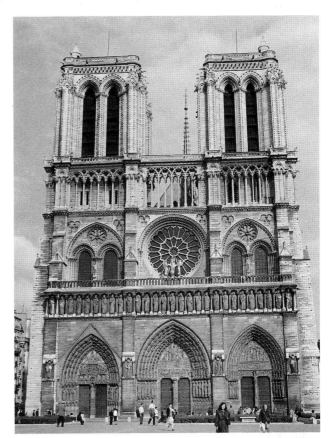

**Figure 13.22** West facade of Notre Dame, Paris, ca. 1200–1250. Photo: © Museum of Notre Dame de Paris.

Figures 13.21 and 13.24), and sculptural details became more numerous. But, like an Aquinan proposition, the final design represents the reconciliation of all individual parts into a majestic and harmonious synthesis.

## Stained Glass

Stained glass was to the Gothic cathedral what mosaics were to the early Christian church: a source of religious edification, a medium of divine light, and a delight to the eye. Produced on the site of the cathedral by a process of mixing metal oxides into molten glass, colored sheets of glass were cut into fragments to fit preconceived designs. They were then fixed within lead bands, bound by a grid of iron bars, and set into stone **mullions** (vertical frames). Imprisoned in this lacelike armature, the glass vibrated with color, sparkling in response to the changing natural light and casting rainbows of color that seemed to dissolve the stone walls. The faithful of the High Middle Ages regarded the cathedral windows as precious objects—glass tapestries that clothed the House of God with radiant light. They especially treasured the windows that were filled with rich blues, which, in contrast to other colors, required a cobalt oxide that came from regions outside France.

**Figure 13.23** Grotesques and a gargoyle waterspout on a tower terrace of Notre Dame, Paris, as restored in the nineteenth century. Alinari/Art Resource, New York.

Legend had it that Abbot Suger, the first churchman to exploit the aesthetic potential of stained glass, produced blue glass by grinding up sapphires—a story that, although untrue, reflects the popular equation of precious gems with sacred glass.

Suger exalted stained glass as a medium that filtered divine truth. To the medieval mind, light was a symbol of Jesus, who had proclaimed to his apostles, "I am the light of the world" (John 8.12). Drawing on this mystical bond between Jesus and light, Suger identified the *lux nova* ("new light") of the Gothic church as the symbolic equivalent of God and the windows as mediators of God's love. But for Suger, light—especially as it passed through the stained glass windows of the church—also signified the sublime knowledge that accompanied the progressive purification of the human spirit as it ascended to God (compare Canto 33 of Dante's "Paradiso," Reading 2.19). Suger's mystical interpretation of light, inspired by his reading of neoplatonic treatises (see chapter 8, page 3), sustained his belief that contemplation of the "many-colored gems" of church glass could transport the Christian from "the slime of this earth" to "the purity of heaven." On the wall of the ambulatory at Saint-Denis, Abbot Suger had these words inscribed: "That which is united in splendor, radiates in splendor/And the magnificent work inundated with the new light shines."

The light symbolism that Suger embraced was as distinctive to medieval sermons and treatises as it was to the everyday liturgy of the church; recall the words of Ambrose's sixth-century song of praise, the "Ancient Morning Hymn" (see Reading 2.6, page 18),

> O Splendor of God's glory bright,
> O Thou who bringest light from light,
> O Light of light, light's living spring,
> O Day, all days illumining!

## The Windows at Chartres

The late twelfth and early thirteenth centuries were, without doubt, the golden age of stained glass. At Chartres, the 175 surviving glass panels with representations of more than four thousand figures comprise a cosmic narrative of humankind's religious and secular history. Chartres' windows, which were removed for safekeeping during World War II and thereafter returned to their original positions, follow a carefully organized theological program designed, as Abbot Suger explained, "to show simple folk . . . what they ought to believe." Like most Gothic cathedrals, Chartres was dedicated to the Virgin Mary. Chartres housed the tunic Mary was said to have worn when she gave birth to Jesus; and since that tunic had survived the late twelfth-century fire that destroyed most of the old church—a

**Figure 13.24** West facade of Notre Dame of Amiens, France, ca. 1220–1288. Height of nave 144 ft. Scala/Art Resource, New York.

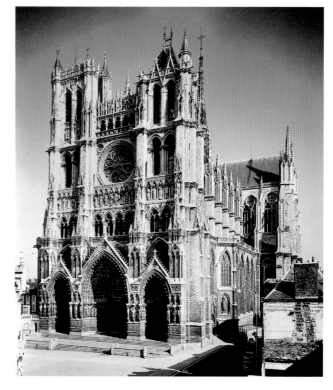

**Figure 13.25** *Notre Dame de la Belle Verrière* ("Our Lady of the Beautiful Glass"), Chartres Cathedral, twelfth century. Stained glass. Photo: Sonia Halliday, Weston Turville, U.K.

miracle that was taken to indicate the Virgin's desire to see the cathedral rebuilt—her image dominated the iconographic program. In one of Chartres' oldest windows, whose vibrant combination of red and blue glass inspired the title *Notre Dame de la Belle Verrière* ("Our Lady of the Beautiful Glass"), the Virgin appears in her dual role as Mother of God and Queen of Heaven (Figure **13.25**). Holding the Christ child on her lap and immediately adjacent to her womb, she also symbolizes the Seat of Wisdom. In the lancet windows below the rose of the south transept wall (Figure **13.26**), Mary and the Christ child are flanked by four Old Testament prophets who carry on their shoulders the four evangelists, a symbolic rendering of the Christian belief that the Old Dispensation upheld the New (compare Figure 13.12). Often, the colors chosen for parts of the design carry symbolic value. For instance, in scenes of the Passion from the west-central lancet window, the cross carried by Jesus is green—the color of vegetation—to symbolize rebirth and regeneration.

**Figure 13.26** (opposite)  South rose and lancets, Chartres Cathedral, thirteenth century. Photo: © Hirmer Fotoarchiv, Munich.

**Figure 13.27** Sainte Chapelle, Paris, from the southwest, 1245–1248. Photo: A. F. Kersting, London.

Many of Chartres' windows were donated by members of the nobility, who are frequently shown kneeling in prayer below the images of the saints (see Figure 13.26)—and by guilds of craftspeople and merchants. Scenes depicting the activities of bakers, butchers, stonemasons, and other workers often appear among the windows commemorating the patron saints of each guild (see Figure 11.17).

## Sainte Chapelle: Medieval "Jewelbox"

The art of stained glass reached its highest point in Sainte Chapelle, the small palace chapel commissioned for the Ile de France by King Louis IX ("Saint Louis") (Figure **13.27**). Executed between 1245 and 1248, the chapel was designed to hold the Crown of Thorns, a relic that Christian Crusaders claimed to have recovered along with other symbols of Christ's Passion. The lower level of the chapel is richly painted with frescoes that imitate the canopy of Heaven, while the upper level consists almost entirely of 49-foot-high lancet windows dominated by ruby red and purplish blue glass (Figure **13.28**). More than a thousand individual stories are

**Figure 13.28** Upper chapel of Sainte Chapelle, Paris. Height of lancet windows 49 ft. © Ciccione/Photo Researchers, Inc.

depicted within the stained glass windows that make up two-thirds of the upper chapel walls. In its vast iconographic program and its dazzling, ethereal effect, this medieval "jewelbox" is the crowning example of French Gothic art.

## Gothic Sculpture

The sculpture of the Gothic cathedral was an exhaustive compendium of Old and New Testament history, classical and Christian precepts, and secular legend and lore. Like the stained glass of the Gothic cathedral, the sculptural program—that is, the totality of its carved representations—conveyed Christian doctrine and liturgy in terms that were meaningful to both scholars and laity. Learned churchmen might glean from these images a profound symbolic message, while less educated Christians might see in them a history of their faith and a mirror of daily experience. Designed to be "read" by the laity, the Gothic facade was both a "bible in stone" and an encyclopedia of the religious and secular life of an age of faith.

In the sculpture of the cathedral, as in the stained glass window scenes, the Virgin Mary holds a prominent place. At Chartres, the west portal—called the Royal Portal for its figures of kings and queens from the Old Testament (Figure 13.29)—takes as its central motif Christ in Majesty; but on the right tympanum, the Mother of God is honored as Queen of the Liberal Arts (Figure 13.30). She appears as the Seat of Wisdom (compare *La Belle Verrière*, Figure 13.25), and is framed by **archivolts** (the relief bands framing the tympanum) that include allegorical representations of grammar, rhetoric, arithmetic, and the other four Liberal Arts. Each of the disciplines is accompanied by the appropriate historical authority. For instance, the inner archivolt on the lower right shows Music, who, holding a **psaltery** (a stringed instrument; see also Figure 13.37) and striking a set of bells, stands just above Pythagoras (celebrated for having discovered the numerical relation between the length of strings and musical notes), shown hunched over his lap desk.

On cathedral facades, the Virgin Mary appears frequently as Mother of God and Queen of Heaven (Figure 13.31). The central trumeau of the west portal at Notre Dame in Paris shows the regal Mary carrying the Christ child (Figure 13.32). Beneath her feet is an image of the fallen Eve, depicted alongside Adam in the Garden of Eden. The conjunction of Mary and Eve alluded to the popular medieval idea that Mary was the "new Eve," who brought salvation as a remedy for the sentence of death resulting from the disobedience of the "old Eve."

The thousands of individually carved figures on the facades of the cathedrals at Chartres, Paris, Amiens, and

**Figure 13.29** Royal Portal, west facade, Chartres Cathedral, ca. 1140–1150.

**Figure 13.30** Scenes from the life of the Virgin Mary, between 1145 and 1170. Right tympanum of the royal portal, west facade, Chartres Cathedral. Photo: © James Austin, London.

**Figure 13.31** *Coronation of the Virgin*, ca. 1225. Central tympanum of the north portal, Chartres Cathedral. © Hirmer Fotoarchiv, Munich.

**Figure 13.32** Virgin and Child (above) and Temptation of Adam and Eve (below), thirteenth century. Central trumeau of the west portal, Notre Dame, Paris. Photo: Bulloz, Paris.

elsewhere required the labor of many sculptors working over long periods of time. Often, the variety of styles on a single facade reflects the efforts of different workshops and different eras. The present cathedral at Chartres, at least the fifth on that site, was the product of numerous building campaigns: Its west portal survived the devastating fire of 1194, while its north and south portals were added in the early thirteenth century. The Royal Portal retains the linear severity of the Romanesque style (see Figure 13.29). In the central tympanum sits a rigidly posed Christ in Majesty flanked by symbols of the four evangelists and framed by the Elders of the Apocalypse in the outer archivolts. In the lintel below, the apostles are ordered into formal groups of threes. Yet, if one compares this late twelfth-century portal with that at Autun, carved only a few decades earlier (see Figure 13.9), it is apparent that medieval sculpture was moving in the direction of greater repose and heightened realism.

During the thirteenth century, figural representation became gradually more detailed and lifelike. The figures on Chartres' north portal (1200–1220)—a veritable throng of angels, prophets, kings, and patriarchs— assume natural poses, their robes shifting with the positions of their bodies and their gestures varied and subtle. Rather than conform stiffly to the architectural framework, they seem to detach themselves from the stone, a fact quickly grasped when one observes the live pigeons darting in and out of the spaces behind and between the stone representations of the Virgin Mary and Jesus seated on the central tympanum (see Figure 13.31). The trend toward greater realism in Gothic sculpture accompanied the proliferation of religious imagery and architectural details—indeed, at Amiens, the entire west facade seems to dissolve into a lacy skein of stone (see Figure 13.24).

## Medieval Painting

Medieval painting shared the graphic character of Romanesque sculpture. Responsive to the combined influence of Germanic, Islamic, and Byzantine art, medieval artists developed a taste for decorative abstraction through line. In fresco, manuscript illumination, and panel painting, line worked to flatten form, eliminate space, and enhance the symbolic nature of the image. Line also helped to emphasize gesture, an important symbolic device. In an age dominated by sermons, liturgical chant, and other oral genres, a single, symbolic gesture was truly "worth a thousand words."

Graceful draftsmanship characterizes the illustrations in the thirteenth-century Psalter of Saint Swithin (Figure 13.33). Like the figures at Moissac and Autun, those depicted in the *Capture and Flagellation of Christ* are tall, thin, and lively, their gestures and facial expressions exaggerated to emphasize the contrasting states of

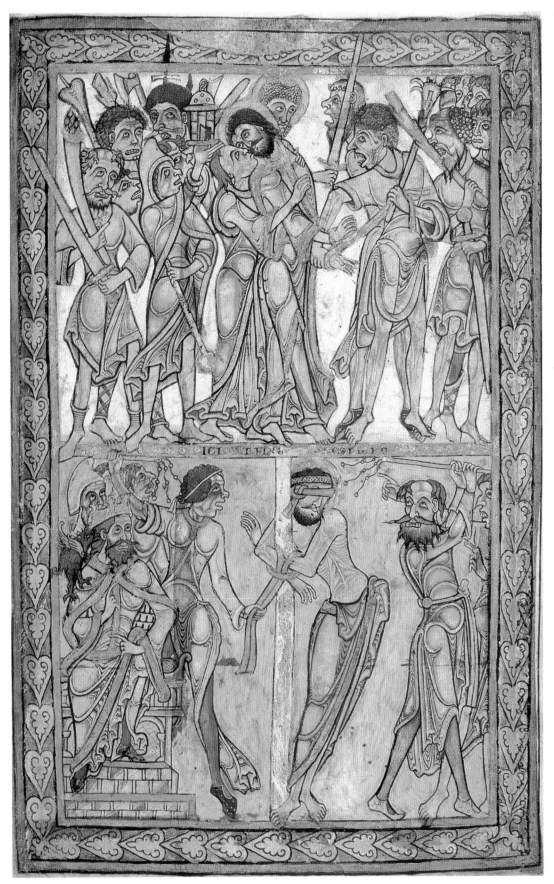

**Figure 13.33** Capture of Christ and the Flagellation, from the *Psalter of Saint Swithin*, ca. 1250. Reproduced by permission of the British Library, London.

**Figure 13.34** Crucifixion and Deposition of Christ with the Church and the Synogogue, from the *Psalter of Blanche of Castile*, ca. 1235. Bibliothèque de l'Arsenal, Paris, MS 1186, f.24.

arrogance and humility. The artist who painted the *Crucifixion and Deposition of Christ* for the Psalter of Blanche of Castile (the mother of Saint Louis) imitates the geometric compositions and strong, simple colors of stained glass windows (Figure 13.34). To the right and left of Jesus are depicted the Church (representing the New Dispensation) and the Synagogue (representing the Old Dispensation). Book illuminators often used pattern books filled with stock representations of standard historical and religious subjects, a practice that encouraged stylistic conservatism. Nevertheless, in the preparation of thousands of miniatures and marginal illustrations for secular and religious manuscripts, the imagination of medieval artists usually prevailed.

Some of the finest examples of medieval painting appear on thirteenth-century altarpieces. The typical Gothic altarpiece consisted of a wooden panel or panels covered with **gesso** (a chalky white plaster), on which images were painted in **tempera** (a powdered pigment that produces dry, flat surface colors), and embellished with gold leaf. Installed on or behind the church altar, the altarpiece usually displayed scenes from the Life of Jesus, the Virgin Mary, or a favorite saint or martyr. A late thirteenth-century altarpiece by the Florentine painter Cimabue (1240–1302) shows the Virgin and Child elevated on a monumental seat that is both a throne and a tower (Figure 13.35). Angels throng around the throne, while, beneath the Virgin's feet, four Hebrew prophets display scrolls predicting the coming of Jesus. To symbolize their lesser importance, angels and prophets are pictured considerably smaller than the enthroned Mary. Such hierarchic grading, which was typical of medieval art, also characterized Egyptian and Byzantine compositional design.

Cimabue's lavishly gilded devotional image has a schematic elegance: Line elicits the sharp, metallic folds of the Virgin's dark blue mantle, the crisp wings of the angels, the chiseled features of the Christ child, and the decorative surface of the throne. The figure of the Virgin combines the hypnotic grandeur of Byzantine icons (by which many Italian artists were influenced) and the weightless, hieratic clarity of Gislebertus' Christ in Majesty at Autun (see Figure 13.9). Although Cimabue's Virgin is more humanized than the Autun Jesus, she is every bit as regal an object of veneration.

Medieval artists often imitated the ornamental vocabulary of Gothic architecture and the bright colors of stained glass windows. The Sienese painter Simone Martini (1284–1344) made brilliant use of Gothic architectural motifs in his *Annunciation* altarpiece of 1333 (Figure 13.36). The frame of the altarpiece consists of elegant Gothic spires and heavily gilded **ogee** arches (pointed arches with S-shaped curves near the apex) sprouting finials and crockets. Set on a gold leaf ground, the petulant Virgin, the Angel Annunciate, and the vase of lilies (symbolizing Mary's purity) seem suspended in time and space. Martini's composition depends on a refined play of lines: The graceful curves of the Angel Gabriel's wings are echoed in his fluttering vestments, in the contours of the Virgin's body as she shrinks from the angel's greeting, and in the folds of her mantle, the pigment for which was ground from semiprecious lapis lazuli.

## *Medieval Music*

### Early Medieval Music and Liturgical Drama

The major musical developments of the Early Middle Ages, like those in architecture, came out of the monasteries. In Charlemagne's time, monastic reforms in Church liturgy and in sacred music accompanied the renaissance in the visual arts. One early medieval monk wrote in the margin of his songbook, "The tedious plainsong grates my tender ears." Perhaps to remedy such complaints, the monks at Saint-Gall enlarged the range of expression of the classical Gregorian chant by adding **antiphons**, or verses sung as responses to the text. Carolingian monks also embellished plainsong with the **trope**, an addition of music or words to the established liturgical chant. Thus, "Lord, have mercy upon us" became "Lord, *omnipotent Father, God, Creator of all*, have mercy upon us." A special kind of trope, called a **sequence**, added words to the long, melismatic passages—such as the alleluias and amens—that occurred at the end of each part of the Mass.

By the tenth century, singers began to divide among themselves the parts of the liturgy for Christmas

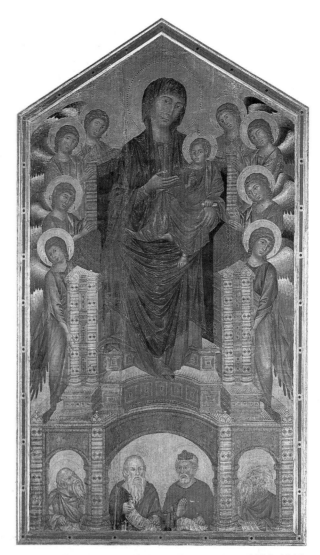

**Figure 13.35** Cimabue, *Madonna Enthroned*, ca. 1280–1290. Tempera on wood, 12 ft. 7½ in. × 7 ft. 4 in. Uffizi Gallery, Florence. Scala/Art Resource, New York.

and Easter, now embellished by tropes and sequences. As more and more dramatic incidents were added to the texts for these Masses, full-fledged music-drama emerged. Eventually, liturgical plays broke away from the liturgy and were performed in the intervals between the parts of the Mass. Such was the case with the eleventh-century *Play of Herod*, whose dramatic "action" brought to life the legend of the three Magi[6] and the massacre of the innocents by King Herod of Judea—incidents surrounding the Gospel story of the birth of Christ appropriate to the Christmas season. By the twelfth century, as spoken dialogue and possibly musical instruments were introduced, Church drama moved outside the walls of the church itself.

---

[6]See Music Listening Selections at end of chapter.

**Figure 13.36** Simone Martini, *Annunciation*, 1333. (Saints in side panels by Lippo Memmi.) Tempera on wood, 8 ft. 8 in. × 10 ft. Uffizi Gallery, Florence. Scala/Art Resource, New York.

## Medieval Musical Notation

Musical notation was invented in the monasteries. As with Romanesque architecture, so with medieval musical theory and practice, Benedictine monks at Cluny and elsewhere were especially influential. During the eleventh century, they devised the first efficient Western system of musical notation, thus facilitating the performance and transmission of liturgical music. They arranged the tones of the commonly used scale in progression from A through G and developed a formal system of notating pitch. The Italian Benedictine Guido of Arezzo (ca. 990–ca. 1050) introduced a staff of colored lines (yellow for C, red for F, etc.) on which he registered neumes—marks traditionally written above the words to indicate tonal ascent or descent (see chapter 9). Guido's system established a precise means of indi-

cating shifts in pitch. Instead of relying on memory alone, singers could consult songbooks inscribed with both words and music. Such advances encouraged the kinds of compositional complexity represented by medieval polyphony.

## Medieval Polyphony

Although our knowledge of early medieval music is sparse, there is reason to believe that, even before the year 1000, choristers were experimenting with multiple lines of music as an alternative to the monophonic style of Gregorian chant. **Polyphony** (music consisting of two or more lines of melody) was a Western invention; it did not make its appearance in Asia until modern times. The earliest polyphonic compositions consisted of Gregorian melodies sung in two parts simultaneously, with both voices moving note-for-note in parallel motion (parallel **organum**),[♪] or with a second voice moving in contrary motion (free organum),[♪] perhaps also adding many notes to the individual syllables of the text (melismatic organum).[♪] Consistent with rules of harmony derived from antiquity, and with the different ranges of men's voices, the second musical part was usually pitched a fourth or a fifth above or below the first, creating a pure, hollow sound.

Throughout the High Middle Ages, Northern France—and the city of Paris in particular—was the center of the art of polyphonic composition. From the same area that produced the Gothic cathedral came a new musical style that featured several lines of melody arranged in counterpoised rhythms. The foremost Parisian composer toward the end of the twelfth century was Pérotin. A member of the Notre Dame School, Pérotin enhanced the splendor of the Christian Mass by writing three- and four-part polyphonic compositions based on Gregorian chant. Pérotin's music usually consisted of a principal voice or "tenor" (from the Latin *tenere*, meaning "to hold") that sang the "fixed song" (Latin, *cantus firmus*) and one or more voices that moved in shorter-phrased and usually faster tempos.[♪] The combination of two or three related but independent voices, a musical technique called **counterpoint**, enlivened late twelfth- and thirteenth-century music. Indeed, the process of vertical superimposition of voice on voice enhanced sonority and augmented the melodic complexity of medieval music much in the way that the counterbalanced parts of the Gothic structure enriched its visual texture.

As medieval polyphony encouraged the addition of voices and voice parts, the choir areas of Gothic cathedrals were enlarged to accommodate more singers. Performed within the acoustically resonant bodies of such cathedrals as Notre Dame in Paris, the polyphonic Mass produced an aural effect as resplendent as the multicolored glass that shimmered throughout the interior. Like the cathedral itself, the polyphonic Mass was a masterful synthesis of carefully arranged parts—a synthesis achieved in *time* rather than in *space*.

## The "Dies Irae"

One of the best examples of the medieval synthesis, particularly as it served the Christian immortality ideology, is the "Dies irae" ("Day of Wrath"). The fifty-seven-line hymn, which originated among the Franciscans during the thirteenth century, was added to the Roman Catholic **requiem** (the Mass for the Dead) and quickly became a standard part of the Christian funeral service. Invoking a powerful vision of the end of time, the "Dies irae" is the musical counterpart of the sermons (see Reading 2.17) and *Last Judgment* portals (see Figure 13.9) that issued forth solemn warnings of final doom. The hymn opens with the words:

> Day of Wrath! O day of mourning!
> See fulfilled the prophets' warning,
> Heaven and earth in ashes burning!

But, as with most examples of apocalyptic art, including Dante's *Commedia*, the hymn holds out hope for absolution and deliverance:

> With Thy favored sheep, oh, place me!
> Nor among the goats abase me,
> But to Thy right hand upraise me.
>
> While the Wicked are confounded,
> Doomed to flames of woe unbounded,
> Call me, with Thy saints surrounded.

Like so many other forms of medieval expression, the "Dies irae" brings into vivid contrast the destinies of sinners and saints. In later centuries, it inspired the powerful requiem settings of Mozart, Berlioz, and Verdi, and its music became a familiar symbol of apocalyptic death and damnation.

## The Motet

The thirteenth century also witnessed the invention of a new religious musical genre, the **motet**—a short, polyphonic choral composition based on a sacred text. Performed both inside and outside the church, it was the most popular kind of medieval religious song. Like the trope, the motet (from the French word *mot*, meaning "word") developed from the practice of adding words to the melismatic parts of a melody. Medieval motets usually juxtaposed two or more uncomplicated themes, each with its own lyrics and metrical pattern, in a manner that was lilting and lively.[♪] Motets designed to be sung outside the church often borrowed secular tunes with vernacular words. A three-part motet might combine a love song in the vernacular, a well-known hymn of praise to the Virgin, and a Latin liturgical text in the *cantus firmus*. Thirteenth-century motets were thus polytextual as well as polyphonic and polyrhythmic. A stock of melodies (like the stock of images in medieval pattern books) was available to musicians for use in secular and sacred songs, and the same one might serve both types of song. Subtle forms of symbolism occurred in many medieval motets, as for instance where a popular song celebrating spring might be used to refer to the Resurrection of Jesus, the awakening of romantic love, or both.

---

[♪]See Music Listening Selections at end of chapter.

[♪]See Music Listening Selections at end of chapter.

## Instrumental Music of the Middle Ages

Medieval music relied upon the human voice. Musical instruments first appeared in religious music not for the purpose of accompanying songs, as with *troubadour* poems and folk epics, but to substitute for the human voice in polyphonic compositions. Medieval music depended on **timbre** (tone color) rather than volume for its effect, and most medieval instruments produced sounds that were gentle and thin by comparison with their modern (not to mention electronically amplified) counterparts. Medieval string instruments included the harp, the psaltery, and the lute (all three are plucked), and bowed fiddles such as the vielle and the rebec (Figure **13.37**). Wind instruments included portable pipe organs, recorders, and bagpipes. Percussion was produced by chimes, cymbals, bells, tambourines, and drums. Instrumental music performed without voices accompanied medieval dancing. Percussion instruments established the basic rhythms for a wide variety of high-spirited dances, including the estampie,♭ a popular round dance consisting of short, repeated phrases.

## *SUMMARY*

Medieval churches and cathedrals were the monumental expressions of an age of faith. In Carolingian times, the abbey church became the focal point of monastic life as well as the repository of sacred relics that drew pilgrims from neighboring areas. After the year 1000, Romanesque pilgrimage churches were constructed in great numbers throughout Western Europe. They feature all-stone masonry with round arches and thick barrel and groin vaults. The sculptures on their stone portals and capitals illustrate the Christian themes of redemption and salvation.

While the Romanesque church was essentially a rural phenomenon, the Gothic cathedral was the focus and glory of the medieval town. First developed in the region of Paris, the cathedral was an ingenious synthesis of three structural elements—rib vaults, pointed arches, and flying buttresses—the combination of which permitted the extensive use of stained glass. Raised to breathtaking heights, the Gothic cathedral was, in the words recited at the Mass for the consecration of a Catholic church, "the Court of God and the Gate of Heaven." The sculptural facade, a "bible in stone," presented a panorama of Old and New Testament history, medieval lore, and everyday life. Medieval sculpture and painting styles were generally abstract, symbolic, and characterized by expressive linearity, the use of bright colors, and a decorative treatment of form. Gradually,

♭See Music Listening Selections at end of chapter.

**Figure 13.37** Music and Her Attendants, from Boethius, *De Arithmetica*, fourteenth century. Scala/Art Resource, New York. Holding a portable pipe organ, the elegant lady who symbolizes the civilized art of courtly music is surrounded by an ensemble of female court musicians. In the circle at the top, King David plays a psaltery, the instrument named after the Psalms (Psaltery) of David. Clockwise from right: lute, clappers, trumpets, nakers (kettledrums), bagpipe, shawm, tambourine, rebec (viol).

however, medieval art moved in the direction of greater realism and descriptive detail.

As in the visual arts, the music of the Middle Ages was closely related to religious ritual. In Carolingian times, tropes and sequences came to embellish Christian chant, a process that led to the birth of liturgical drama. In the eleventh century, Benedictine monks devised a system of musical notation that facilitated performance and made possible the accurate transmission of music from generation to generation. At about the same time, polyphony—a uniquely Western form of musical expression—emerged. In polyphonic compositions, up to three further melodic lines provided counterpoint to the fixed melody. Polyphonic religious compositions known as motets often borrowed vernacular texts and secular melodies.

Like the Gothic cathedral, the polyphonic motet may be said to illustrate the medieval practice of juxtaposing and reconciling opposing elements. Collectively, all of the arts worked to form a coherent whole—a synthesis that projected the medieval view of nature as the expression of a preordained, divine order.

# GLOSSARY

**antiphon** a verse sung in response to the text; see also "antiphonal" in Glossary, chapter 9

**archivolt** a molded or decorated band around an arch or forming an archlike frame for an opening

**bay** a regularly repeated spatial unit of a building; in medieval architecture, a vaulted compartment

**counterpoint** a musical technique that involves two or more independent melodies; the term is often used interchangeably with "polyphony"

**crocket** a stylized leaf used as a terminal ornament

**finial** an ornament, usually pointed and foliated, that tops a spire or pinnacle

**gargoyle** a waterspout usually carved in the form of a grotesque figure

**gesso** a chalky white plaster used to prepare the surface of a panel for painting

**historiated capital** the uppermost member of a column, ornamented with figural scenes

**lancet** a narrow window topped with a pointed arch

**lintel** a horizontal beam or stone that spans an opening (see Figure 13.10)

**motet** a short, polyphonic religious composition based on a sacred text

**mullion** the slender, vertical pier dividing the parts of a window, door, or screen

**ogee** a pointed arch with an S-shaped curve on each side

**organum** the general name for the oldest form of polyphony: In *parallel organum*, the two voices move exactly parallel to one another; in *free organum* the second voice moves in contrary motion; *melismatic organum* involves the use of multiple notes for the individual syllables of the text

**polyphony** (Greek, "many voices") a musical texture consisting of two or more lines of melody that are of equal importance

**psaltery** a stringed instrument consisting of a flat soundboard and strings that are plucked

**quadripartite** consisting of or divided into four parts

**refectory** the dining hall of a monastery

**reliquary** a container for a sacred relic or relics

**requiem** a Mass for the Dead; a solemn chant to honor the dead

**rose** (from the French *roue*, "wheel") a large circular window with stained glass and stone tracery

**sequence** a special kind of trope consisting of words added to the melismatic passages of Gregorian chant

**sexpartite** consisting of or divided into six parts

**tempera** a powdered pigment that produces dry, flat colors

**timbre** tone color; the distinctive tone or quality of sound made by a voice or a musical instrument

**triforium** in a medieval church, the shallow arcaded passageway above the nave and below the clerestory (see Figure 13.19)

**tripartite** consisting of or divided into three parts

**trope** an addition of words, music, or both to Gregorian chant

**trumeau** the pillar that supports the superstructure of a portal (see Figure 13.10)

**tympanum** the semicircular space enclosed by the lintel over a doorway and the arch above it (see Figure 13.10)

**voussoir** (French, "wedge") a wedge-shaped block or unit in an arch or vault

**westwork** (from the German, *Westwerk*) the elaborate west end of a Carolingian or Romanesque church

# SUGGESTIONS FOR READING

Boney, Jean. *French Gothic Architecture of the Twelfth and Thirteenth Centuries*. Berkeley, Calif.: University of California Press, 1983.

Calkins, Robert. *Monuments of Medieval Art*. Ithaca, N.Y.: Cornell University Press, 1989.

Dodwell, C. R. *The Pictorial Arts of the West 800–1200*. New Haven: Yale University Press, 1993.

Gimpel, Jean. *The Cathedral Builders*, translated by D. King. Ithaca, N.Y.: Cornell University Press, 1980.

Macauley, David. *Cathedral: The Story of its Construction*. Boston: Houghton Mifflin, 1973.

Mâle, Emile. *The Gothic Image: Religious Art in France of the Thirteenth Century*, trans. Dora Nussey. New York: Harper, 1973.

Martindale, Andrew. *Gothic Art from the Twelfth to the Fifteenth Century*. New York: Praeger, 1974.

Seay, Albert. *Music in the Medieval World*. 2nd ed. Englewood Cliffs, N.J.: Prentice-Hall, 1991.

Simson, Otto von. *The Gothic Cathedral*. New York: Harper, 1964.

Snyder, James. *Medieval Art*. New York: Abrams, 1989.

# MUSIC LISTENING SELECTIONS

**Cassette I Selection 6** Medieval liturgical drama, *The Play of Herod*, Scene 2, "The Three Magi."

**Cassette I Selection 7** Three examples of early medieval polyphony: parallel organum, "Rex caeli, Domine"; free organum, trope, "Agnus Dei"; melismatic organum, "Benedicamus Domino"; ca. 900–1150.

**Cassette I Selection 8** Pérotin, Three-part organum, "Alleluya" (Nativitas), twelfth century.

**Cassette I Selection 9** Anonymous, Motet, "En non Diu! Quant voi; Eius in Oriente," thirteenth century, excerpt.

**Cassette I Selection 10** French dance, "Estampie," thirteenth century.

# PART
# III
# THE WORLD BEYOND THE WEST

Western students often overlook the fact that Europe—home of the culture that is most familiar to them—occupies only a tiny area at the far western end of the vast continental landmass of Asia. At the eastern end of that landmass lie two geographic and cultural giants, India and China, and the small but mighty Japan (see Maps 14.1 and 14.2). During the European Middle Ages, East and West had little contact with each other, apart from periodic exchanges of goods and technology facilitated by Muslim intermediaries. Although neither India nor China nor Japan had a direct impact on the West, their indirect influence was considerable, especially in the areas of science and technology.

Between 500 and 1300 C.E., India produced some of the finest Sanskrit literature ever written. Hindu temple architecture and sculpture reached new levels of imagination and complexity, and Indian music flour-ished. In China, during roughly the same period, the Tang and Song dynasties fostered a golden age in poetry and painting. The Chinese surpassed the rest of the world in technological invention and led global production in fine pottery and textiles. Even at the peak of productivity in medieval Europe, and especially between the years 1250 and 1350, China's technical sophistication, naval power, and cultural fertility exceeded that of any country in the West. Medieval Japan originated the world's oldest prose fiction and cultivated a style governed by beauty of effect in art and life. Deeply infused with the values of Buddhism and other Asian religions, the artistic record of India, China, and Japan provides a holistic view of nature that works broadly to universalize the human experience. A brief examination of these achievements puts our study of the humanistic tradition in a global perspective and provides a basis for the appreciation of three of Asia's most notable cultures.

(opposite) Standing Court Lady, Tang dynasty, mid-seventh century. Pottery with painted decoration, height 15⅛ in. The Metropolitan Museum of Art, New York. Anonymous gift, in memory Louise G. Dillingham, 1978 (1978.345). Photo: Lynton Gardiner, © 1989 The Metropolitan Museum of Art.

# 14

# Asian Civilizations:
# The Artistic Record

## The Medieval Period in India

Although the term "medieval" does not apply to the history of India in the Western sense of an interlude between classical and early modern times, scholars have used that term to designate the era between the end of the Gupta dynasty (ca. 500) and the Mongol conquest of India in the fourteenth century—a thousand-year period that roughly approximates the Western Middle Ages. The dissolution of the Gupta Empire at the hands of Central Asian Huns, an event that paralleled the fall of Rome in the West and the collapse of the Han Empire in China, destroyed the remains of South Asia's greatest culture. Following this event, amidst widespread political turmoil and anarchy, India became a conglomeration of fragmented, rival local kingdoms dominated by a warrior caste (not unlike the feudal aristocracy of medieval Europe). Ruling hereditary chiefs or *rajputs* ("sons of kings") followed a code of chivalry that set them apart from the lower classes. The caste system (see chapter 3), which had been practiced in India for many centuries, worked to enforce the distance between rulers and the ruled. And as groups were subdivided according to occupation and social status, caste distinctions became more rigid and increasingly fragmented. Extended families of the same caste were ruled by the eldest male, who might take a number of wives. Children were betrothed early in life and women's duties—to tend the household and raise children (preferably sons)—were carefully prescribed. In a society where males were masters, a favorite Hindu proverb ran, "A woman is never fit for independence." The devotion of the upper-caste Hindu woman to her husband was dramatically expressed in *sati*, a custom by which the wife threw herself on her mate's funeral pyre.

Early in the eighth century, Arab Muslims entered India and began to convert members of the native population to Islam. Muslim authority took hold in Northern India, and Muslims rose to power as members of the ruling caste. During the tenth century, the invasions of Turkish Muslims brought further chaos to India, resulting in the capture of Delhi (Map 14.1) in 1192 and the destruction of the Buddhist University of Nalanda in the following year. Muslim armies destroyed vast numbers of Hindu and Buddhist religious statues, which they regarded as idols, and Islam supplanted Hinduism and Buddhism in the Indus valley (modern Pakistan) and in Bengal (modern Bangladesh). Elsewhere,

Map 14.1 India in the Eleventh Century.

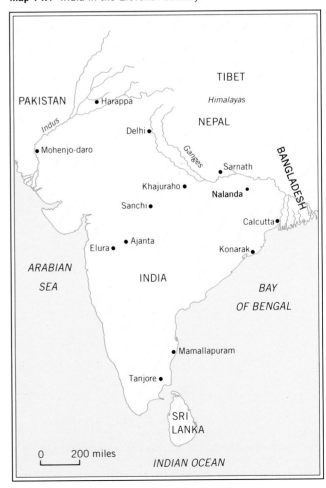

however, the native traditions of India and the Hindu religion itself prevailed. Indeed, most of India—especially the extreme south, which held out against the Muslims until the fourteenth century—remained profoundly devoted to the Hindu faith. Today, approximately eighty-five percent of India's population is Hindu. Buddhism, on the other hand, had virtually disappeared from India by the twelfth century.

## Hinduism in Medieval India

In the medieval period, the philosophic aspects of Hinduism (as defined in the principal religious writings, the *Upanishads* and the *Bhagavad-Gita*; see chapter 2) were overshadowed by growing devotion to the gods and goddesses of Hindu mythology. These personal deities, rooted in India's most ancient texts—the *Vedas*—are personifications of the powerful, life-giving forces of nature. Although the worship of them suggests that Hindus are polytheistic, it is more accurate to say that Hinduism, fundamentally pantheistic, perceives all of nature—divine, human, and animal—as one. At the very core of Indian civilization, Hinduism confirms the oneness of nature. It teaches that all individual aspects of being belong to the same divine substance: the impersonal, all-pervading Absolute Spirit known as Brahman. Hindus view regional deities and the gods of ancient India as **avatars** (Sanskrit, "incarnations") of Brahman, much in the way that Christians regard Jesus as the incarnate form of God. Indeed, since Hindus believe that the avatars of Brahman may assume different names and forms (even those of animals), they freely honor the Buddha and Jesus as human guises of the Divine Reality. Having no single founder, no spokesman, and no priesthood comparable with that of medieval Christianity, nor any uniform set of sacred practices, Hinduism encourages its devotees to seek union with Brahman in their own fashion, whether through meditation or by worshiping the many gods and spirits of Hindu myth and legend. The plural character of Hinduism contrasts sharply with Judaism, Christianity, and Islam, all of which hold divinity as a singular concept. The many gods of the Hindus—like the facets of a diamond—exist only, however, as individual aspects (or manifestations) of the Whole.

In medieval India, three principal gods dominated the Hindu pantheon: Brahma, Vishnu, and Shiva. Hindus associated this "trinity" with the three main expressions of Brahmanic power: creation, preservation, and destruction. They honored Brahma—his name is the masculine form of Brahman—as the creator of the world. They prized Vishnu (identified with the sun in ancient Vedic hymns) as the preserver god. Hindu mythology recounts Vishnu's appearance on earth in nine different incarnations, including that of Krishna,

the hero-god of the *Mahabharata* (see chapter 2). Icons of Vishnu often resemble those of the Buddha, who is accepted by Hindus as an avatar of Vishnu (Figure **14.1**). Such ritual images, cast in bronze by the lost-wax method (see chapter 1), are among the finest freestanding figural sculptures executed since golden-age Greece. Produced in large numbers in tenth-century Tamil Nadu in South India, bronze effigies of the god were often bedecked with flowers and carried in public processions. (Note the rings at the four corners of the base of the *Standing Vishnu*, which once held poles for transporting the statue.)

The third god of the trinity, Shiva, is the Hindu lord of fertility and regeneration. A god of destruction and creation, of disease and death, and of sexuality and rebirth, Shiva symbolizes the dynamic rhythms of the

**Figure 14.1** *Standing Vishnu*, from Southern India, Chola dynasty, tenth century C.E. Bronze, with greenish-blue patination, height 33¾ in. The Metropolitan Museum of Art, New York, Purchase 1962. Gift of Mr. and Mrs. John D. Rockefeller.

universe. While often shown in a dual male and female aspect, Shiva is most commonly portrayed as Lord of the Dance, an image that evokes the Hindu notion of time. Unlike the Western view of time, which is linear and progressive, the Hindu perception of time is cyclical; it moves like an ever-turning cosmic wheel. Hindus believe that the worship of Shiva and Vishnu, their avatars, and their female consorts is an expression of intense personal devotion by which one gains the blessing of the divine. Hindus perceive the god to be present in its representation; hence the act of worship puts one in direct physical and visual contact with the god: "Beholding the image is an act of worship."*

The four-armed figure of Shiva as Lord of the Dance is one of medieval India's most famous Hindu icons (Figure **14.2**)—so popular, in fact, that Tamil

*Diana L. Eck, *Darśan: Seeing the Divine Image in India*. Chambersburg, Pa.: Anima Books, 1981, 3.

sculptors cast multiple versions of the image. Framed in a celestial circle of fire, Shiva seems to gyrate, thus symbolizing cosmic creation and destruction, the living cycle of birth and death. His serpentine body bends at the neck, waist, and knees in accordance with specific and prescribed dance movements (Figure **14.3**). Every part of the statue has symbolic meaning: In one right hand Shiva carries a small drum, the symbol of creation; a second right hand (the arm wreathed by a snake, ancient symbol of regeneration) forms the *mudra* meaning protection (see chapter 9); one left hand holds a flame, the symbol of destruction; the second left hand points toward the feet, the left one "released" from the earth, the right one crushing a dwarf that symbolizes ignorance. Utterly peaceful in countenance, Shiva displays the five activities of the godhead: creation, protection, destruction, release from destiny, and enlightenment. By these activities, the god dances the universe in and out of existence.

**Figure 14.2** *Shiva Nataraja, Lord of the Dance*, from Southern India, Chola period, eleventh century. Copper, height 43⅞ in. The Cleveland Museum of Art. Purchase from the J. H. Wade Fund, 30.331.

**Figure 14.3** Temple sculptures. Classical dance postures, inspired by the *Karanas*, from the Devi temple, Chidambaram, India, thirteenth century.
© Government of India, Department of Archeology.

## Indian Religious Literature

Medieval Indian literature drew heavily on the mythology and legends of early Hinduism as found in the Vedic hymns and in India's two great epics, the *Mahabharata* and the *Ramayana* (see chapter 2). This body of classic Indian literature was recorded in Sanskrit, the language of India's educated classes. Serving much the same purpose that Latin served in the medieval West, Sanskrit functioned for centuries as a cohesive force amidst India's diverse groups of regional vernacular dialects.

Among the most popular forms of Hindu literature in the medieval period were the *Puranas* (Sanskrit, "old stories"), a collection of eighteen religious books that preserved the myths and legends of the Hindu gods. Many of the tales in the *Puranas* illustrate the special powers of Vishnu and Shiva or their avatars. In the *Vishnu Purana*, for instance, Krishna is pictured as a lover who courts his devotees with sensual abandon, seducing them to become one with the divinity. In contrast to medieval Christianity's somber condemnation of the sensual life, Hinduism regards the physical union of male and female as symbolic of the eternal mingling of flesh and spirit, a sublime metaphor for the fusion of the Self (Atman) and the Absolute Spirit (Brahman) that culminates in *nirvana*. The *Upanishads* make clear the analogy:

> In the embrace of his beloved a man forgets the whole world—everything both within and without. In the same manner, he who embraces the Self knows neither within nor without.

The Hindu view of human sexuality as a metaphor for spiritual knowledge recalls the rituals of pre-Christian fertility cults, which exalted the life-affirming and regenerative aspects of erotic love. In the following passage from the *Vishnu Purana*, Krishna's cajoling and sensuous courtship, culminating in the circle of the dance, symbolizes the god's love for the human soul and the soul's unswerving attraction to the One.

### READING 2.21

## From the *Vishnu Purana*

. . . [Krishna], observing the clear sky, bright with the       1
autumnal moon, and the air perfumed with the fragrance
of the wild water-lily, in whose buds the clustering bees
were murmuring their songs, felt inclined to join with the
milkmaids [Gopis] in sport. . . .

Then Madhava [Krishna], coming amongst them,
conciliated some with soft speeches, some with gentle
looks; and some he took by the hand: and the illustrious
deity sported with them in the stations of the dance. As
each of the milkmaids, however, attempted to keep in one      10
place, close to the side of Krishna, the circle of the dance
could not be constructed; and he, therefore, took each by
the hand, and when their eyelids were shut by the effects
of such touch, the circle was formed. Then proceeded the
dance, to the music of their clashing bracelets, and songs
that celebrated, in suitable strain, the charms of the
autumnal season. Krishna sang of the moon of autumn—
a mine of gentle radiance; but the nymphs repeated the
praises of Krishna alone. At times, one of them, wearied
by the revolving dance, threw her arms, ornamented with    20
tinkling bracelets, round the neck of the destroyer of
Madhu [Krishna]; another, skilled in the art of singing his
praises, embraced him. The drops of perspiration from the
arms of Hari [Krishna] were like fertilizing rain, which
produced a crop of down upon the temples of the
milkmaids. Krishna sang the strain that was appropriate to
the dance. The milkmaids repeatedly exclaimed "Bravo,
Krishna!" to his song. When leading, they followed him;
when returning they encountered him; and whether he
went forwards or backwards, they ever attended on his      30
steps. Whilst frolicking thus, they considered every instant
without him a myriad of years; and prohibited (in vain) by
husbands, fathers, brothers, they went forth at night to
sport with Krishna, the object of their affection.

Thus, the illimitable being, the benevolent remover of
all imperfections, assumed the character of a youth
among the females of the herdsmen of [the district of]
Vraja; pervading their natures and that of their lords by
his own essence, all-diffusive like the wind. For even as
the elements of ether, fire, earth, water, and air are      40
comprehended in all creatures, so also is he everywhere
present, and in all. . . .

———————◆———————

## Indian Poetry

If the religious literature of India is sensuous in nature,
so too is the secular literature, much of which is devoted
to physical pleasure. Sanskrit lyric poetry is the most
erotic of all world literatures. Unlike the poetry of other
ancient cultures, that of India was meant to be spoken,
not sung. On the other hand, Sanskrit poetry shares
with most ancient Greek and Latin verse a lack of
rhyme. It also exploits such literary devices as **alliteration** (the repetition of initial sounds in successive words,
as in "panting and pale") and **assonance** (similarity
between vowel sounds, as in "lake" and "fate").

In Sanskrit verse, implication and innuendo are
more important than direct statement or assertion. The
multiplicity of synonyms in Sanskrit permits a wide
range of meanings, puns, and verbal play. And although
this wealth of synonyms and near-synonyms contributes to the richness of Indian poetry, it makes English translation quite difficult. For example, there are
some fifty expressions in Sanskrit for "lotus"; in English
there is but one. Sanskrit poets employ a large number
of stock similes: The lady's face is like the moon, her
eyes resemble lotuses, and so on. Sanskrit poems are
rarely intimate or personal; rather, they describe general
and universal conditions. But classical rules of style dictate that every poem must exhibit a single characteristic
sentiment, such as anger, courage, wonder, or passion.
Grief, however—the emotion humans seek to avoid—
may not dominate any poem or play.

A great flowering of Indian literature occurred
between the fourth and tenth centuries, but it was not
until the eleventh century and thereafter that the
renowned anthologies of Sanskrit poetry appeared. One
of the most honored of these collections, an anthology
of 1,739 verses dating from between 700 and 1050, was
produced by the twelfth-century Buddhist monk
Vidyakara. It is entitled *The Treasury of Well-Turned Verse*.
As with most Indian anthologies, poems on the subject
of love outnumber those in any other category, and
many of the love lyrics feature details of physical passion.
As suggested by the selection that follows, Indian poetry
is more frank and erotic than ancient or medieval European love poetry and less concerned with the romantic
aspects of courtship than most Islamic verse.

### READING 2.22

## From *The Treasury of Well-Turned Verse*

**"When we have loved, my love"**

When we have loved, my love,
Panting and pale from love,
Then from your cheeks my love,
Scent of the sweat I love:
And when our bodies love
Now to relax in love
After the stress of love,
Ever still more I love
Our mingled breath of love.

**"When he desired to see her breast"**

When he desired to see her breast
She clasped him tight in an embrace;
And when he wished to kiss her lip
She used cosmetics on her face.
She held his hand quite firmly pressed
Between her thighs in desperate grip;
    Nor yielded to his caress,
    Yet kept alive his wantonness.

**"If my absent bride were but a pond"**

If my absent bride were but a pond,
her eyes the water lilies and her face the lotus,
her brows the rippling waves, her arms the lotus stems;
then might I dive into the water of her loveliness
and cool of limb escape the mortal pain
exacted by the flaming fire of love.

————————— ◆ —————————

## Indian Architecture

The medieval period generated some of the finest works of Hindu art and architecture in India's long history. Buddhist imagery influenced the style of medieval Hindu art, and Buddhist rock-cut temples and shrines provided models for Hindu architects. Between the sixth and fourteenth centuries, Hindus built thousands of temple-shrines to honor Vishnu and Shiva. These structures varied in shape from region to region, but generally they took the shape of a mound (often square or rectangular) topped with lofty towers or spires. Such structures were built of stone or brick with iron dowels frequently substituting for mortar. As with the early Buddhist *stupa* (see Figure 9.21), the medieval Hindu temple symbolized the sacred mountain. Some temples were even painted white to resemble the snowy peaks of the Himalayas. The Buddhist *stupa* was invariably a solid mound; however, the Hindu temple, more akin to the *chaitya* hall (see Figures 9.22. 9.23), enclosed a series of interior spaces leading to a shrine—the dwelling place of the god on earth. Devotees entered the temple by way of an ornate porch or series of porches, each porch having its own roof and spire. Beyond these areas stood a large hall designed for sacred dancing, and, finally, the dim, womb-like sanctuary that enshrined the cult image of the god. The Hindu temple did not serve as a place for congregational worship (as did the medieval church); rather, it functioned as a place of private, individual devotion, a place in which the devotee might contemplate or make offerings to the god. The design of the Hindu temple is based on a cosmic diagram and governed by divine numerology. The sacred square or womb at the center is the primordial Brahman; the surrounding squares correspond to the protective gods. Although the Hindu temple and the Gothic cathedral were very different in terms of design and building function, both signified the profoundly human impulse to forge a link between Heaven and earth and between matter and spirit.

499 Indian mathematicians complete a compilation of known mathematical and astronomical principles
ca. 600 the decimal system is in use in India
876 the symbol for "zero" is first used in India

**Figure 14.4** Kandariya Mahadeo temple, Khajuraho, India, ca. 1000. Height approx. 102 ft. Archeological Survey of India. Reproduced by courtesy of the British Library, London.

**Figure 14.5** Plan of Kandariya Mahadeo temple, Khajuraho.

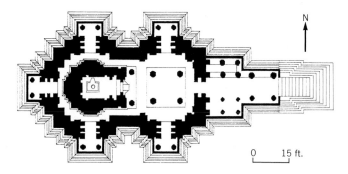

0    15 ft.

The Kandariya Mahadeo temple in Khajuraho is but one of twenty-five remaining Hindu temple-shrines that rise like stone mountains out of the dusty plains of Central North India (see Map 14.1). Dedicated in the early eleventh century to the god Shiva, the temple rests on a high masonry terrace and is entered through an elevated porch (Figures **14.4**, **14.5**). Like most Indian temples, Kandariya Mahadeo consists of a series of extensively ornamented horizontal cornices that ascend in narrowing diameter to their lotus-shaped peaks. At each tier of the beehivelike tower is a row of figures: Human beings and animals drawn from India's great epics appear at the lower levels, while divine nymphs and celestial deities adorn the upper sections. The ensemble consists of a total of some six hundred figures (Figure **14.6**).

Like the Gothic cathedral, the Hindu temple hosted a multitude of high-relief sculptures that covered almost

**Figure 14.6** Celestial deities, ca. 1000. Stone. Kandariya Mahadeo temple, Khajuraho. Photo: © Richard Lucas/The Image Works, Inc.

the entire building to create a richly textured surface. Yet conceptually, no two artistic enterprises could have been further apart: Whereas the medieval Church discouraged the representation of nudity as symbolic of sexual pleasure and sinfulness, Hinduism exalted the human body as symbolic of abundance, prosperity, and regeneration. The sinuous nudes that animate the surface of the Kandariya Mahadeo temple assume languid, erotic poses. Deeply carved, and endowed with supple limbs and swelling breasts and buttocks, their bodies signify the divine attributes of life breath and "fullness." The loving couples (known as *mithunas*)—men and women locked in passionate embrace (Figure 14.7)—call to mind the imagery of the dance in the *Vishnu Purana*, symbolic of regenerative bliss and the ultimate oneness of human and divine energy.

## Indian Music and Dance

As noted in chapter 9, the music of India is inseparable from religious practice. Moreover, a single musical tradition—one that goes back some three thousand years—dominates both secular and religious music. In ancient times, India developed a system of music

**Figure 14.7** *Mithuna* couple, from Orissa, India, twelfth–thirteenth centuries. Stone, height 6 ft. The Metropolitan Museum of Art, New York. Florence Waterbury Fund, 1970.

**Figure 14.8** Ravi Shankar playing the sitar (right); others with tabla (hand drums) and tamboura (plucked string instrument). Photo:. © Silverstone/Magnum Photos, Inc.

characterized by specific melodic forms (*ragas*) and rhythms (*talas*). The centuries have produced thousands of *ragas*, sixty of which remain in standard use; nine are considered primary. Each *raga* comprises a series of seven basic notes arranged in a specific order. The performer may improvise on a chosen *raga* in any manner and at any length. As with the Greek modes (see chapter 6), each of the basic Indian *ragas* is associated with a different emotion, mood, or time of day. A famous Indian anecdote tells how a sixteenth-century court musician, entertaining at midday, once sang a night *raga* so beautiful that darkness instantly fell where he stood. Governing the rhythmic pattern of an Indian musical composition is the *tala* which, in union with the *raga*, shapes the mood of the piece. Indian music divides the octave into twenty-two principal tones and many more microtones, all of which are treated equally. There is, therefore, no tonal center and no harmony in traditional Indian music. Rather, the character of a musical composition depends on the choice of the *raga* and upon its exposition. A typical *raga* opens with a slow portion that establishes a particular mood, moves into a second portion that explores rhythmic variations, and closes with rapid, complex, and often syncopated improvisations that culminate in a frenzied finale.⸹

India developed a broad range of stringed instruments that were either bowed or plucked. The most popular of these was the **sitar**, a long-necked stringed instrument with a gourd resonator, which came into use during the thirteenth century (Figure 14.8). Related to the cithara, an instrument used in ancient Greece (see chapter 6), the sitar provided a distinctive rhythmic "drone," while its strings were plucked for melody. Accompanied by flutes, drums, bells, and horns, sitar players were fond of improvising patterns of notes in quick succession against a resonating bass sound.

The Sanskrit word for music (*sangeeta*) means both "sound" and "rhythm," suggesting that the music of India, like that of ancient Greece, was inseparable from the art of the dance. Indian dance, like the *raga* that

accompanied it, set a mood or told a story by way of rigidly observed steps and hand gestures (*mudra*). India trained professional dancers to achieve difficult leg and foot positions (see Figure 14.3), some of which may be seen on the facades of Indian temples (see Figure 14.6). Each of some thirty traditional dances requires a combination of complex body positions, of which there are more than one hundred. The close relationship among the arts of medieval India provides something of a parallel with the achievement of the medieval synthesis in the West. On the other hand, the sensual character of the arts of India distinguishes them sharply from the arts of Christian Europe.

## The Medieval Period in China

Nowhere else in the world has a single cultural tradition dominated so consistently over so long a period as in China. When European merchants visited China in the thirteenth century, the Chinese had already enjoyed 1,700 years of civilization. China's agrarian landmass, rich in vast mineral, vegetable, and animal resources, readily supported a large and self-sufficient population, the majority of which constituted a massive land-bound peasantry. Despite internal shifts of power and repeated barbarian attacks, China experienced a single form of government—imperial monarchy—and a large degree of political order until the invasion of the Mongols in the thirteenth century. But even after the establishment of Mongol rule under Kublai Khan (1215–1294), the governmental bureaucracy on which China had long depended remained intact, and Chinese culture continued to flourish. The wealth and splendor of early fourteenth-century China inspired the awe and admiration of Western visitors, such as the famous Venetian merchant-adventurer Marco Polo (1254–1342). Indeed, in the two centuries prior to Europe's rise to economic dominion (but especially between 1250 and 1350), China was "the most extensive, populous, and technologically advanced region of the medieval world."*

---

⸹See Music Listening Selections at end of chapter.

*Janet L. Abu-Lughod, *Before European Hegemony: The World System A.D. 1250–1350*. New York: Oxford University Press, 1989, 316.

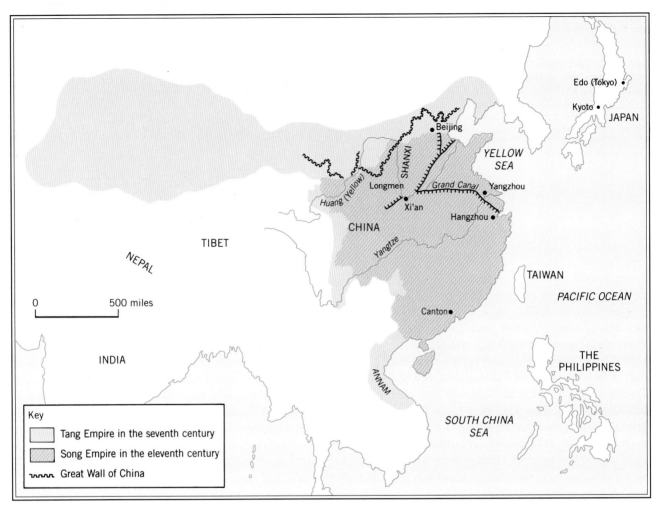

**Map 14.2** East Asia.

## China During the Tang Era

Tang China (618–907 C.E.) was a unified, centralized state that had no equal in India or the West. In contrast with India, class distinctions in China were flexible and allowed a fair degree of social mobility: Even commoners could rise to become members of the ruling elite. Nevertheless, as in all Asian and European civilizations of premodern times, the great masses of Chinese peasants had no voice in political matters.

Despite the success of Buddhism in China (see chapters 8 and 9), Confucianism remained China's foremost moral philosophy. Confucian teachings encouraged social harmony and respect for the ruling monarch, whom the Chinese called the "Son of Heaven." The Confucian equation of virtue and authority, which linked the destiny of the community with the ruler's obedience to moral law (see chapter 3), and Confucian respect for the universal order (expressed in the creative interaction of *yin* and *yang*) were humanizing forces in Chinese culture. Confucianism was generally tolerant of all religious creeds, though it disapproved of the Buddhist commitment to celibacy, which contravened the Confucian esteem for family. The growth of Buddhist sects and the popularity of a religion that attracted large

numbers of talented men to the cloister encouraged eighth-century emperors to restrict the number of Buddhist monasteries and to limit the ordination of new monks and nuns. In contrast to medieval Europe, however, where transcendental Christianity guided the soul's journey to the hereafter, China held firmly to a secular ethic that emphasized proper conduct (*li*) and the sanctity of human life on earth. These Confucian tenets—renewed in the neo-Confucian movement of the eleventh century—challenged neither the popular worship of a large number of Chinese nature deities nor ancient rites that honored the souls of the dead. Likewise, Confucian ideals of order, harmony, and filial duty were easily reconciled with holistic Daoism (see chapter 2). Tolerant of all religions, the Chinese never engaged in religious wars or massive crusades of the kind that disrupted both Christian and Islamic civilizations.

| | |
|---|---|
| **700** | the Chinese perfect the making of porcelain, which reaches Europe as "china" |
| **725** | the Chinese build a water clock with a regulating device anticipating mechanical clocks |
| **748** | the first printed newspaper appears in Beijing |
| **868** | the *Diamond Sutra*, the first known printed book, is produced |

Under the rule of the Tang emperors, China experienced a flowering of culture that was unmatched anywhere in the world. Often called the greatest dynasty in Chinese history, the Tang brought unity and wealth to a vast Chinese empire (Map 14.2). Tang emperors perpetuated the economic policies of their immediate predecessors, but they employed their vast powers to achieve a remarkable series of reforms. They completed the Grand Canal connecting the lower valley of the Yellow River to the eastern banks of the Yangzi, a project that facilitated shipping and promoted internal cohesion and wealth. They initiated a full census of the population (some four centuries before a similar survey was undertaken in Norman England), which was repeated every three years. They also humanized the penal code and tried to guarantee farmlands to the peasants. They stimulated agricultural production, encouraged the flourishing silk trade, launched a tax reform that based assessments on units of land rather than agricultural output, and they commuted payments from goods to coins.

The Tang Empire dwarfed the Carolingian Empire in the West not only by its geographic size and population but also by its intellectual and educational accomplishments. Tang bureaucrats, steeped in Confucian traditions and rigorously trained in the literary classics, were members of an intellectual elite that rose to service on the basis of merit. Beginning in the seventh century (but rooted in a long tradition of leadership based on education and ability), every government official was subject to a rigorous civil service examination. A young man gained a political position by passing three levels of examinations (district, provincial, and national) that tested his familiarity with the Chinese classics as well as his grasp of contemporary political issues. For lower-ranking positions, candidates took exams in law, mathematics, and calligraphy. As in the Islamic world and the Christian West, higher education in China required close familiarity with the basic religious and philosophical texts. But because Chinese characters changed very little over the centuries, students could read 1,500-year-old texts as easily as they could read contemporary ones. Chinese classics were thus accessible to Chinese scholars in a way that the Greco-Roman classics were not accessible to Western scholars. Training for the arduous civil service examinations required a great degree of memorization and a thorough knowledge of the Chinese literary tradition, but originality was also important: Candidates had to prove accomplishment in the writing of prose and poetry, as well as in the analysis of administrative policy. Strict standards applied to grading, and candidates who failed the exams (only one to ten percent passed the first level) could take them over and over, even into their middle and old age.

During the seventh century, the imperial college in the capital city of Chang'an (present-day Xi'an) prepared some three thousand men for the civil service examinations. (As in the West, women were excluded from education in colleges and universities.) Such scholar

**Figure 14.9** Attributed to the Song emperor Huizong (reigned 1101–1125), but probably by court academician, after a lost painting by Zhang Xuan (fl. 713–741 C.E.), Women Combing Silk, detail of *Court Ladies Preparing Newly Woven Silk*, Northern Song dynasty, early twelfth century. Ink, color, and gold on silk handscroll, height 14½ in., length 57¼ in. Courtesy, Museum of Fine Arts, Boston. Chinese and Japanese Special Fund.

officials constituted China's highest social class. And while the vast population of Chinese peasants lived in relative ignorance and poverty, the aristocratic bureaucracy of the Tang generally enjoyed lives of wealth and position. Nowhere else in the world (except perhaps Baghdad) was such prestige attached to scholarship and intellectual achievement. Despite instances in which family connections influenced political position, the imperial examination system remained the main route to official status in China well into the twentieth century.

Another traditional Chinese practice survived into the modern period: the binding of women's feet. From earliest times, Chinese women participated in agricultural activities as well as in the manufacture of silk (Figure 14.9); many were trained in dance and musical performance (Figure 14.10). In the early 900s, however, as women seem to have assumed a more ornamental role in Chinese society, footbinding became common among the upper classes. To indicate that their female offspring were exempt from common labor, prosperous urban families bound the feet of their infant daughters—a practice that broke the arch and dwarfed the foot to half its normal growth. Footbinding, a cruel means of signifying social status, persisted into the early twentieth century.

## China in the Song Era

After a brief period of political turmoil resulting from the attacks of nomadic tribes, the Song dynasty (960–1279) restored stability to China. The three centuries of Song rule corresponded roughly to the golden age of Muslim learning, the waning of the Abbasid Empire and the era of Norman domination in Europe

| | | |
|---|---|---|
| 1000 | the magnetic needle compass is developed in China |
| 1009 | the Chinese first use coal as fuel |
| ca. 1040 | three varieties of gunpowder are described by Zeng Kongliang |
| 1041 | movable type is utilized in China |

(see chapters 10, 11). The Song Era was a period of population growth, agricultural productivity, and vigorous commercial trade centering on the exportation of tea, silk, and porcelain. China's new economic prosperity caused a population shift from the countryside to the city, where social mobility was on the rise. The port city of Hangzhou (see Map 14.2), with a population of almost two million people, boasted a variety of restaurants, teahouses, temples, gardens, and shops, including bookstores and pet shops (Figure 14.11). Chinese cities were larger and more populous than those in the West and city dwellers enjoyed conditions of safety that are enviable even today—in Hangzhou, the streets were patrolled at night, and bridges and canals were guarded and fitted with balustrades to prevent drunken revelers from falling into the water.

Although the Song Era was a time of peace, a ready army was a necessity. However, mercenaries came to replace peasant-soldiers in the ranks. Whereas medieval Islam and the feudal West prized heroism and the art of war, the Chinese despised military life. A Chinese proverb claimed that "superior" men should no more serve as soldiers than high-grade iron should serve to forge common nails. Chinese poets frequently lamented the disruption of family life as soldiers left home to defend remote

**Figure 14.10** Attributed to Zhou Wenju, detail of a girls' ensemble performing court banquet music during the reign of Emperor Xuanzong, with (upper group, left to right) lute, angular harp, long zither, stone-chime, mouth organ, hourglass drum, transverse flute, and clapper, Song dynasty. Ink and color on silk handscroll, 16⅜ in. × 71⅞ in. The Art Institute of Chicago. Kate S. Buckingham Purchase Fund, 1950. Photograph © 1998 The Art Institute of Chicago. All rights reserved.

**Figure 14.11** *Lady Wenqi's Return to China*, Northern Song dynasty, ca. 1100. Ink, gold, and color on silk. The Museum of Fine Arts, Boston. Denman Waldo Ross Collection. © 1998. All rights reserved.

regions of the Empire. In combat, the Chinese generally preferred starving out their enemies to confronting them in battle. The peaceful nature of the Chinese impressed its first Western visitors: Arriving in China a half century after the end of the Song Era, Marco Polo observed with some astonishment that no one carried arms.

## Technology in the Tang and Song Eras

Chinese civilization is exceptional in the extraordinary number of its technological inventions, many of which came into use elsewhere in the world only long after their utilization in China. A case in point is printing, which originated in ninth-century China but was not perfected in the West until the fifteenth century. The earliest printed document, the *Diamond Sutra*, dated 868, is a Buddhist text produced from large woodcut blocks (Figure **14.12**). In the mid-eleventh century, the Chinese invented movable type and, by the end of the century, the entire body of Buddhist and Confucian classics, including the commentaries, were available in printed editions. One such classic (a required text for civil service candidates) was *The Book of Songs*, a venerable collection of over three hundred poems dating from the first millennium B.C.E. By the twelfth century, the Chinese were also printing paper money—a practice that inevitably gave rise to the "profession" of counterfeiting. Although in China movable type did not inspire a revolution in the communication of ideas (as it would in Renaissance Europe), it encouraged literacy, fostered scholarship, and facilitated the preservation of the Chinese classics.

Chinese technology often involved the intelligent application of natural principles to produce labor-saving devices. Examples include the water mill (devised to grind tea leaves and to provide power to run machinery), the wheelbarrow (used in China from at least the third century but not found in Europe until more than ten centuries later), and the stern-post rudder and magnetic compass (Song inventions that facilitated maritime trade). The latter two devices had revolutionary consequences for Western Europeans, who used them to inaugurate an age of exploration and discovery (see chapter 19). Gunpowder, invented by the Chinese as early as the seventh century and used in firework displays, was employed (in the form of fire-arrow incendiary devices) for military purposes in the mid-tenth century, but arrived in the West only in the fourteenth century. Other contrivances, such as the abacus and the hydro-mechanical clock, and such processes as iron-casting (used for armaments, for suspension bridges, and for the construction of some Tang and Song pagodas) were unknown in the West for centuries or were invented independently of Chinese prototypes. Not until the eighteenth century, for instance, did Western Europeans master the technique of steel-casting, which had been in use in China since the sixth century C.E.; and the seismograph (invented in China around 100 B.C.E.) remained unknown to Europe until modern times.

Some of China's most important technological contributions, such as the foot stirrup (in use well before the fifth century) and gunpowder, improved China's ability to withstand the attacks of Huns, Turks, and other tribal peoples who repeatedly attacked China's northern frontiers. In the West, however, the foot stirrup and gunpowder had revolutionary results: The former ushered in the military aspect of medieval feudalism; and the latter ultimately undermined siege warfare and inaugurated modern forms of combat. While thirteenth-century China was far ahead of the medieval

**Figure 14.12** The *Diamond Sutra*, the world's earliest printed book, dated 868 C.E. 72 × 30 in. Reproduced by courtesy of the British Library, London. Department of Oriental Manuscripts and Books.

West in science and technology, its wealth in manpower—a population of some hundred million people—may have made a technology of industrial power (like that pursued in the early modern West) unnecessary.

In addition to being ingenious in engineering and metallurgy, the Chinese were in the forefront in the practice of medicine. From the eleventh century on, they used vaccination to prevent diseases, thus establishing the science of immunology. Their understanding of human anatomy and their assumption that illness derives from an imbalance of *qi* (life energy) gave rise to acupuncture—the practice of applying needles to specific parts of the body to regulate and restore proper energy flow. Chinese medical encyclopedias dating from the twelfth century were far in advance of any produced in the medieval West. In both India and China, the belief that the mind and the body are one generated healing practices (such as meditation and yoga) that have met positive reception in the West only in recent decades.

| | | |
|---|---|---|
| | **1045** | the Chinese perform the first anatomical dissection of the human body |
| | **1100** | the Chinese use coke in iron smelting |
| | **1145** | illustrations of the internal organs and circulatory vessels are published in China |
| | **1221** | the Chinese devise shrapnel bombs with gunpowder |

## Chinese Literature

Chinese literature owes little to other cultures. It reflects at every turn a high regard for native traditions and for the concepts of universal harmony expressed in Confucian and Daoist thought. Philosophic in nature, it is, however, markedly free of religious sentiment. Even between the fifth and ninth centuries, when Buddhism was at its height in China, Chinese literature was largely secular, hence very different from most of the writings of medieval Europe and the rest of Asia.

The literature of the Tang and Song eras embraced a wide variety of genres including treatises on history, geography, religion, economics, and architecture; monographs on botany and zoology; essays on administrative and governmental affairs; drama, fiction, and lyric poetry. Experts in the art of compiling information, the Chinese produced a vast assortment of encyclopedias, manuals of divination and ritual, ethical discourses, and anthologies based on the teachings of Confucius and others. Like the medieval scholastics in the West, Chinese scholars esteemed their classical past, but, unlike the Europeans, they acknowledged no conflict between (and therefore no need to reconcile) faith and reason.

During the twelfth and thirteenth centuries, in Song urban centers, storytelling flourished, and popular theater arose in the form of dramatic performance. Popular genres included comedy, historical plays, and tales of everyday life—many of which featured love stories. As dramatists began to adapt literary plots to music, **opera** (musical drama)† became the fashionable entertainment among ordinary townspeople and at the imperial court. The first Chinese **novels**—products of a long tradition of oral narrative—also appeared during the twelfth century, their themes focusing on the adventures of contemporary heroes.

The novel, however, was not original to China. Rather, it was a product of the aristocratic and feudal culture of medieval Japan (discussed later in this chapter). In China, early fiction writing reached a high point with the monumental historical novel entitled *Three Kingdoms* (attributed to the fourteenth-century playwright Luo Guanzhong). This one thousand-page work, filled with hundreds of characters and lengthy, epic descriptions of martial prowess, brings alive the turbulent era that followed the breakup of the Han dynasty (168–265 C.E.).

## Chinese Music and Poetry

To the Chinese, music functioned to imitate and sustain the harmony of nature (see chapter 7). Both Daoists and Confucians regarded music as an expression of cosmic order, and Daoists even made distinctions between *yin* and *yang* notes. Like most of the music of the ancient world, that of China was monophonic, but it assumed a unique timbre produced by nasal tones that were often high in pitch and subtle in inflection. The sliding nasal tones that typify Chinese music resemble those of the zither. Frequently used for Buddhist chant (see chapter 9), the zither was the favorite Chinese instrument, and musical notation to guide the performer was devised as early as the second century B.C.E. The Chinese employed the zither, along with the short-necked lute and various flutes, bells, and chimes in instrumental ensembles (see Figure 14.10). But the most popular Chinese musical genre was the solo song, performed with or without instrumental accompaniment.

A close kinship between Chinese music and speech was enforced by the unique nature of the Chinese language. Consisting of some fifty thousand characters, it demands subtle intonations of its speaker: The pitch or tonal level at which any word is pronounced gives it its meaning. A single word, depending on how it is uttered, may have more than a hundred meanings. In this sense, all communication in the Chinese language is musical—a phenomenon that has particular importance for Chinese poetry. Chinese poetry is a kind of vocal music: A line of spoken poetry is—like music—essentially a series of tones that rise and fall in various rhythms. Moreover,

since Chinese is a monosyllabic language with few word endings, rhyme is common to speech. All Chinese verse is rhymed, often in long runs that are almost impossible to imitate in English. And, finally, it is characterized by extraordinary kinds of condensation and innuendo that most English translations cannot capture.

During the Tang Era, China produced some of the most beautiful poetry in world literature. The poems of the eighth and ninth centuries—an era referred to as the golden age of Chinese poetry—resemble diary entries that record the intimate experience of everyday life. Unlike the poetry of India, Chinese lyrics are rarely sensuous or erotic and only infrequently attentive to either physical affection or romantic love. Restrained and sophisticated, the poetry of the Tang period was written by scholar-poets (the so-called *literati*) who considered verse making, along with calligraphy and painting, the mark of educated and intellectual refinement. From earliest times, nature and natural imagery played a large part in Chinese verse. Tang poets continued this long tradition: Their poems are filled with the meditative spirit of Daoism and a sense of oneness with nature.

Two of the greatest poets of the Tang period, Li Bo (ca. 700–762) and Du Fu (712–770), belonged to the group of cultivated individuals who made up China's cultural elite. Although Li Bo was not a scholar-official, as was his friend Du Fu, he was familiar with the Chinese classics. Both Li Bo and Du Fu were members of the Eight Immortals of the Wine Cup, an informal association of poets who celebrated the kinship of ink and drink and the value of inebriation to poetic inspiration. Du Fu, often regarded as China's greatest poet, wrote some 1,400 poems, many of which are autobiographical reflections that impart genuine emotion and humor. In contrast with these Tang poets, the ninth-century poet Bo Zhu-yi, who headed the Bureau of War, brought to his poetry a note of cynicism and worldliness that is particularly typical of the Song Era. Like most of the poets of his time, he was a statesman, a calligrapher, an aesthetician, and a moralist. He thus epitomized the ideal well-rounded individual long before that concept became important among Renaissance Europeans.

## READING 2.23
### Poems of the Tang and Song Eras

**Li Bo's "Watching the Mount Lushan Waterfall"**

| | |
|---|---:|
| Incense-Burner Peak shimmers in the sun, | 1 |
| Purple mist slowly rising. | |
| A flying stream, seen from below, | |
| Hangs like clouds down the crag. | |
| The waterfall pours itself | 5 |
| Three thousand feet straight down, | |
| Roaring like the Milky Way | |
| Tumbling from high heaven. | |

†See Music Listening Selections at end of chapter.

**Figure 14.13** Mi Yujen, *Cloudy Mountains*, 1130. Ink, white lead, and slight touches of color on silk handscroll, 13 ft. 6 in. × 6 ft. 3 in. The Cleveland Musuem of Art. Purchase from the J. H. Wade Fund.

### Li Bo's "Zhuang Zhou and the Butterfly"

Zhuang Zhou[1] in dream became a butterfly,                    1
And the butterfly became Zhuang Zhou at waking.
Which was the real—the butterfly or the man?
Who can tell the end of the endless changes of things?
The water that flows into the depth of the distant sea        5
Returns anon to the shallows of a transparent stream.
The man, raising melons outside the green gate of the city,
Was once the Prince of the East Hill,[2]
So must rank and riches vanish.
You know it, still you toil and toil,—What for?                10

### Du Fu's "Spring Rain"

Oh lovely spring rain!                                         1
You come at the right time, in the right season.
Riding the night winds you creep in,
Quietly wetting the world.
Roads are dark, clouds are darker.                            5
Only a light on a boat, gleaming.
And in the morning the city is drunk with red flowers,
Cluster after cluster, moist, glistening.

### Du Fu's "Farewell Once More"
### (To my friend Yan at Feng Ji Station)

Here we part.                                                  1
You go off in the distance,
And once more the forested mountains
Are empty, unfriendly.
What holiday will see us                                      5
Drunk together again?
Last night we walked
Arm in arm in the moonlight,
Singing sentimental ballads
Along the banks of the river.                                 10
Your honor outlasts three emperors.
I go back to my lonely house by the river,
Mute, friendless, feeding the crumbling years.

### Bo Zhu-yi's "On His Baldness"

At dawn I sighed to see my hairs fall;                        1
At dusk I sighed to see my hairs fall.
For I dreaded the time when the last lock should go . . .
They are all gone and I do not mind at all!
I have done with that cumbrous washing and getting dry;       5
My tiresome comb forever is laid aside.
Best of all, when the weather is hot and wet,
To have no topknot weighing down on one's head!
I put aside my dusty conical cap;
And loose my collar fringe,                                   10
In a silver jar I have stored a cold stream;
On my bald pate I trickle a ladle-full.
Like one baptized with the Water of Buddha's Law,
I sit and receive this cool, cleansing joy.
*Now* I know why the priest who seeks repose                  15
Frees his heart by first shaving his head.

### Bo Zhu-yi's "Madly Singing in the Mountains"

There is no one among men that has not a special failing:     1
And my failing consists in writing verses.
I have broken away from the thousand ties of life:
But this infirmity still remains behind.
Each time that I look at a fine landscape:                    5
Each time that I meet a loved friend,
I raise my voice and recite a stanza of poetry
And am glad as though a god had crossed my path.
Ever since the day I was banished to Xunyang
Half my time I have lived among the hills.                    10
And often, when I have finished a new poem,
Alone I climb the road to the Eastern Rock.
I lean my body on the banks of white stone:
I pull down with my hands a green cassia[1] branch.
My mad singing startles the valleys and hills:               15
The apes and birds all come to peep.
Fearing to become a laughing-stock to the world,
I choose a place that is unfrequented by men.

———————————◆———————————

[1]A fourth-century follower of Laozi (see chapter 2), whose writings describe how, in a dream, he became a butterfly.
[2]The Marquis of Dongling, a third-century-B.C.E. official, lost his exalted position at court after the fall of the Qin dynasty, and retired to grow melons outside of the city of Chang'an.

[1]A tree whose bark is used as a source of cinnamon.

## Chinese Landscape Painting

During the Tang Era, figural subjects dominated Chinese art (see Figure 14.9), but by the tenth century, landscape painting became the favorite genre. The Chinese, and especially the *literati* of Song China, referred to landscape paintings as wordless poems and poems as formless paintings; such metaphors reflect the intimate relationship between painting and poetry in Chinese art. In subjects dealing with the natural landscape, both Chinese paintings and Chinese poems seek to evoke a mood rather than provide a literal, objective description of reality. Chinese landscapes work to convey a spirit of harmony between heaven and earth. This cosmic approach to nature, fundamental to both Daoism and Buddhism, asks the beholder to contemplate, rather than simply to view the painted image. The contemplative landscape may require the beholder to integrate multiple viewpoints, and to shift between foreground, middleground, and background in ways that resemble the mental shifts employed in reading lines of poetry.

Chinese paintings generally assume one of three basic formats: the handscroll, the hanging scroll, or the album leaf (often used as a fan). Between one and forty feet long, the handscroll is viewed continuously from right to left (Figure **14.13**). Like a poem, the visual "action" unfolds in time—an object of lingering contemplation and delight. The hanging scroll, on the other hand, is vertical in format and is meant to be read from the bottom up—from earth to heaven, so to speak (see Figure **14.14**). The album leaf usually belongs to a book that combines poems and paintings in a sequence. Both leaves and scrolls are made of silk or paper and ornamented with ink or thin washes of paint applied in monochrome or in muted colors. An interesting Chinese practice is the addition of the seals or signatures of collectors who have owned the work of art. These appear along with occasional marginal comments or brief poems inspired by the visual image. The poem may also serve as an extension of the content of the work of art. The Chinese painting, then, is a repository of the personal expressions of both artist and art lover.

By comparison with medieval and Renaissance art in the West, much of which is religious in subject matter, Chinese painting draws heavily on the visual world and the everyday activities of men, women, and children. Whereas Western artists exalt the heroic deeds and historical achievements of individuals, Chinese artists rarely glorify human accomplishments. Indeed, in Chinese paintings, the landscape often dwarfs the figures so that human occupations seem mundane and incidental within the vast sweep of nature.

*A Solitary Temple Amid Clearing Peaks,* attributed to Li Cheng (active 940–967), is meditative in mood and subtle in composition (Figure **14.14**). There is no single

**Figure 14.14** Attributed to Li Cheng, *A Solitary Temple Amid Clearing Peaks,* Northern Song dynasty, ca. 950 C.E. Ink and slight color on silk hanging scroll, 44 × 22 in. The Nelson-Atkins Museum of Art, Kansas City, Missouri. Purchase: Nelson Trust. 47–71.

viewpoint from which to observe the mountains, trees, waters, and human habitations. Rather, we perceive the whole from what one eleventh-century Chinese art critic called the "angle of totality." We look down upon some elements, such as the rooftops, and up to others, such as the mountains. The lofty mountains and gentle waterfall seem protective of the infinitely smaller images of houses and people. Misty areas act as transition points between foreground, middleground, and background, but each plane—even the background—is delineated with identical precision. The visual voyage

**Figure 14.15** Ma Yuan, *Apricot Blossoms*, late twelfth or early thirteenth century. Ink and color on silk fan, mounted as album leaf, 9⅞ × 10 in. National Palace Museum, Taipei, China. Photo: Bruce White.

through discontinuous space engages our recognition of the subtle relationships between all parts of the painting, putting us in touch with the physical and spiritual energies of nature. As with Chinese poetry, in which a few well-chosen words may convey a distinct mood, the Chinese painting displays a remarkable economy of line and color—that is, the artist has evoked a memorable image by means of a limited number of brushstrokes and tones. Li Cheng has fulfilled the primary aim of the Chinese landscape painter (as defined by Song critics): to capture the whole universe within a few inches of space.

Equally brilliant in detail and in its organization of positive and negative space, *Apricot Blossoms* by Ma Yuan (ca. 1160–1225) reflects the Song taste for decorative works featuring floral motifs (Figure 14.15). Refined nature studies like this one, executed in ink and color on silk, dwell on a single element in nature (the "broken branch") rather than the expansive landscape. The couplet at the right (added by the artist's patron) extends the "message" of the image as fragile, elegant, fleeting:

> Meeting the wind, they offer their artful charm;
> Moist with dew, they boast their pink beauty.*

The earliest treatises on Chinese painting appeared in the Song Era. They describe the artist's practice of integrating complementary pictorial elements: dark and light shapes, bold and muted strokes, dense and sparse textures, large and small forms, and positive and negative shapes, each pair interacting in imitation of the *yin/yang* principle that underlies cosmic wholeness. Specific brushstrokes, each bearing an individual name, are prescribed for depicting different natural phenomena: pine needles, rocks, mountains, and so forth. A form of calligraphy, the artist's brushstrokes are the "bones" of

---

*Maxwell Hearn, *Splendors of Imperial China: Treasures from the National Palace Museum, Taipei*. New York: The Metropolitan Museum of Art, 1996, 33.

the Chinese painting. Economy, gestural expressiveness, and spontaneity are hallmarks of the finest Chinese paintings, as they are of the best Chinese poems. In premodern China, tradition rather than originality governed creativity: Artists freely copied the works of the masters and honored their forebears by "quoting" from their poems or paintings.

## Chinese Crafts

From earliest times, the Chinese excelled in the production of ceramic wares. They manufactured fine terracotta and stoneware objects for everyday use and for burial in the tombs of the dead (see chapter 7). During the Tang Era, Chinese craftspeople produced thousands of realistic clay images : A terra-cotta court dancer wears an elegant dress with long sleeves designed to sway with her body movements (see Part Opener, p. 142). Replicas of horses—the treasured animals of China—appear in great numbers in Tang graves. Such figures were usually cast from molds, assembled in sections, and glazed with green, yellow, and brown (Figure **14.16**).

**Figure 14.16** *Horse and Rider*, Tang dynasty, early eighth century. Pottery with three-color glaze and painted decoration, height 15 in. The Metropolitan Museum of Art, New York. Rogers Fund, 1954. 54.169.

**Figure 14.17** Flower vase, Northern Song dynasty. *Cuzhou* ware, glazed stoneware with *sgraffito* decoration, 22⅜ × 10 in. The Nelson-Atkins Museum of Art, Kansas City, Missouri. Purchase: Nelson Trust.

In addition to earthenware pottery, Tang and Song craftspeople produced sophisticated stoneware (Figure **14.17**). The crowning achievement was **porcelain**—a hard, translucent ceramic ware fired at high heat. Describing the magnificent porcelain vessels of the Tang Era, a ninth-century merchant observed that one could see the sparkle of water through Chinese bowls that were "as fine as glass." Exported along with silk, lacquerware, and carved ivory, porcelain became one of the most sought-after of Chinese luxury goods—indeed, it was so popular that Westerners still refer to dishes and plates as "china." Noted for their refined contours, some classic Chinese ceramics look back to early bronze receptacles, while the gray-green glazes of others recall the color and texture of Chinese jades. Other types, such as the blue and white porcelains that influenced

Islamic art, originated in the Tang Era. In subtlety of design, Chinese ceramics compare favorably with the most sublime Chinese landscape paintings.

The somber restraint of Chinese pottery stands in sharp contrast to the profuse richness of Chinese metalwork, inlaid wood, carved lacquers, and textiles. So famous was Chinese silk that the 8,000-mile overland trade route connecting West and East (from Constantinople on the Atlantic to Chang'an on the Pacific) was dubbed "the Silk Road." Between roughly 500 B.C.E. and 1450 C.E., this route (and the nomadic peoples who traversed it) facilitated the exchange of goods and ideas between China and the great cities of Southwest Asia (see chapters 7, 10).

## Chinese Architecture

Chinese architects embraced a system of design that reflected the ancient Daoist quest for harmony with nature. Structures were emphatically horizontal—built to hug the earth—and both whole towns and individual buildings were laid out according to a cosmic axis that ran from north to south. Celestial symbolism governed Chinese palace design: for instance, four doors represented the four seasons, eight windows signified the eight winds, and twelve halls stood for the number of months in the year. House doors faced the "good"

**Figure 14.18** Seven-tiered bracket for a Chinese palace hall, from the Song dynasty architectural manual, *Yingzao fashih* (1925 edition). Woodcut.

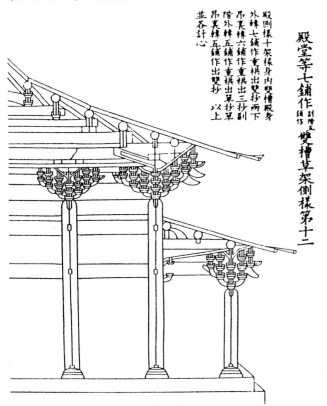

southerly direction of the summer sun, and rear walls were closed to the cold North, homeland of barbarian hordes that had threatened China throughout its history. Chinese residences were normally self-enclosed and looked inward to courtyards or gardens.

During the Tang and Song Eras, the multiroofed pagoda, a shrine sheltering the relics of the Buddha or the *bodhisattvas*, remained the principal center of Buddhist worship (see chapter 9). From earliest times, pagodas were constructed of wood, a building material that was plentiful in China and one that was highly valued for its natural beauty. Chinese architectural ingenuity lay in the invention of a unique timber frame that—in place of walls—bore the entire weight of the roof while making the structure earthquake-resistant (Figure 14.18). Perfected during the Tang Era, the Chinese system of vaulting consisted of an intricate series of wooden cantilevers (horizontal brackets extending beyond the vertical supports) that provided support for centrally pitched, shingled, or glazed-tile roofs. By the tenth century, the aesthetics of wood construction were firmly established and, during the following century, scholars enshrined these principles in China's first manual on architecture. Since wooden buildings were highly vulnerable to fire—almost all examples of early Chinese shrines had been destroyed by the end of the first millennium—Chinese architects also built in brick and in cast iron. Regardless of medium, however, Chinese pagodas, pavilions, and domestic structures, with their projecting upturned eaves, were masterful achievements in elegant design. And, as indicated by the many magnificent pagodas found throughout Japan and Southeast Asia, China was influential in disseminating an architectural style that, in its dependence on the wooden cantilever and its harmonious relationship with the natural site, remains stylistically distinct from that of the West.

## The Medieval Period in Japan

Buddhism entered Japan in the early sixth century, bringing in its wake the basic elements of Chinese culture. The Chinese system of writing, record-keeping, and governing, as well as the fundamentals of Chinese art and architecture, had a profound influence upon the Japanese. In the eighth century, the aristocratic Fujiwara clan ascended to the imperial Japanese throne. For roughly four centuries (794–1185) a sophisticated Japanese court ruled from the capital city of Heian (modern Kyoto), from which came Japan's first wholly original literature and a set of aesthetic norms that left a permanent mark on Japanese culture.

It was Japan that introduced to world literature the prose form known as the novel. *The Tale of Genji* (ca. 1004), a Japanese classic, tells the story of the "shining prince" of the Heian court. Because the novel exposes the inner life of Genji and other characters, it has been called the world's first psychological novel. However, it also paints a detailed picture of Japanese life within a small segment of the population: the aristocracy. The men and women of this class prized elegant clothes (women usually wore five to twelve layers of silk robes), refined manners, and poetic versatility: Inability to compose the appropriate on-the-spot poem was considered a social deficiency. They also regarded as essential education in the (Chinese) classics, and the cultivation of dance, music, and fine calligraphy—in all, a set of values that prefigured the Renaissance ideal of the well-rounded courtier by some five hundred years (see chapter 16). The author of *The Tale of Genji*, Murasaki Shikibu (978–1016), was one of a group of outstanding female writers and members of Heian court society. Upper-class women like Murasaki were unique in East Asian literary history: Their fame in writing polished intimate prose was so great that one tenth-century male diarist pretended his work had been penned by a woman. The achievement of medieval Japanese women is all the more remarkable in that (like their Chinese counterparts) they were excluded from the world of scholarly education and, hence, from training in written Chinese. Nevertheless, using a system of phonetic symbols derived from Chinese characters, these women produced the outstanding monuments of medieval Japanese prose.

*The Tale of Genji*—in English translation some six volumes long—cannot be represented adequately here. But it is possible to gain insight into both the talents of Murasaki Shikibu and the character of the Heian court by means of a brief look at Shikibu's *Diary*, which she wrote between the years 1008 and 1010. Her keen eye for visual detail, for instance, is revealed in her vivid descriptions of court attire:

> . . . the older women wore plain jackets in yellow-green or dark red, each with five damask cuffs. The brightness of the wave pattern printed on their trains caught the eye, and their waistlines too were heavily embroidered. They had white robes lined with dark red in either three or five layers but of plain silk. The younger women wore jackets with five cuffs of various colors, white on the outside with dark red on yellow-green, white with just one green lining, and pale red shading to dark red with one white layer interposed; they were all arranged most intelligently.*

Beyond its importance as a historical record, Lady Murasaki's *Diary* is significant as an exercise in self-analysis. Not an autobiography, it is, rather, a series of reminiscences, anecdotes, and experiences. Nevertheless, it documents the author's quest to understand her role as a writer and her place in the highly artificial Heian court. As such, the *Diary* displays a dimension of self-consciousness that has long been considered an exclusively Western phenomenon.

## READING 2.24
## From Murasaki's *Diary*

. . . The wife of the Governor of Tanba is known to everyone in the service of Her Majesty and His Excellency as Masahira Emon. She may not be a genius but she has great poise and does not feel that she has to compose a poem on everything she sees merely because she is a poet. From what I have seen, her work is most accomplished, even her occasional verse. People who think so much of themselves that, at the drop of a hat, they compose lame verses that only just hang together or produce the most pretentious compositions imaginable are quite odious and rather pathetic. [10]

Sei Shōnagon,[1] for instance, was dreadfully conceited. She thought herself so clever, and littered her writings with Chinese characters, but if you examined them closely, they left a great deal to be desired. Those who think of themselves as being superior to everyone else in this way will inevitably suffer and come to a bad end, and people who have become so precious that they go out of their way to be sensitive in the most unpromising situations, trying to capture every moment of interest, [20] however slight, are bound to look ridiculous and superficial. How can the future turn out well for them?

I criticize other women like this, but here is one who has managed to survive this far without having achieved anything of note and has nothing to rely on in the future that might afford her the slightest consolation. Yet, perhaps because I still retain the conviction that I am not the kind of person to abandon herself completely to despair, on autumn evenings, when nostalgia is at its most poignant, I go out and sit on the veranda to gaze in reverie. "Is this [30] the moon that used to praise my beauty?" I say to myself, as I conjure up memories of the past. Then, realizing that I am making precisely that mistake which must be avoided, I become uneasy and move inside a little, while still, of course, continuing to fret and worry.

I remember how in the cool of the evening I used to play the koto[2] to myself, rather badly; I was always worried lest someone were to hear me and realize that I was just "adding to the sadness of it all." How silly of me, and yet how sad! So now my two kotos, one of thirteen [40] strings and the other of six, stand in a miserable little closet blackened with soot, ready tuned but idle. Through neglect—I forgot, for example, to ask that the bridges be removed on rainy days—they have accumulated the dust and lean there now against a

---

*Murasaki Shikibu, Her Diary and Poetic Memoirs*, translated by Richard Bowring. Princeton, N. J.: Princeton University Press, 1982, 79.

[1]Female writer (ca. 968–1025) famous for her *Pillow Book*, a long collection of notes, stories, and descriptions of everyday life among members of the Heian upper class.
[2]A Japanese musical instrument of the zither family.

cupboard, their necks jammed between that and a pillar, with a biwa standing on either side.

There is also a pair of large cupboards crammed full to bursting point. One is full of old poems and tales that have become the home for countless silverfish that scatter in such an unpleasant manner that no one cares to look at them any more; the other is full of Chinese books which have lain unattended ever since he who carefully collected them passed away. Whenever my loneliness threatens to overwhelm me, I take out one or two of them to look at. But my women gather together behind my back. "It's because she goes on like that that she is so miserable. What kind of lady is it who reads Chinese books?" they whisper. "In the past it was not even the done thing to read sutras!"[3] "Yes," I feel like replying, "but I've never seen anyone who lived longer just because they obeyed a prohibition!" But that would be inconsiderate of me, for what they say is not unreasonable.

Everyone reacts differently. Some are cheerful, open-hearted, and forthcoming; others are born pessimists, amused by nothing, the kind who search through old letters, carry out penances, intone sutras without end, and clack their beads, all of which I find most unseemly. So aware am I of my women's prying eyes that I hesitate to do even those things a woman in my position should allow herself to do. How much more so at court, where I do have many things I wish to say but always think better of it. There would be no point, I tell myself, in explaining to people who would never understand, and as it would only be causing trouble with women who think of nothing but themselves and are always carping, I just keep my thoughts to myself. It is very rare that one finds people of true understanding; for the most part they judge everything by their own standards and ignore everyone else's opinion.

So I seem to be misunderstood, and they think that I am shy. There have been times when I have been forced to sit in their company, and on such occasions I have tried to avoid their petty criticisms, not because I am particularly shy but because I consider it all so distasteful; as a result, I am now known as somewhat of a dullard.

"Well, we never expected this!" they all say. "No one liked her. They all said she was pretentious, awkward, difficult to approach, prickly, too fond of her tales, haughty, prone to versifying, disdainful, cantankerous, and scornful. But when you meet her, she is strangely meek, a completely different person altogether!"

How embarrassing! Do they really look upon me as such a dull thing, I wonder? But I am what I am and so act accordingly. Her Majesty too has often remarked that she had thought I was not the kind of person with whom she could ever relax, but that now I have become closer to her than any of the others. I am so perversely standoffish; if only I can avoid putting off those for whom I have genuine respect.

The key to everything is to be pleasant, gentle, properly relaxed, and self-possessed; this is what makes for charm and composure in a woman. No matter how amorous or capricious one may be, as long as you are well-meaning at heart and refrain from anything that might cause embarrassment to others, you will be forgiven.

On the other hand, women who think too highly of themselves and act in a pretentious and overbearing manner become the object of attention, even when they take great care over their least move, and, once this happens, people are bound to find fault with whatever they say or do, going so far as to criticize how they sit down or how they take their leave. Those, of course, who tend to contradict themselves when they talk and disparage their companions are watched and listened to all the more. As long as one is free from such faults, people will be prepared to give you the benefit of the doubt and show you good will, no matter how superficial it might be.

Those who go out of their way to hurt others, as well as those who do stupid things by mistake, deserve, I think, to be ridiculed. Some people are so good-natured they can still care for someone even though that person hates them, but most people are just not capable of such magnanimity. Does the compassionate Buddha himself ever teach that taking the name of the three treasures in vain is merely a trivial offense? How much more so in this sullied world of ours should he who is hard on others be hardly done by. And yet one can clearly tell the differences in people's natures in the way that some glare at you openly with malicious intent and spread the most dreadful rumors, hoping to enhance themselves thereby, whereas others hide their feelings and appear on the surface to be quite friendly. . . .

---◆---

## Buddhism in Japan

As Buddhism spread throughout Japan, it inspired the construction of hundreds of shrines and temples, the oldest of which are found just outside Japan's early capital city of Nara. The site of the oldest wooden buildings in the world, this eighth-century temple complex with its graceful five-storied pagoda (Figure 14.19) preserves the timber style that originated in China. The Buddhism that arrived in sixth-century Japan was of the Mahayana variety, which regarded the Buddha as a savior and recognized the existence of many *bodhisattvas* (see chapter 9). Mahayana Buddhism gradually absorbed Japan's native Shinto religion, which venerated the nature spirits of the countryside. Indeed, the two faiths, Buddhism and Shintoism, formed a vigorous amalgam that accommodated many local beliefs and practices. One popular branch of Mahayana Buddhism, the Pure Land sect, worshiped the *bodhisattva* known as Amitabha (or Amida), who was thought to preside over the western paradise (the "pure land"). According to his followers, simply uttering the name of Amitabha many times a day was an aid to salvation and a means of assuring that the merciful Amida would deliver their dying souls to Paradise. Mahayana Buddhism assimilated the divine

[3]Buddhist discourses (see chapter 8).

**Figure 14.19** East pagoda of Yakushiji, Nara, Japan, ca. 720 C.E. Photo: Ancient Art and Architecture, Middlesex, U.K.

beings of India and China as well as those of Japan and honored them in painting and sculpture. Kichijoten, for instance, a female Buddhist deity of Indian derivation, is represented in a richly polychromed wooden statue of the Late Heian period (Figure 14.20). The popular goddess of abundance and good fortune, she is shown dressed in the elegant robes and jewelry of a Heian aristocrat.

## The Age of the *Samurai*: The Kamakura Shogunate (1185–1333)

Toward the mid-twelfth century, Heian authority gave way to a powerful group of local clans that competed for political and military preeminence. The strength of any clan depended on the *samurai* (literally, "those who serve"), skilled warriors who held land in return for military service to aristocratic lords—a system of local protection not unlike that of feudalism in the West. Outfitted with warhorses and elaborate armor made of iron plated with lacquer to protect against the rain (Figure 14.21), and trained in the arts of archery and swordsmanship, the *samurai* were a class of warrior aristocrats. They upheld values similar to those of the European knight

(see chapter 11) and embraced a code of conduct called *bushido* ("the way of the warrior"), which required selflessness in battle, fierce loyalty to one's superior, and a disdain for death. (Unlike the Western code of chivalry, however, *bushido* was little concerned with the warrior's behavior toward women.) The code demanded ritual suicide, usually by disembowelment, for any *samurai* warrior who fell into dishonor. Not surprisingly, the sword was the distinctive symbol of this warrior class.

By 1192, Japan's civil wars came to an end as a single powerful general-in-chief, or *shogun*, replaced the emperor as the most powerful figure in Japanese government. The clan ruler who established the shogunate at Kamakura, Minamoto no Yoritomo (1147–1199), is pictured on a silk scroll in magnificent ceremonial dress,

**Figure 14.20** *Kichijoten*, Late Heian period, late twelfth century. Painted wood, height 35½ in. Joruriji, Kyoto, Japan.

**Figure 14.21** *Samurai* armor with blue yarns from Taira clan, twelfth century. Height 3 ft. 3½ in. Itsukushima Shrine, Hiroshima, Japan.

the stiff formality of which provides a startling contrast with the personalized features of the head and face (Figure 14.22). The blend of naturalism and abstraction in this painting is typical of Japanese portraiture at its best. During the thirteenth century, Japanese sculptors—master woodcarvers—moved toward a more intense pictorial realism. The artist Jokei executed a series of painted wood temple guardians that reveal the Japanese fascination with the human figure in violent action (Figure 14.23). By means of exaggeration and forthright detail, he achieved a balletic union of martial-arts grace and *samurai* fierceness. The Kamakura shogunate remained the source of Japanese government only until 1333, but the values of the *samurai* would prevail well into modern times.

## The Nō Drama

Nō drama, the oldest form of Japanese theater, evolved from performances in dance, song, and mime popular in the Heian era and possibly even earlier. Like Greek drama, the Nō play treats serious themes drawn from a legacy of history and literature. Just as the plays of Sophocles recounted the story of the House of Thebes,

so Nō playwrights recalled the civil wars of the *samurai* and episodes from *The Tale of Genji*. Nō drama, however, was little concerned with character development or the realistic reenactment of actual events. Rather, by means of a rigidly formalized selection of text, gestures, dance, and music (usually performed on flute and drum), the play explored a given story to expose its underlying meaning.

Nō drama—still flourishing in modern-day Japan—is performed on a square wooden stage that opens to the audience on three sides and is connected by a raised passageway to an offstage dressing room. Though roofed, the stage holds almost no scenery and that which does appear serves a symbolic function. As in ancient Greek drama, all roles are played by men. Elegant costumes and masks, often magnificently carved and painted (Figure 14.24), may be used to represent individual characters. This mask of a young woman reveals the classic Heian preference for the white-powdered face, plucked eyebrows, and blackened

**Figure 14.22** Attributed to Fujiwara Takanobu, *Minamoto no Yoritomo*, Kamakura period, second half of twelfth century. Ink and color on silk hanging scroll, height 4 ft. 6¾ in. Jingoji, Kyoto, Japan.

including a high regard for beauty of effect, an emphasis on refinement of form, and a melancholic sensitivity to the pathos of human life.

## READING 2.25

### From Zeami's *Kadensho*

*Yūgen* is considered to be the mark of supreme        1
attainment in all of the arts and accomplishments. In the
art of the Nō in particular the manifestation of *yūgen* is
of the first importance. In general, a display of *yūgen* in
the Nō is apparent to the eye, and it is the one thing
which audiences most admire, but actors who possess
*yūgen* are few and far between. This is because they do
not in fact know the true meaning of *yūgen*. There are
thus none who reach that stage.

In what sort of place, then, is the stage of *yūgen*        10
actually to be found? Let us begin by examining the
various classes of people on the basis of the appearance
that they make in society. May we not say of the
courtiers, whose behavior is distinguished and whose
appearance far surpasses that of other men, that theirs is
the stage of *yūgen*? From this we may see that the
essence of *yūgen* lies in a true state of beauty and
gentleness. Tranquility and elegance make for *yūgen* in
personal appearance. In the same way, the *yūgen* of
discourse lies in a grace of language and a complete        20
mastery of the speech of the nobility and gentry, so that

**Figure 14.23** Jokei, *Kongorikishi*, Kamakura period, ca. 1288. Painted wood, height 5 ft. 4 in. Kofukuji, Nara, Japan.

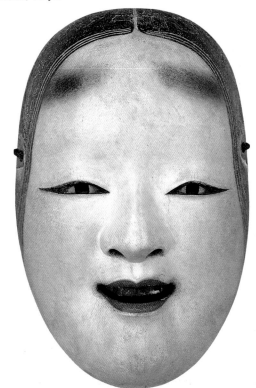

**Figure 14.24** *Ko-omote* Nō mask, Ashikaga period, fifteenth century. Painted wood, height approx. 10 in. Kongo Family Collection, Tokyo.

teeth—marks of high fashion among medieval Japanese females. A chorus sits at the side of the stage and expresses the thoughts of the actors but, unlike the Greek chorus, the Japanese one does not advance the dramatic action. A single program of Nō drama (which lasts some six hours) consists of a group of plays, with a selection from each of the play-types, such as god-plays, warrior-plays, and women-plays. Comic interludes are provided between them to lighten the serious mood.

The formalities of Nō drama were not set down until the early fifteenth century, when the playwright and actor Zeami Motokiyo (1363–1443) wrote an instructional manual for Nō actors. Zeami's manual, the *Kadensho*, prescribed demanding training exercises for the aspiring actor; it also analyzed the philosophic and aesthetic purposes of Nō theater. In the excerpt that follows, certain hallmarks of Japanese culture emerge, even the most casual utterance will be graceful. With respect to a musical performance, it may be said to possess *yūgen* when the melody flows beautifully and sounds smooth and sensitive. In the dance there will be *yūgen* when the discipline has been thoroughly mastered and the audience is delighted by the beauty of the performer's movements and by his serene appearance. In acting, there will be *yūgen* when the performance of the Three Roles is beautiful. If the characterization calls for a display of anger or for the representation of a devil, the actions may be somewhat forceful, but as long as the actor never loses sight of the beauty of the effect and bears in mind always the correct balance between his mental and physical actions and between the movements of his body and feet, his appearance will be so beautiful that it may be called "the *yūgen* of a devil."

All these aspects of *yūgen* must be kept in mind and made a part of the actor's body, so that whatever part he may be playing *yūgen* will never be absent. . . . It is through the use of intelligence that the above principles are thoroughly grasped; that poetry is learned so as to impart *yūgen* to his discourse; that the most elegant costuming is studied so as to impart *yūgen* to his bearing: though the characterization varies according to the different parts, the actor should realize that the ability to appear beautiful is the seed of *yūgen*. It is all too apt to happen that an actor, believing that once he has mastered the characterization of the various parts he has attained the highest stage of excellence, forgets his appearances and therefore is unable to enter the realm of *yūgen*. Unless an actor enters the realm of *yūgen* he will not attain the highest achievements. If he fails to attain the highest achievements, he will not become a celebrated master. That is why there are so few masters. The actor must consider *yūgen* as the most important aspect of his art and study to perfect his understanding of it.

The "highest achievement" of which I have spoken refers to beauty of form and manners. The most careful attention must therefore be given to the appearance presented. Accordingly, when we thoroughly examine the principles of *yūgen* we see that when the form is beautiful, whether in dancing, singing, or in any type of characterization, it may properly be called the "highest achievement." When the form is poor, the performance will be inferior. The actor should realize that *yūgen* is attained when all of the different forms of visual or aural expression are beautiful. It is when the actor himself has worked out these principles and made himself their master that he may be said to have entered the realm of *yūgen*. If he fails to work out these principles for himself, he will not master them, and however much he may aspire to attain *yūgen*, he will never in all his life do so.

. . . . . . . . . . . .

Sometimes spectators of the Nō say, "The moments of 'no-action' are the most enjoyable." This is an art which the actor keeps secret. Dancing and singing, movements and the different types of miming are all acts performed by the body. Moments of "no-action" occur in between. When we examine why such moments without actions are enjoyable, we find that it is due to the underlying spiritual strength of the actor which unremittingly holds the attention. He does not relax the tension when the dancing or singing come to an end or at intervals between the dialogue and the different types of miming, but maintains an unwavering inner strength. This feeling of inner strength will faintly reveal itself and bring enjoyment. However, it is undesirable for the actor to permit this inner strength to become obvious to the audience. If it is obvious, it becomes an act, and is no longer "no-action." The actions before and after an interval of "no-action" must be linked by entering the state of mindlessness in which one conceals even from oneself one's intent. This, then, is the faculty of moving audiences, by linking all the artistic powers with one mind.

> Life and death, past and present—
> Marionettes on a toy stage.
> When the strings are broken,
> Behold the broken pieces.

This is a metaphor describing human life as it transmigrates between life and death. Marionettes on a stage appear to move in various ways, but in fact it is not they who really move—they are manipulated by strings. When these strings are broken, the marionettes fall and are dashed to pieces. In the art of the Nō too, the different sorts of miming are artificial things. What holds the parts together is the mind. This mind must not be disclosed to the audience. If it is seen, it is just as if a marionette's strings were visible. The mind must be made the strings which hold together all the powers of the arts. If this is done the actor's talent will endure. This resolution must not be confined to the times when the actor is appearing on the stage. Day or night, wherever he may be, whatever he may be doing, he should not forget this resolution, but should make it his constant guide, uniting all his powers. If he unremittingly works at this his talent will steadily grow. This article is the most secret of the secret teachings. . . .

———————◆———————

# SUMMARY

Between roughly 500 and 1300, India, China, and Japan produced arts and ideas that, although markedly different from those of the European West, contributed richly to the corpus of the humanistic tradition. Asian art of this period reveals a profound respect for the interdependence of natural and divine forces, of body and mind, and of matter and spirit. The sacred literature of Hinduism, as well as the rich fund of Sanskrit secular poetry, manifests a distinctly sensual approach to nature. In literature, architecture, and sculpture, the Hindu gods are identified with the creative, cyclical, and regenerative forces of the Absolute Spirit. The Hindu notion that nature and humankind belong to one and the same unifying, organic order differs sharply from the medieval Christian view that humankind was distinct and separate from both lower (animal) and higher (divine) forms of reality. In Indian visual art, as in Indian music and dance, the holistic view is expressed as a celebration of cyclical and natural universal rhythms.

The arts of China blossomed under the centralized leadership of the Tang and Song dynasties. Chinese religious philosophy—a synthesis of Buddhist, Confucian, and Daoist precepts—emphasized natural harmony and the unity of all living things. These concepts found sublime expression in Chinese poetry and landscape painting—two of China's greatest contributions to world culture. The Chinese imperial examination system produced an elite class of scholar-officials, while China's high regard for scholarship also generated a class of scholar-poets known as *literati*. China manufactured high-quality luxury goods and exported these to the rest of the world. Until at least the fourteenth century, China's technological and commercial achievements (such as the invention of printing, the magnetic compass, gunpowder, and the manufacture of magnificent porcelains and silks) far outstripped those of the West.

Japan's artistic record bears the stamp of Chinese culture. In the Heian period, however, a literary form unique to medieval Japan—the psychological novel—made its way into world literature. The *samurai* culture of the Kamakura shogunate and a rich heritage of Mahayana Buddhism played distinctive roles in the arts:

The former commissioned magnificent weapons, armor, and palace portraiture, while the latter supported a flourishing industry in shrine architecture and sculpture. The medieval Japanese preference for refined form and beauty of effect is illustrated in the visual arts, in literature, and perhaps most distinctively in Nō theater, the classic drama of Japan.

Deeply committed to the concept of natural harmony, the civilizations of India, China, and Japan produced an extraordinary fund of arts and ideas. As modern forms of communication have worked to bring all parts of the world closer together, the Asian contributions to the humanistic tradition have gained greater recognition, better understanding, and deeper appreciation among Westerners.

---

## GLOSSARY

**alliteration**   a literary device involving the repetition of initial sounds in successive or closely associated words or syllables

**assonance**   a literary device involving a similarity in sound between vowels followed by different consonants

**avatar**   (Sanskrit, "incarnation") the incarnation of a Hindu deity

*mithuna*   the Hindu representation of a male and a female locked in passionate embrace

**novel**   an extended fictional prose narrative

**opera**   a drama set to music and making use of vocal pieces with orchestral accompaniment

**porcelain**   a hard, translucent ceramic ware made from clay fired at high heat

*raga*   a mode or melodic form in Hindu music; a specific combination of notes associated with a particular mood or atmosphere

**sitar**   a long-necked stringed instrument popular in Indian music

*tala*   a set rhythmic formula in Hindu music

---

## SUGGESTIONS FOR READING

Bhavnani, Enakshi. *The Dance in India*, 2nd ed. Bombay: Taraporevala, 1970.
Cahill, James. *The Painter's Practice: How Artists Lived and Worked in Traditional China*. New York: Columbia University Press, 1994.
Clunas, Craig. *Art in China*. New York: Oxford University Press, 1997.
Coomaraswamy, Ananda. *The Dance of Shiva*. New York: Sunwise Turn, 1913.
Dawson, Robert, ed. *The Legacy of China*. New York: Oxford University Press, 1964.
Hookham, Hilda. *A Short History of China*. New York: New American Library, 1972.
Massey, Reginald. *The Music of India*. New York: Crescendo, 1977.
Morris, Ivan. *The World of the Shining Prince: Court Life in Ancient Japan*. New York: Knopf, 1964.
Murck, Alfreda, and Wen Fong. *Words and Images: Chinese Poetry, Calligraphy, and Painting*. Princeton, N.J.: Princeton University Press, 1991.
Rawson, Jessica, ed. *The British Museum Book of Chinese Art*. New York: Thames and Hudson, 1992.
Wu, N. I. *Chinese and Indian Architecture*. New York: Braziller, 1963.
Yoshikawa, Itsuji. *Major Themes in Japanese Art*. New York: Weatherhill/Heibonsha, 1976.

---

## MUSIC LISTENING SELECTIONS

**Cassette I Selection 11**   Indian music, *Thumri*, played on the sitar by Ravi Shankar.
**Cassette I Selection 12**   Chinese music: Cantonese music drama for male solo, zither, and other instruments, "Ngoh wai heng kong" ("I'm Mad About You").

# Selected General Bibliography

Adas, Michael, ed. *Islamic and European Expansion: The Forging of a Global Order*. Philadelphia: Temple University Press, 1993.

Baker, Herschel. *The Image of Man: A Study in the Idea of Human Dignity in Classical Antiquity, the Middle Ages, and the Renaissance*. New York: Harper, 1961.

Baker, Joan Stanley. *Japanese Art*. London: Thames and Hudson, 1984.

Bechert, Heinz, and Richard Gombrich. *The World of Buddhism: Buddhist Monks and Nuns in Society and Culture*. London: Thames and Hudson, 1984.

Bentley, Jerry H. *Old World Encounters: Cross-Cultural Contacts and Exchanges in Pre-Modern Times*. New York: Oxford University Press, 1993.

Clark, Kenneth. *Civilisation: A Personal View*. New York: Harper, 1970.

Clunas, Craig. *Art in China*. New York: Oxford University Press, 1997.

Craven, Roy C. *Indian Art*. London: Thames and Hudson, 1985.

Devisse, Jean, and Michel Mollat. *The Image of the Black in Western Art*. Vol. 2, *From the Early Christian Era to the "Age of Discovery,"* translated by William G. Ryan. Houston, Tex.: Menil Foundation, 1990.

Esposito, John L. *Islam: The Straight Path*. New York: Oxford University Press, 1992.

Ferguson, George. *Signs and Symbols in Christian Art*. New York: Oxford University Press, 1966.

Gernet, Jacques. *A History of Chinese Civilization*. Cambridge, UK: Cambridge University Press, 1996.

Gies, Frances, and Joseph Gies. *Cathedral, Forge and Waterwheel: Technology and Invention in the Middle Ages*. New York: HarperCollins, 1995.

Goldstein, Thomas. *The Dawn of Modern Science: From the Arabs to Leonardo da Vinci*. Boston: Houghton Mifflin, 1980.

al-Hassan, Ahmad Y., and Donald R. Hill. *Islamic Technology: An Illustrated History*. Cambridge, U.K.: Cambridge University Press, 1986.

Hibbert, Christopher. *Cities and Civilizations*. London: Weidenfeld and Nicolson, 1986.

Hiskett, Mervyn. *The Course of Islam in Africa*. Edinburgh: University of Edinburgh Press, 1994.

Hopfe, L. M. *Religions of the World*, 4th ed. New York: Macmillan, 1987.

Kostoff, Spiro. *A History of Architecture: Settings and Rituals*, 2nd ed. New York: Oxford University Press, 1995.

Lee, Sherman E. *A History of Far Eastern Art*, 5th ed. New York: Abrams, 1994.

Lund, Erik, Mogens Pihl, and Johannes Sløk. *A History of European Ideas*, translated by W. G. Jones. Reading, Mass.: Addison-Wesley, 1962.

May, Elizabeth, ed. *Music of Many Cultures*. Berkeley, Calif.: University of California Press, 1980.

Morton, W. Scott. *China: Its History and Culture*. New York: Cromwell, 1980.

——. *Japan: Its History and Culture*. New York: Cromwell, 1970.

Nuttgens, Patrick. *The Story of Architecture*. Englewood Cliffs, N.J.: Prentice-Hall, 1983.

O'Faolain, Julia, and Lauro Martines, eds. *Not in God's Image: Women in History from the Greeks to the Victorians*. New York: Harper, 1973.

Quadir, C. A. *Philosophy and Science in the Islamic World: From Origins to the Present Day*. London: Routledge, Chapman, and Hall, 1988.

Rahman, Fazlur. *Islam*. London: Weidenfeld and Nicolson, 1966.

Schirokauer, Conrad. *A Brief History of Chinese and Japanese Civilizations*, 2nd ed. San Diego: Harcourt Brace, 1988.

Skord, Virginia, ed. *Tales of Tears and Laughter: Short Fiction of Medieval Japan*. Honolulu: University of Jawaii Press, 1995.

Sorrell, Walter. *The Dance Through the Ages*. New York: Grosset and Dunlap, 1967.

Spencer, Harold. *The Image Maker: Man and His Art*. New York: Scribner, 1975.

Sternfeld, F. W. *Music from the Middle Ages to the Renaissance*. Vol. 1 of *The History of Western Music*. New York: Praeger, 1973.

Stokstad, Marilyn. *Medieval Art*. New York: Harper Collins, 1986.

Sullivan, Michael. *The Arts of China*, 3rd ed. Berkeley, Calif.: University of California Press, 1984.

Tidworth, Simon. *Theatres: An Architectural and Cultural History*. New York: Praeger, 1973.

Tregear, Mary. *Chinese Art*. London: Thames and Hudson, 1985.

Williams, John A., ed. *Themes of Islamic Civilization*. Berkeley, Calif.: University of California Press, 1971.

Zimmer, Heinrich. *Myths and Symbols in Indian Art and Civilization*. Princeton, N.J.: Princeton University Press, 1992.

## BOOKS IN SERIES

*Daily Life in the Five Great Ages of History*. The Horizon Books of Daily Life. New York: American Heritage Pub. Co., 1975.

*Great Ages of Man: A History of the World's Cultures*. New York: Time-Life Books, 1965–1969.

*Time-Frame*. 25 vols. (projected). New York: Time-Life Books, 1990–.

# Credits

The author and publishers wish to thank the following for permission to use copyright material. Every effort has been made to trace the copyright holders, but if any have been inadvertently overlooked the publishers will be pleased to make the necessary arrangement at the first opportunity.

Reading 2.1 (p. 4) Excerpts from *Metamorphoses*, vol. II, trs. J. Arthur Hanson. Loeb Classical Library, 1989, by permission of Harvard University Press and the Loeb Classical Library

Reading 2.2 (p. 6) Excerpts from *The Jerusalem Bible*. Copyright © 1966 by Darton, Longman & Todd Ltd. and Doubleday, a division of Bantam Doubleday Dell Publishing Group, Inc., by permission of Doubleday

Reading 2.3 (p. 8) Excerpts from *The Jerusalem Bible*. Copyright © 1966 by Darton, Longman & Todd Ltd. and Doubleday, a division of Bantam Doubleday Dell Publishing Group, Inc., by permission of Doubleday

Reading 2.5 (p. 17) From 'The Nicene Creed', in *Documents of the Christian Church*, ed. Henry Bettensen, 2nd ed. 1963. Reprinted by permission of Oxford University Press

Reading 2.7 (p. 19) Excerpts from *Confessions of Saint Augustine*, trs. Rex Warner. Translation copyright © 1963 by Rex Warner, renewed 1991 by F. C. Warner. Introduction copyright © 1963, renewed 1991 by Vernon J. Bourke, by permission of Dutton Signet, a division of Penguin Books USA Inc.

Reading 2.8 (p. 20) Excerpts from *City of God Against the Pagans*, vol. IV. trs. Philip Levine. Loeb Classical Library, 1966, by permission of Harvard University Press and the Loeb Classical Library

Reading 2.9 (p. 46) Excerpts from *The Qur'an*, trs. M. H. Shakir, by permission of Tahrike Tarsile Qur'an

Reading 2.10 (p. 53) 'Ibn Zaydun: Two Fragments' and 'Ibn Abra: The Beauty Spot' from James Kritzeck, *Anthology of Islamic Literature from the Rise of Islam to Modern Times*. Copyright © 1962 by James Kritzeck, by permission of Henry Holt & Co., Inc.

Reading 2.11 (p. 54) 'The Man of God' and 'Empty the Glass of Your Desire' from *Love Is a Stranger*, trs. Rabir Edmund Helminski, 1993, by permission of Threshold Books

Reading 2.12 (p. 55) 'Prince Behram and the Princess Al-Datma' from *Arabian Nights*, trs. Jack Zipes. Translation copyright © 1991 by Jack Zipes, by permission of Dutton Signet, a division of Penguin Books USA Inc.

Reading 2.13 (p. 68) Excerpts from *Beowulf*, trs. Burton Raffel. Translation copyright © 1963 by Burton Raffel. Afterword © 1963 by New American Library, by permission of Dutton Signet, a division of Penguin Books USA Inc.

Reading 2.14 (p. 76) Excerpts from *The Song of Roland*, trs. Patricia Terry. Copyright © 1965 by permission of Prentice-Hall, Inc.

Reading 2.15 (p. 84) Excerpts from Chrétien de Troyes, *Lancelot*, trs. W. W. Comfort, Everyman, 1970, by permission of David Campbell Publishers Ltd.

Reading 2.17 (p. 93) Excerpts from Pope Innocent III, *On the Misery of the Human Condition*, ed. Donald R. Howard. Copyright © 1969 by permission of Prentice-Hall, Inc.

Reading 2.19 (p. 104) Excerpts from Dante Alighieri, *Divine Comedy*, trs. John Ciardi. Translation copyright © 1954, 1957, 1959, 1960, 1961, 1965, 1967, 1970 by the Ciardi Family Publishing Trust, by permission of W. W. Norton & Company, Inc.

Reading 2.20 (p. 111) Excerpts from *Basic Writings of Saint Thomas Aquinas*, vol. I, ed. Anton C. Pegis, by permission of the Anton C. Pegis Estate

Reading 2.22 (p. 148) Excerpts from *An Anthology of Sanskrit Court Poetry*, trs. Daniel H. Ingalls, nos. 575, 690, 784. Copyright © 1988 by the President and Fellows of Harvard College, by permission of Harvard University Press

Reading 2.23 (p. 157) 'Farewell Once More' by Tu Fu from *One Hundred Poems from the Chinese*, ed. Kenneth Rexroth. Copyright © 1971 by Kenneth Rexroth, by permission of New Directions Publishing Corp.

Reading 2.25 (p. 167) Excerpts from Zeami, 'Kadensho' in *Sources of Japanese Tradition*, by William Theodore de Bary. Copyright © 1958 by Columbia University Press, by permission of Columbia University Press

# Index